The Folklore of Cornwall

By considering the folklore of Cornwall in a Northern European context, this book casts light on a treasury of often-ignored traditions. Folklore studies internationally have long considered Celtic material, but scholars have tended to overlook Cornwall's collections. *The Folklore of Cornwall* fills this gap, placing neglected stories on a par with those from other regions where Celtic languages have deep roots. The book shows how the Cornish 'droll tellers' helped to build a unique pattern of legends and folktales, creating Cornwall's distinct body of oral tradition.

"Two books in one: an erudite introduction to Cornish folklore, but the book also stands as an excellent introduction to modern folklore studies more generally."

Simon Young, University of Virginia (Siena, CET)

Ronald M. James is a historian and folklorist. In 2016 he was made a Bard of the Gorsedh Kernow, the Bardic Council of Cornwall, for services to Cornish heritage and culture, taking the name *Carer Henhwedhlow—Lover of Legends*.

"Professor James is extraordinarily well-versed in European folklore, having a seemingly exhaustive array of legends to draw upon for his comparative analysis. His explication of folktale origins is convincing as well as interesting, and his explication of their meanings as a way of explaining pre-modern beliefs is especially intriguing."

Kevin J. Gardner, Professor and Chair, Department of English, Baylor University, USA

"His detailed research in the United States, for example, reveals how emigrant Cornish men and women took their folklore to the mining frontier of the American West, adapting it to local conditions (as in the 'tommyknockers'), yet further evidence of the tradition's continuing vitality and relevance. Cornish folklore has been literally global in its impact and extent, and in this important book Ronald M. James encourages us to look at this fascinating subject in new and innovative ways. It is sure to be the standard volume for many years to come."

Philip Payton, Professor of History, Flinders University, Australia

"Exploring a wealth of interesting and enjoyable tales, James sets the rich folklore of Cornwall—from the indigenous piskie to the emigrant tommy-knocker—within a much wider historic and geographic context. This book is both highly informative and a real pleasure to read."

Ceri Houlbrook, Researcher in the History Group, University of Hertfordshire

"Our first real book on Cornish folklore since 1890 … and, my goodness, it has been worth the wait. You can count the great names in Cornish folklore studies on the fingers of one hand: Bottrell, Courtney, Hunt, Tregarthen … and now, a century after Tregarthen put down her pen, Ron James. He has confirmed his membership of the club with this remarkable new work. *The Folklore of Cornwall* will prove an inspiration not only for Cornish scholars, but for folklorists more generally."

Simon Young, University of Virginia (Siena, CET)

The Folklore
of Cornwall

The Oral Tradition of a Celtic Nation

RONALD M. JAMES

UNIVERSITY
of
EXETER
PRESS

First published in 2018 by
University of Exeter Press
Reed Hall, Streatham Drive
Exeter EX4 4QR
UK
www.exeterpress.co.uk

British Library Cataloguing in Publication Data
A catalogue record for this book is available from the British Library.

Hardback ISBN 978 0 85989 470 8

Typeset in Perpetua 11½ point on 14 point by BBR Design, Sheffield

Contents

Illustrations

Cover The folklore of Cornwall is more than cute pixies and quaint legends: serious concerns about terrifying encounters with the supernatural fill the narratives. W.H.C. Groome (1854–1913), a noted illustrator, portrays piskies tormenting a horse. 'Night-riders, Night-riders, please stop!' appeared in Enys Tregarthen's *North Cornwall Fairies and Legends*, published in 1906. Tregarthen's stories often strayed from oral tradition, but here she hits the mark: the Cornish believed piskies sometimes troubled horses during the hours of darkness.

Back cover 'The Zennor Poet', by Richard T. Pentreath, depicts Henry Quick (1792–1857), often called the last of the Cornish droll tellers. Quick, to the far left, is reading one of his compositions to a receptive audience. Pentreath (1806–1869) received the Bronze Medal for the painting at the Royal Cornwall Polytechnic Society in 1842. Lost for decades, 'The Zennor Poet' was rediscovered by Viv Hendra at the Lander Gallery in 2015. Courtesy of the Zennor Parish Council with thanks to Penlee House Gallery and John Nicholson's Fine Art Auctioneers and Valuers.

Acknowledgements

Firstly, it is important to thank Philip Payton, the former director of the Institute for Cornish Studies, who published two of my articles about indigenous folklore in *Cornish Studies*. His input during the 2009 International Gatherings of Cornish Cousins in Grass Valley, California, helped inspire the completion of this book. In addition, special thanks to Professor Payton for writing a preface for this volume; it is an honour to have a contribution from such a distinguished authority on Cornwall.

Secondly, Garry Tregidga, the current director of the Institute for Cornish Studies, also encouraged the development of this book. He reviewed a preliminary chapter outline and offered general support. In addition, Dr Tregidga published one of my articles on folklore in *Cornish Studies*. Thanks as well to Simon Baker and Helen Gannon of the University of Exeter Press for their expert efforts in guiding this book into print. In this context, gratitude must be expressed to the anonymous reviewers who provided excellent suggestions for the process of revision. Appreciative recognition is also due to Tim Absalom, Geomapping Unit, University of Plymouth, for the drafting of the map used in this volume. In addition, my thanks to Melanie James for heroic assistance with the copy-editing and to Amanda Thompson of BBR Design for talent and perseverance during the typesetting process.

I have benefited from the opportunity to give presentations at International Gatherings of Cornish Cousins in North America. The chance to meet Cornish enthusiasts and scholars and to receive feedback on topics dealing with the folklore of Cornwall was invaluable. Along this line, thanks as well to the California Cornish Cousins and particularly to Gage McKinney for kind support for this project over the years.

I gratefully acknowledge the International Telephone and Telegraph Corporation and the Institute of International Education for funding my fellowship to Ireland, 1981–1982, during which I initiated research on this project at the Department of Irish Folklore (now the National Folklore

Collection). This facility houses the enormous library of Carl Wilhelm von Sydow (1878–1952), which includes nineteenth-century books dealing with Cornish folklore, allowing for my first chance to read on this topic. In addition, attending an excellent presentation in 1982 at the Department of Irish Folklore by Ríonach Uí Ógaín and Anne O'Connor was an inspiration. It began my considering how their Irish variants of 'The Spectre Bridegroom' might compare with those of Cornwall. That line of thinking shaped how this volume would unfold.

Decades of discussions about folklore with my friend, William Kersten, deserve recognition and thanks for all he contributed to these pages. Simon Young of the University of Virginia Program (CET) Siena, read draft articles, which transformed into chapters, offering useful suggestions. More importantly, he shared drafts of his excellent work, affording me the opportunity to have access to his research often before publication. Philip Hayward of Kagoshima University, Research Center for the Pacific Islands, read a draft of my article on mermaids, the core of Chapter 7. He provided valuable comments. Similarly, Paul Manning of Trent University offered an ingenious way to consider Cornish mining spirits; the opportunity to have conversations with him in emails and in person was helpful and much appreciated. Thanks to the editors of *Western Folklore* for providing suggestions in the late 1980s that improved my work about the knockers and their American descendants, research that was initiated during my Irish sojourn.

A word about my teachers: while I attended folklore classes from five instructors with very different approaches, I studied more directly under two folklorists of related but divergent branches of the Swedish academic family. My mentor of five years was Sven S. Liljeblad (1899–2000). I was his only student from 1976 to 1981 (aside from his teaching a folklore class one semester, during which I served as his assistant). Sven gave me years of warm support and insightful guidance; he also helped with my research and early interpretation of the Cornish mining spirits.

In addition, I studied under Bo Almqvist (1931–2013) while conducting research in Ireland. Almqvist was a conservative adherent of the Finnish Historic Geographic Method, which stresses the comprehensive comparative analysis of folktale types to understand their individual histories. His bibliography is filled with eloquent essays that breathe meaning into folklore while resting on the soundest of detailed research. Almqvist's 1991 collection of essays, *Viking Ale: Studies on folklore contacts between the Northern and the Western World*, is particularly inspirational.

Although I benefited from studying with Almqvist and subsequently learnt a great deal from his publications, I was not his student in the strictest sense. I am the protégé of Sven Liljeblad, himself trained by the formidable theoretician von Sydow. Among von Sydow's students was Elisabeth Hartmann (1912–2004), a German scholar who went north to study under the best folklorists of the time. Liljeblad and von Sydow directed her 1936 doctoral dissertation, *Die Trollvorstellungen in den Sagen und Märchen der Skandinavischen Völker—The Troll Beliefs in the Legends and Folktales of the Scandinavian Folk.*

Not surprisingly, my studies with Sven included many discussions about Hartmann's research. In addition, she and I engaged in an epistolary relationship during the final five years of her life, granting me insight into her work, which is particularly important in a comparative analysis of northern European legends dealing with supernatural beings. She, like Sven, provided suggestions and insights about many aspects of folklore. I cherish the memory of these two scholars and friends.

Special thanks as always to my wife and son, Susan and Reed, for years of encouragement. Susan's expert editing is always an asset when it comes to polishing the written word. Most of all, thanks to both for patiently dealing with me during the years devoted to this project.

Preface

In the late 1960s and early 1970s, as a budding schoolboy Cornish enthusiast, I eagerly awaited the latest additions to the Tor Mark Press range. An imprint of the Truro publishers, D. Bradford Barton, the Tor Mark booklets were for me, and countless others, I imagine, a priceless introduction to the world of Cornish studies.

By the early 1970s, the series had reached almost forty separate titles, with topics as diverse as *The Story of the Cornish Language* and *Industrial Archaeology of Cornwall*. Most were written by contemporary authors, some instantly recognizable as existing contributors to the Cornish scene, and others (I guessed) *noms de plume* of D. Bradford Barton himself, the Tor Mark publisher. Three volumes, however, were of distinctly different provenance, and were windows into an entirely new (for me) subject, Cornish folklore. In 1969 I first stumbled across *Cornish Legends*, its cover depicting that curious rock-pile on Bodmin Moor, the Cheesewring. Turning to the title page, it became apparent that here was a selection of stories from a much earlier publication, a book entitled *Popular Romances of the West of England* which had appeared almost a century before, in 1871, its author one Robert Hunt (1807–1887). Although there was no Introduction to explain who Hunt was, or what had prompted his folkloric collection, I divined that he was an antiquarian writer who, at the height of the mid-Victorian period, had decided to record for posterity the folklore then still extant in Cornwall. Intriguing tales with strangely evocative titles, this 1969 Tor Mark reprint included stories such as 'The Fairy Miners—The Knockers', 'The Witch of Treva', and 'The Voice from the Sea'. Although presented without context or interpretation, the pamphlet hinted at a wonderfully rich reservoir of further material, ripe for investigation.

As if to prove the point, later in 1969 Tor Mark Press published *Cornish Folklore*, a further selection from Hunt's 1871 collection, again without explanation. This time the cover illustration was Mên-an-Tol, the well-known Penwith ancient monument, and the stories ranged from 'The Spriggans of Trencrom Hill' and

'The Mermaid's Rock' to 'The Lovers of Porthangwartha' and 'The Fairy Revels on the Gump, St Just'. A couple of years later a third volume appeared (undated), again attributed to Hunt but this time with no mention of his 1871 book. Entitled *Cornish Customs and Superstitions*, its cover depicting an eerie wind-blown tree atop a Cornish hedge, probably somewhere in north Cornwall, this further collection included items such as 'The Zennor Charmers' and 'King Arthur's Stone'. As ever, Hunt's imaginative prose added much to the atmosphere and excitement of these stories: 'if tales tell true, it is probable long years must pass before the Englishman can banish the Celtic powers who here hold sovereign sway'.

The three Tor Mark Press booklets together were an important attempt to bring Cornish folklore to as wide an audience as possible, Cornish as well as tourist, and was surely successful in that aim, the titles readily available in bookshops up and down Cornwall for many years. Although, as I discovered later, there had been some earlier attempt at a scholarly evaluation of Cornish folklore, notably by Charles Thomas, the Tor Mark volumes were the first, certainly since the Second World War, to place the subject before a broad readership, often amateur but always well informed. Since then, a number of authors, academic and popular, has been drawn to the subject of Cornish folklore, and there have been facsimile reprints of Hunt's (and others') work. But it is remarkable that only now, nearly forty years since the first of the Tor Mark booklets appeared, there is at last a full academic exploration of this significant subject, from the capable pen of Ronald M. James. We have had to wait a long time for such a book, and he is to be congratulated for grasping the nettle with such alacrity. My appetite was whetted all those years ago by the Tor Mark pamphlets, and in a sense, I have been waiting for Ronald's book all my life.

Ronald M. James needs little introduction to devotees of Cornish studies. Historian, folklorist and former heritage officer, he studied Northern European folklore during an extended sojourn in Ireland, and has published widely, both in his native North America and in the series *Cornish Studies*. Adept at writing for interested and informed readers, as well as purely scholarly audiences, he gives us for the very first time extensive comparative treatment of Cornish folklore, putting Cornwall in its Northern European context and offering explanations that draw from the frameworks of other folklorists, many of them distinguished scholars, including those under whom he had studied in Ireland. But in doing so, he points out the features that make Cornwall distinctive, giving Cornish folklore that 'unique cultural fingerprint', as he puts it.

Importantly, Ronald M. James argues that folklore is in constant flux, not least in Cornwall, so that the tales recorded in the nineteenth century by Hunt and other collectors were not a direct window to some remote Iron-Age Celtic society (as some had insisted in an Irish context, for example) but reflected instead the contact of the pre-modern and modern worlds, of the impact of industrialization upon tradition. Ronald is careful to examine the motives of Hunt and the other collectors, noting their anxiety to record folklore before it became 'lost', but he also identifies their desire to present Cornwall and Cornish folklore as 'Celtic', a cultural proto-nationalism that anticipated the more overtly Celtic nationalist project of W. B. Yeats in Ireland, such as his *Fairy and Folk Tales of the Irish Peasantry*, published in 1888.

Ronald is equally careful to examine the role of the Cornish droll tellers of the nineteenth century, those who kept the stories alive by constant retelling. These droll tellers embellished their stories with each retelling, adding new elements to suit their fancy or to tailor the 'drolls' for particular audiences. Some folklorists, Ronald explains, have regarded this tendency to elaborate and embroider as a sign of folkloric degeneration, an indication that the strict rules of storytelling that obtained in other areas, that one should never deviate from the inherited oral 'script', had broken down in Cornwall as folklore lost its cultural roots. On the contrary, argues Ronald, the imaginative intervention of the droll tellers in their stories was evidence of the continuing vitality of the tradition and its ability to adapt to cultural change.

Intriguingly, Robert Morton Nance (1873–1959) and other leaders of the early twentieth-century Cornish Revival argued that the decline of the Cornish language had stunted Cornish folklore, leaving only fragments to be gathered up. It was a view that echoed the opinion of some academic folklorists, who saw Cornish folklore as essentially limited and little more than a pale reflection of a wider English folklore. It is a position that Ronald M. James firmly refutes, and he turns instead to Merv Davey's more recent (and entirely convincing) insistence that the widely held assumption that 'Cornish folklore is neither distinctive nor to be taken seriously' is simply wrong.

Ronald M. James shows us exactly why this is so, and his range is impressive. His detailed research in the United States, for example, reveals how emigrant Cornish men and women took their folklore to the mining frontier of the American West, adapting it to local conditions (as in the 'tommyknockers'), yet further evidence of the tradition's continuing vitality and relevance. Cornish folklore has been literally global in its impact and extent, and in this important book Ronald M. James encourages us all to look at this fascinating subject in new and innovative ways. It is sure to be the standard volume for many years to come.

Philip Payton
Flinders University
Adelaide, Australia

Introduction

The folklore of Cornwall is often overlooked when compared to collections from elsewhere in Europe, and yet Cornish volumes of legends and folktales represent some of the first to appear in Britain. These publications preserve outstanding expressions of belief and story. Neglect of this material has been in part because it is typically lumped together with the traditions of English-speaking Britain. Indeed, the question of whether Cornwall should be regarded as just another English county or as separate from England is at the heart of why the consideration of its folklore is often diminished: it is the position here that Cornish folklore is distinct from traditions gathered in what can be called 'England' or 'the rest of England' depending on one's point of view.

Complicating the perception that Cornish folklore can be disregarded is the fact that many felt industrialization prematurely disrupted the pre-modern world of Cornwall. The peninsula was at the heart of changes that precipitated the industrial revolution; it did not seem to be a typical, sleepy agricultural land removed from the pressures of the modern world. In addition, nineteenth-century sources described its droll tellers, the indigenous raconteurs, as delighting in altering stories they had heard. This is yet another factor that may have caused folklorists to ignore Cornwall.

Underpinning these concerns is the inspiration behind the word 'folklore'; William Thoms (1803–1885) invented the term in 1846 to designate a variety of popular traditions as well as a field of study initially tangled with the ambitions of nineteenth-century Romanticism.[1] Folklorists of the period hoped to peer through a window on the Iron Age, as linguist Kenneth H. Jackson (1909–1991) eloquently suggested as late as 1964.[2] Cornwall seemed to have little to offer in this regard. It was easy to dismiss its folklore as mutated, diluted and overwhelmed by changing times, at best an imperfect lens through which to view a distant past.

Setting aside antiquated ambitions, the analysis here demonstrates that Cornish folklore is distinct, but it is important to keep early documentation in

perspective. Folklorists now understand that traditions are in constant flux.[3]
Nineteenth-century collections offer snapshots of cultural elements that are
both an inheritance from previous generations and a living organism, serving
the moment. In the case of Cornwall this is vividly demonstrated by its droll
tellers, who breathed life into ever-changing narratives. With creativity to be
celebrated, these artists kept their stories flourishing, passing them on with
their own special stamp.

Regardless of how some might view Cornwall, all can agree that it is
geographically removed from the core of England, situated as it is in the far
south-west of Britain. In addition, it was home to native speakers of a Celtic
language, struggling for linguistic survival into the eighteenth century. In
fact, Cornwall was one of six 'nations' recognized by the Pan-Celtic Congress
during the first decade of the twentieth century, joining Ireland, Scotland,
Wales, the Isle of Man and Brittany in the north-west of France. Remoteness
and distinct cultural roots provide additional means to see Cornwall as having
a separate heritage. The study of folklore presents an opportunity to consider
how stories told in an out-of-the-way place compare with those collected
elsewhere, shedding light on Cornwall and the experience of its people. At
the same time, its nineteenth-century traditions, with their special adaptation
to the environment, open the door to a better understanding of northern
European folklore in general.

It has long been known that legends and folktales found elsewhere in Europe
also appeared in Cornwall. Katharine Mary Briggs (1898–1980) classified
many Cornish stories from nineteenth-century collections in her compendium
of British oral tradition.[4] Despite efforts along this line, Cornish variants do
not appear in most discussions of comparative analysis. This is not to discount
previous work: others have grappled with these narratives. Nevertheless, by
employing internationally accepted methods and indexes more can be accomplished and Cornish collections can take their place next to the folklore of
their neighbours.

The folktales and legends of Cornwall serve to illuminate three aspects
of local and regional folklore. The first of these was previously mentioned,
namely that the homegrown droll tellers shed light on the role of creativity as
opposed to the conservative transmission of traditional narratives. These storytellers employed inventiveness in a way that was not necessarily attempted
or valued elsewhere. The Irish *seanchaithe* (English, seanachies or shanachies),
for example, claimed a degree of fidelity as they repeated stories they heard.
Setting aside the veracity of this assertion, there is no correct way to transmit
folklore. Furthermore, it appears that the flexible attitude of Cornish droll

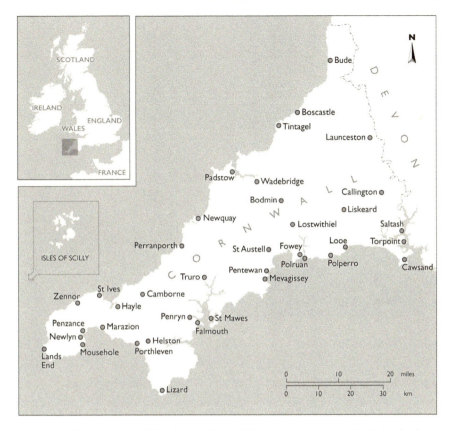

Cornwall is part of the 'Celtic fringe'. Other Celtic nations include Ireland, Scotland,
Wales and the Isle of Man, as well as Brittany in the far north-west of France.
Courtesy of Tim Absalom, Geomapping Unit, University of Plymouth.

tellers caused imported stories to adapt quickly, granting the peninsula many
unusual variants.

Secondly, various factors acted upon Cornish tradition, giving it a unique
fingerprint. This often meant that stories changed to suit a land surrounded
by the sea: boats occasionally replaced horses, for example. This process of
adaptation supports the thesis that Carl Wilhelm von Sydow (1878–1952)
advanced with the term 'ecotype'.[5] His approach to oral tradition borrows a
term from biology, maintaining that the environment and local culture affect
legends and folktales as they migrate from one place to another. Considered
together, a group of stories will exhibit this sort of mutation, and this is
apparent with Cornish folklore.

Finally, it is important to underscore again that Cornwall is a distant place.
How narratives arrived there and transformed offers an opportunity to consider a

1. Carl Wilhelm von Sydow
(1878–1952) arrived at an approach
to folklore known as the 'Ecotype
Method', a Swedish variation on the
technique devised in Finland. Von Sydow
encouraged the international study of oral
tradition from Celtic-speaking areas.

central aspect of isolated societies. Several folklorists have observed that far-flung locations often exhibit peculiarities in their oral traditions. For example, Einar Ólafur Sveinsson (1899–1984) in his classic work, *The Folk-Stories of Iceland*, suggests that his homeland's narratives can be partially understood with the term 'periphery phenomena', which he says occurs 'when a story reaches the limit of its range of dissemination'. Cornwall is no Iceland, but it is a far-off peninsula, and the effect of remoteness likely caused some of its idiosyncrasies. Sveinsson suggests, for example, that because a legend or folktale may arrive as a single variant, there is less chance for it to be 'corrected' by other storytellers if it is outside the norm elsewhere. In short, an outlying place may receive a version of a story that is different in some way. With no means to bring this deviant back to its original form, it can become standard in this peripheral land.[6] This is yet another way to understand how the folklore of Cornwall developed.

These three points can illuminate aspects of Cornish heritage. Unfortunately, understanding is hampered by the limited number of primary sources. In addition, early folklore publications were not based on audio recordings and precise transcriptions. Just as it is impossible to collect more material, nothing can purify what exists. It would be better if there were more variants of stories and if documents more reliably captured the spoken word. That said, unless it can be demonstrated that the published legends and folktales are flawed beyond redemption, analysis can proceed.

Examples may not be plentiful, but this study addresses the deficit by considering a wide variety of narratives. As a result, trends become apparent in a way that may not be obvious when examining one tale type at a time. With this approach, Cornish folklore emerges as something that was at once like its neighbours and yet also different. This is in keeping with historical perspective: Philip Payton (1953–), describes the Cornish as something of an oddity, as industrialized Celts. The role of underground mining, but also of a maritime environment, influenced oral tradition as it diffused from predominantly agricultural regions. A comparative examination of nineteenth-century Cornish folklore reveals a collection of stories with unusual adaptations.[7]

With this approach in hand, this volume addresses Cornish folklore in the context of northern European oral traditions. The first chapter places early collectors in a historical setting, and it provides an overview of their activity in the peninsula. This is followed in Chapter 2 by a discussion of the droll tellers, the professional storytellers of Cornwall who shaped their homeland's legends and folktales. The third chapter considers various forms of Cornish folklore and how they might be interpreted, particularly when employing a comparative method. Parts of these first three chapters are based on my article that appeared in *Cornish Studies* in 2011.[8]

The fourth chapter introduces the subject of piskies, the land-dwelling supernatural beings. Cornwall shared in the northern European predilection for perceiving these extraordinary neighbours as living in communities that mirrored those of humanity. This idea of social supernatural beings is relatively rare internationally, so it is important at the outset to realize how the Cornish pisky and its relations fit into a broader framework.

Chapter 5 explores various migratory legends associated with piskies. These include stories dealing with the fairy cow, the helpful barn fairy and several other narratives that are common throughout the region. Chapter 6 addresses migratory legends about supernatural beings abducting or seeking the company of people. The discussion reveals, here and in subsequent chapters, that Cornish variants are at once like and yet distinct from those recorded elsewhere.

Chapter 7 considers sea-based supernatural beings, comparing Cornish traditions with those of other places. Cornwall exhibited a belief in fish-tailed mermaids, with stories like those in other European maritime cultures. This chapter is based on another of my articles that appeared in *Cornish Studies*.[9]

The eighth chapter deals with a widespread story involving the spectre bridegroom. This romantic tale provides another opportunity to explore the remarkable nature of Cornish folklore. The account of the spectre bridegroom has appeared in literature for a millennium, following a familiar pattern, but in Cornwall, a sailor lost at sea often replaces the dead lover buried in an earthly grave; instead the man seeks to bring his living bride to his cold, watery abode. This chapter is based on yet another of my articles in *Cornish Studies*.[10]

Chapter 9 focuses on giants, a topic that is often associated with Cornwall. Indeed, there are English stories about giants in Cornwall that were not recorded in the peninsula. Narratives about these enormous supernatural beings introduce the need to separate the indigenous traditions of Cornwall from accounts that others told about the place. This distinction is also useful in understanding the topic of the following two chapters.

Chapters 10 and 11 address the Cornish knockers, the underground mine spirits, which changed with industrialization and emigration. The transformation of the knocker into the American tommyknocker demonstrates the vitality of the tradition. These chapters improve upon my 1992 publication in *Western Folklore*, incorporating insights gained over the subsequent quarter century of additional research on the topic.[11]

A concluding section discusses how Cornish folklore can be understood in context. This body of narrative and belief is part of the northern European family of tradition, but it followed its own path. How this occurred is an important part of Cornwall's story.

Finally, an appendix presents a type index of traditional Cornish folklore. This uses the folktale type index initially developed by the Finnish scholar Antti Aarne (1867–1925) and his American successor Stith Thompson (1885–1976). Because folktales are relatively rare in the Cornish collections, Reidar Th. Christiansen's (1886–1971) work on the migratory legend is of greater importance here. The Cornish type index is not definitive; it is offered to facilitate research and with the expectation that future work will augment it.[12]

With the hope of looking to the future, it is important to acknowledge the past. Charles Thomas (1928–2016), noted archaeologist and the first director of the Institute of Cornish Studies of the University of Exeter, took a significant step in fitting oral tradition into a broader understanding of Cornish culture. His publications in the 1950s, *Studies in the Folk-Lore of Cornwall: I. The Taboo* and *II. The Sacrifice*, challenged others to consider the topic. Unfortunately, too few followed.[13] This survey of Cornish folklore follows in the wake of Thomas and others, but even with this, much more needs to be done.

Topics not adequately considered here include King Arthur, sunken communities, ships in the clouds, witches, festivals and folkways and many other subjects, not to mention material from people today who define aspects of a changing society in the twenty-first century. All these subjects warrant attention. One of the principal reasons for their absence is that the focus here is on stories that are easily compared with those which exist elsewhere. For several reasons, Cornish variants of folktales and legends exploring these other topics tend to be absent in international indexes of legends and folktales. Indeed, many Cornish stories that are part of this discussion concentrate on the supernatural such that it may seem to be a preoccupation. That is not the intent; rather it is a by-product of seeking narratives that lend themselves to comparison. An exception to this are stories related to Cornish mining spirits, which are not presented here with the same extent of comparative sources; belief in these entities serves its own purpose, revealing something of the character of local folklore while also showing how it evolved, particularly through emigration.

I hope this volume helps readers understand a topic that is popularly found to be intriguing; the world of Celtic folklore has long held fascination for many. This is also an invitation to the larger folklore community to look to Cornwall for comparative insight by demonstrating that its oral tradition is a full-fledged peer of its neighbours. As I undertook this study, I did not expect to find in Cornish folklore anything more than a poorly collected, pale echo of traditions found elsewhere. Analysis reveals an exceptional body of material crafted by local storytellers. With this in hand, perhaps those who hold Cornwall dear will have yet another reason to take pride in the peninsula beyond the River Tamar.

CHAPTER ONE

The Collectors

A brief story in *Popular Romances of the West of England*, by Robert Hunt (1807–1887), describes a man who was drowned in the ocean:

> A fisherman or a pilot was walking one night on the sands at Porth-Towan, when all was still save the monotonous fall of the light waves upon the sand.
>
> He distinctly heard a voice from the sea exclaiming,—'The hour is come, but not the man'.
>
> This was repeated three times, when a black figure, like that of a man appeared on the top of the hill. It paused for a moment, then rushed impetuously down the steep incline, over the sands and was lost in the sea.[1]

Without anything to provide context, this brief account of eighty-eight words is nonsensical and easily ignored as a subliminal oddity.

Hinting that this is more than a bizarre, isolated anecdote, Hunt adds, 'in different forms this story is told all around the Cornish coast'. At this point, the novice might suspect that this is a traditional story. Considering the nature of these four sentences, however, would be a challenge without something more to guide an analysis.

Fortunately, folklorists have the tools to place Hunt's story into a larger framework. It is, in fact, a variant of a widespread legend.[2] By drawing on the larger body of scholarship, it is possible to learn a great deal from that which Hunt preserved for posterity. At this point, it is not necessary to discuss insight to be gained from this eerie voice that demands the drowning of some poor victim; that will come later. What is important here is that the material collected in Cornwall can be seen in perspective as part of European, pre-industrial culture. That realization opens a door to an understanding of nineteenth-century Cornish culture and its place in northern Europe. A first step in this process is to provide a context for the collectors and their traditional storytellers.

2. Robert Hunt (1807–1887) was a scientist and a folklore collector. His two volumes of Cornish folklore, published in 1865, include some of the most valuable evidence of oral tradition from the peninsula. Only two poor-quality photographs of Hunt are known to exist; this one is courtesy of Imperial College London.

The First Cornish Folklore Writers

Scattered throughout Cornish primary sources are references to folklore and its underpinning belief system. A few early documents record snippets of tradition, even though the authors may have viewed oral narrative and folk practices differently from the way later scholars would. O.J. Padel suggests, for example, that Cornish folklore was behind the Tristan cycle of Arthurian literature.[3] In addition, if Geoffrey of Monmouth (*c.*1095–1155), author of *The History of the Kings of Britain*, came from Cornwall as Padel also maintains, the twelfth-century purveyor of Arthurian tradition would represent another early benchmark for the documentation of local folklore. Speculation about these early Cornish connections, however, remains tentative. For authors more reliably recording material from Cornwall, it is necessary to consider subsequent centuries.[4]

The story of Ann Jefferies of St Teath, near the north-east coast of Cornwall, is one of the earlier expressions of Cornish folklore in the written record. Her tale appears in the collection of Hunt, but he relied on earlier documents. Jefferies was acclaimed as having encountered piskies, the fairies of Cornwall. Primary sources include a pamphlet dating back to 1696 in the form of a letter from Moses Pitt to the Bishop of Gloucester. Pitt, a child in the household where Jefferies was a servant, recalled how in 1645 she succumbed to a fit that left her insensible. Upon recovery, Jefferies described being with fairies. Her story is discussed in Chapter 6, but it is sufficient to point out here that the pamphlet is an example of Cornish folklore insinuating itself into the written record before the time of the nineteenth-century collectors.[5]

References to legends, folk belief and traditions occur in the work of other writers who can be grouped under the term 'British antiquarians'. These include Richard Carew whose *Survey of Cornwall* was the second of the English county histories, this one published in 1602.[6] Carew (1555–1629) was a country gentleman who served as High Sheriff of Cornwall and as a Member of Parliament. His eclectic method, writing superficially about a range of topics, was typical of the period. Most references to folk traditions consequently lack details, and the value of information is the simple verification that an aspect of folklore existed when Carew was writing.

More can be gained from Nicholas Boson (1624–1708), a speaker of Cornish and the son of a prosperous family from Newlyn. His *Jowan Chy-an-Horth, py, An try foynt a skyans* (*John of Chyannor, or, The three points of wisdom*) records a version of a 'folktale type', that is, a story that can be found elsewhere. The text was published by Edward Lhwyd (1660–1709) from Wales in 1707, but the manuscript probably dates back to a few decades earlier. Surviving fragments of *The Duchesse of Cornwall's progresse to see the Land's end and to visit the mount* are also likely by Boson; the document exhibits ubiquitous, brief references to traditions. In addition, his important *Nebbaz Gerriau dro tho Carnoack* (*A Few Words about Cornish*), was essential for the later language revival movement.[7]

William Borlase (1696–1772) provides yet another example of an antiquarian who recorded insights concerning Cornish tradition. Born in Pendeen in the far west of Cornwall, he was ordained in 1719. In his 1758 *Natural History of Cornwall*, he includes discussions about the Cornish language and about May Day customs. For celebrations in recognition of the beginning of summer, he notes that 'it is the general custom of Cornwall to make bonfires in every village on the eve of St John Baptist's [June 24] and St Peter's day [June 29] ..., as the remains of part of the Druid superstition'.[8] He also mentions the story of 'Duke Corinaeus wrestling with, and overcoming the giant Gogmagog, and that fable perhaps founded five hundred years since upon the then acknowledged and universal reputation of the people of this country for wrestling'.[9] His observation may have been based on Geoffrey of Monmouth's telling of this story, locating it in Cornwall in his twelfth-century *The History of the Kings of Britain*, hence the reference to the 'fable's' origin five centuries earlier.

A pair of antiquarians at the beginning of the nineteenth century produced yet another book on Cornwall with references to folklore. Fortescue Hitchins (1784–1814) was the son of English astronomer and cleric Malachy Hitchins (1741–1809). The younger Hitchins was born at St Hilary near Penzance and grew up to become a solicitor in St Ives. He published several books on poetry, but his final effort, *The History of Cornwall*, appeared posthumously in two volumes with the help of Methodist theologian, Samuel Drew (1765–1833) of St Austell. As discussed in Chapter 5, this source may have laid the groundwork for a misunderstanding about an indigenous 'Browney', a supernatural helper on the farm, by combining information from elsewhere together with Cornish traditions. As is often the case with this early period, sources require scrutiny.[10]

Anna Eliza Kempe Bray (1790–1883) did not write about Cornwall specifically, but her work on the Devonian border influenced the study of folklore to the west. Born in Surrey, her life meandered until she married Edward Atkyns Bray, the vicar of Tavistock in west Devon. Most of Bray's publications were novels, but her two antiquarian books affected the perception of supernatural beings in the English-speaking world: *Traditions, Legends, Superstitions, and Sketches of Devonshire on the Borders of the Tamar and the Tavy* (1838) and *A Peep at the Pixies; or, Legends of the West* (1854). Bray presents several legends with the elaboration of a novelist. Nevertheless, she was part of the beginning of the transition from the antiquarian gathering of random morsels to a more systematic recording and publishing of oral tradition.[11]

Robert Stephen Hawker of Morwenstow (1803–1875) also made contributions but like many others of his generation and before, he was more antiquarian than folklorist. Hawker focused on stories about shipwrecks and on traditional songs, notably writing 'Trelawny', dear to the hearts of many who count themselves as Cornish. He published numerous books, but of specific note in this context are his 1846 *Echoes from Old Cornwall* and *Footprints of Former Men in Cornwall*, the latter a collection of essays that appeared in 1870. In an 1832 preface to 'Records of the Western Shore', published with his 1869 *The Cornish Ballads and Other Poems*, Hawker wrote that 'the simple legends connected with the wild and singular scenery of my own country appear to me not undeserving of record'. It was an eloquent call that many answered.[12]

John Thomas Blight (1835–1911), artist and antiquarian, had a career cut short with his committal to the Bodmin Mental Asylum in the 1860s. Nevertheless, his *Ancient Crosses and other Antiquities in the West of Cornwall* in 1856 and especially his *A Week at the Land's End*, which appeared in 1861, include snippets of folklore. Given Blight's generation he might have eventually

3. The antiquarian John Thomas Blight (1835–1911) created numerous images of
the far west of Cornwall for his book, *A Week at the Land's End*, published in 1861.
Blight worked during the time when Cornish collectors were gathering folklore
in an increasingly systematic way. His portrait of Penzance (top) provides an
opportunity to consider the importance of the maritime industry to the peninsula.
Mining, farming and the sea framed the setting of the Cornish folklore collectors:
here the Botallack Mine works (bottom) stand atop a bluff overlooking the sea.

joined the ranks of the emerging collectors, but with his work abruptly ended, what he might have achieved is left to the imagination.[13]

The final phase of Cornish antiquarians is dominated by the Couch family whose work represents a transition between early enthusiasts and the more methodical folklorists who followed. Jonathan Couch (1789–1870) practised medicine in his home town of Polperro on the south coast of Cornwall. Although his interests focused on natural history, he also recorded 'words, customs, and remains'. His book, *The History of Polperro: A Fishing Village on the South Coast of Cornwall*, which his son, Thomas Quiller Couch (1826–1884), published after his father's death, includes documentation of local folklore.[14]

T.Q. Couch went on to co-author a volume with the folklorist Margaret Ann Courtney (1834–1920). His work embraces the approach of the new collectors who provided more detail and context. This was part of a shift that was occurring internationally in the study of folklore. A new approach had emerged in Germany with the recording and publishing of traditions by Jacob (1785–1863) and Wilhelm (1786–1859) Grimm, generally known as the Brothers Grimm. The language barrier proved an obstacle for a few years, but eventually, their influence on the English-speaking world affected the way in which scholarship was conducted.

Folklore and Modernism

Jacob and Wilhelm Grimm and those who followed, drew inspiration for gathering oral traditions in part from the dynamics of a changing society. At the risk of over-simplification, rural, agriculturally-based western Europe was transforming into a landscape filled with growing cities that employed factory workers and the multitudes required to serve the needs of urban life. The old ways seemed to be fading.[15]

Much of what motivated collectors was the notion that they needed to salvage oral tradition before it vanished. Folklore constantly evolves, and so the past often seems to be slipping away, enhancing the impression that something valuable is about to be lost. Nineteenth-century modernization heightened the sense that a treasured inheritance was fading. Because change in the agricultural world could be glacial, rural folk culture seemed static and tied to a remote period. Industrialization and the ensuing transformation of society heightened the perceived urgency to preserve these riches. The realization that oral tradition is in constant flux weakens the link of folk culture with a distant time, but the quest to find gems from an ancient past inspired nineteenth-century folklorists.

Although the French collector, Charles Perrault (1628–1703), was a leader in the field during the seventeenth century, Jacob and Wilhelm Grimm are credited with founding the modern discipline of folklore.[16] Jacob applied a rigorous scientific methodology to the study of linguistics and oral tradition. Wilhelm, on the other hand, was more interested in how folktales could inspire a body of German literature to advance a national ethos. That said, the two worked closely in collecting and adapting stories for publication, ultimately releasing their *Kinder- und Hausmärchen* (*Children's and Household Folktales or Grimm's Fairy Tales*) in 1812.[17] Many editions followed.

The Brothers Grimm created a new discipline of the social sciences by carefully gathering and analyzing oral tradition, but they did not fully anticipate where the path would lead. For example, they sometimes altered the material they collected and they initially included folktales published elsewhere. Subsequent editions improved on this, but the brothers still demonstrated a less-than-scholarly stance by today's standards.[18] Jacob and Wilhelm Grimm influenced and inspired folklore studies in other places where it was driven by a reaction to modernism and often linked to support for cultural nationalism.[19]

The Gatherers of Cornish Oral Tradition

Nineteenth-century British folklore enthusiasts worked within this context, inspired at least in part by the example of Jacob and Wilhelm Grimm, whose tales first appeared in English in 1823. Cornish folklore publications are modest compared with those of neighbouring European scholars, but when placed in the context of England, the Cornish collectors were at the cutting edge.[20] Just as Jack Zipes, historian of folklore studies, sees the motivation behind the Brothers Grimm as complex, the same was certainly true for the Cornish collectors, as can be gleaned, in part, from their own writings. Folklorist Amy Hale considers the 1865 work of Hunt, for example, and concludes that, 'we may find the earliest bold assertion of the contemporary Cornish as living Celts, an assertion that was to have a major impact for those in the later Celtic-Cornish Revival'. In a more direct fashion, in 1870 William Bottrell premiered his first volume on Cornish folklore with a title page that included the designation 'An Old Celt' after his name, a clear declaration of his point of view.[21]

In addition, Hale quotes Hunt's call for an effort to 'gather a fragment here, and gather a fragment there', and she finds in this an inspiration of 'the creed and mission of the Old Cornwall Societies: "gather ye the fragments that remain lest nothing be lost"'.[22] Perhaps it is no coincidence that Hunt's phrase echoes the declaration of Jacob Grimm that 'fragments of belief' needed to be gathered up. Grimm likened these snippets of folklore to 'small pieces of a shattered jewel which are lying strewn on the ground all overgrown with grass and flowers, and can only be discovered by the most far-seeing eye'. Nineteenth-century collectors found inspiration in the idea that fragments of an ancient world survived, embedded in traditional culture. They sought to gather them with the hope of reassembling something treasured and all but gone. Hunt's words, like his motivations, were echoed elsewhere.[23]

Given what Hunt and Bottrell wrote and the context of their work, clearly these early Cornish folklorists were responding both to the perceived need to record vanishing traditions and to the idea that their home was a unique place with a Celtic heritage worth promoting. A sense of emergency underscores the books of these two scholars as they describe how the droll tellers, the purveyors of folk narrative, were disappearing from Cornwall. Both collectors mention droll tellers they knew in the early decades of the nineteenth century, but they also note that these storytellers no longer plied their trade by the time the first books of Cornish folklore appeared in print in the 1860s. Besides Hunt and Bottrell, the crisis of disappearing traditions inspired others; an overview of these early Cornish folklorists is warranted.

Hunt was a scientist with an expertise in optics and early photography. Born on the Devon side of the Tamar, he was educated in Cornwall and worked for a time in London. Eventually, Hunt became the secretary of the Royal Cornwall Polytechnic Society in 1840. Although he initially wrote about folklore semi-anonymously in London's literary magazine, *The Athenaeum*, his most significant contribution was his *Popular Romances of the West of England*, appearing in two volumes in 1865. They were subsequently published together in 1871 and 1881 in new editions with some additional material.[24]

Hunt's importance cannot be emphasized enough. The American folklorist, Richard Dorson (1916–1981), in his mammoth study of his British counterparts, notes of the county collectors:

> The one shining example of field exploration was set by Robert Hunt, who in 1829 embarked on a ten-month walking tour of Cornwall to gather up 'every existing tale of its ancient people.' Hunt unearthed a disappearing species in the droll-teller, an itinerant minstrel specializing in long, rambling, episodic narratives interspersed with song, which he often adapted to local situations. As secretary to the Royal Cornwall Polytechnic Society, Hunt further availed himself of the opportunity to elicit old stories

while seated on a three-legged stool near the blazing hearthfire, or
resting on a level after climbing from the depths of a mine.[25]

Dorson points out that in 1862 Hunt employed a postmaster to collect oral
traditions in Cornwall. He suggests that 'these techniques of the protracted
field trip and the paid field-collector were not attempted again within England,
although they would become standard practice in Scotland and Ireland'. He
also notes that Hunt can be regarded as the first of the county collectors,
pursuing a goal of gathering local oral tradition that later became the standard
in England.[26] Dorson would have done well to include Bottrell in his discussions, but it appears he did not know of his work.

William Bottrell (1816–1881) was born at Raftra near Land's End, receiving
his education from Penzance Grammar School. In 1837, he travelled to France
and eventually purchased property in the Basque country, where he collected
folklore. Other travels took him to Canada and Australia, but he eventually
returned to Cornwall to settle for the remainder of his life. Although Bottrell
released his premier volume, *Traditions and Hearthside Stories of West Cornwall*, in
1870, much of his material initially appeared in print in Hunt's books in 1865.
In 1869, Bottrell began writing a column in *The Cornish Telegraph* and in other
publications, documenting his authorship of the folklore he had gathered.
Two additional volumes of his collections appeared in 1873 and 1880, the last
released just before his death.[27]

Margaret Ann Courtney (1834–1920) was a native of Penzance; her book,
Cornish Feasts and Folk-lore, appeared in 1890 based on her articles published by
the Folklore Society in 1886 and 1887. Her co-authored study of the English
dialect in west Cornwall appeared in 1880.[28] Not surprisingly, Courtney's
research on linguistics dominates her work. She drew heavily on Bottrell,
Hunt and on the Shakespearean antiquarian, James Orchard Halliwell-Phillipps
(1820–1889), who also deserves mention in this context.[29] Courtney used
far-ranging material, notably featuring calendar folklore with an extensive list
of seasonal feasts and divination practices employed throughout the year.

The Anglican priest Sabine Baring-Gould (1834–1924), a native of Exeter, in
neighbouring Devon, celebrated the oral tradition of the West Country among his
broad interests. His primary contribution to Cornish folklore studies appeared
between 1889 and 1891 as *Songs and Ballads of the West*. Later compendiums were
published in 1895 and 1907. Although these works are not exclusively Cornish,
they preserve many of its songs that otherwise would have been lost.[30]

Wladislaw Somerville Lach-Szyrma (1841–1915), an Anglican curate, also
made contributions to Cornish folklore with his numerous publications. The

4. William Bottrell (1816–1881), a native of Cornwall, collected folklore for decades. His three volumes, published in 1870, 1873 and 1880, document local traditions and the droll tellers, the conveyors of stories. This small, crude lithograph is the only known image of Bottrell.

son of a Polish professor and Sarah Somerville of Plymouth, in Devon, his work includes collections of local history and folklore. In addition, Lach-Szyrma wrote about remnants of the Cornish language.[31]

William Copeland Borlase (1848–1899) was the great-great-grandson of the previously mentioned William Borlase. The younger Borlase in some ways harkened back to the period of antiquarians, and his interests focused primarily on archaeological ruins, ancient history and prehistory. In 1893, however, he published *The Age of the Saints: A Monograph of Early Christianity in Cornwall with the Legends of the Cornish Saints and an Introduction Illustrative of the Ethnology of the District*. Its contribution to the body of folklore-related Cornish literature was limited.[32]

Nellie Sloggett (1851–1923) had a writing career that differed from that of contemporary collectors. A native of Padstow, she suffered from a spinal infection that left her paralyzed at age seventeen. After writing on numerous subjects in her journal, she took to the folklore of north Cornwall, publishing under the names Enys Tregarthen and Nellie Cornwall. In 1908, *Folklore* published a 'short notice' about her *Legends and Tales of North Cornwall*. British folklorist, Charlotte S. Burne (1850–1923) declared that,

> unfortunately …, [Tregarthen] has chosen to put her material into the shape of fiction, dressing it out with characters, dialogues, descriptions, and bits of word-painting, so that it is absolutely valueless as evidence. A few notes at the end of her first volume show that she could, an [sic] she would, do good work.[33]

Despite the criticism, Tregarthen's publications contain useful information about regional oral tradition. Although Tregarthen did not contribute to the body of folklore in the strictest sense, the path she followed was no less honourable, and within her material, it is possible to discern the legends that inspired her.[34]

The Successors

After the classic period of Cornish collecting, enthusiasts took things in new directions. Henry Jenner (1848–1934) and Robert Morton Nance (1873–1959), focused largely on language. Jenner was a native of Cornwall who spent forty years working at the British Museum in the Department of Ancient Manuscripts. Retiring to Cornwall, he began his efforts in 1909 to promote the heritage of his homeland.

Nance was born in Wales to Cornish parents. He and the older Jenner established the Federation of Old Cornwall Societies. Beginning in 1925, Nance served as the editor of *Old Cornwall*, and in 1928, the two organized the Gorsedh Kernow, the Bardic Council of Cornwall. Jenner served as the first Grand Bard of the Gorsedh Kernow, and then upon his death, Nance succeeded him, holding the title until his death in 1959. Throughout their long careers, both men wrote important articles and books on the Cornish linguistic legacy occasionally contributing material dealing with folklore. Nance and Jenner did not usually focus on oral tradition, but since the time of Jacob Grimm, language studies had been entwined with folklore. More importantly, Nance and Jenner set the stage in the twentieth century for the advocacy of all things Cornish and that included subsequent attention given to its folklore.[35]

Alfred Kenneth Hamilton Jenkin (1900–1980) was born in Cornwall and educated at Oxford. In 1928, he helped found the Gorsedh Kernow, acting as one of its first bards. Jenkin became President of the Federation of Old Cornwall Societies in 1959. For several years, he served in leadership roles at the Royal Institution of Cornwall. Jenkin's valuable publications are comprehensive ethnographic portraits of Cornish life, laced with folklore, preserving more by way of customs than stories.[36]

The American Walter Yeeling Evans-Wentz (1878–1965) is included here although his contribution is unique and specific. He focused on fairy beliefs and traditions throughout the Celtic fringe, where he actively collected during the early 1900s. Much of what he gathered in Cornwall amounted to snippets compared to what had been available before, but his work is significant as a documentation of Cornwall as the twentieth century unfolded. In his book, *The Fairy Faith in Celtic Countries*, he notes that:

> I generally believed that ancient Cornish legends, like the Cornish language, are things of the past only, but I am now no longer of that opinion. Undoubtedly Cornwall is the most anglicized of all Celtic lands ... and its folk-lore is therefore far from being as virile as the Irish folk-lore; nevertheless, through its people, racially mixed though they are, there still flows the blood and the inspiration of a prehistoric ancestry, and among the oldest Cornish men and women of many an isolated village, or farm, there yet remains some belief in fairies and pixies.[37]

Jenner contributed a preface to the section on Cornwall, adding to its value for modern researchers. Evans-Wentz's perception was affected by his interest in mysticism. His later fascination with Tibetan spiritualism caused his career to be viewed by many in a different light.[38]

William Henry Paynter (1901–1976) was primarily interested in witchcraft and the Cornish 'cunning folk', the traditional healers who often relied on magic for their cures. Paynter's focus on a specific aspect of folklore allowed for more detailed documentation, signalling the transition from the comprehensive collections of the nineteenth century to the specialized studies of subsequent decades. Because Paynter worked in the 1920s and 1930s, his efforts signal the end of the gathering of pre-modern Cornish folk traditions. He was made a bard of the Gorsedh Kernow in 1930.[39]

Three more early twentieth-century authors made contributions to the study of Cornish folklore. T.F.G. Dexter (1860–1933) was an eccentric who published several books dealing with folk tradition, but he infused his writings with his own imagined pre-conversion antiquity of Cornwall. He anticipated those who would later take Celtic folklore in mystic tangents, serving a spiritual agenda more than an academic effort to record and understand oral tradition. Margaret Balfour (1898–1940) published stories recalling oral narrative. As to whether Balfour's work remained faithful to the oral narrative is a concern as she leaned toward the fictionalized celebration of folklore. In contrast, Barbara Spooner (1893–1983) worked to advance the study of numerous Cornish traditions including legends dealing with giants and cloud ships, and folk practices such as the Padstow 'Obby 'Oss, a feature of a May Day festival, in which a large hobby horse is part of a parade. Her body of work is limited, but her writing was careful and of value.[40]

Subsequent writers of Cornish folklore moved more solidly into the realm of reprinting or analysis of older material. As discussed in the Introduction, Charles Thomas made numerous contributions including to the field of folklore, but collecting oral tradition was only a small part of his effort. Similarly, the 1975 volume *Folklore of Cornwall* by Tony Deane and Tony Shaw, with a second edition in 2003, introduced little new material. This is typical of works after World War II as the age of collecting pre-modern folk traditions had all but ended in Cornwall.

Conclusion

As he considered his changing world in the mid-nineteenth century, Hunt described how he became convinced that 'the old-world stories were perishing like the shadows on the mist before the rising sun. Many wild tales which I heard in 1829 appear to have been lost in 1835.'[41] He added that 'I cannot but consider myself fortunate in having collected these traditions thirty-five years ago. They could not be collected now.'[42] In addition, he noted that even in his youth, people 'were beginning to be ashamed' of the old stories.[43] Bottrell also wrote about the changing times: 'In a very few years these interesting traditions would have been lost unless they had been preserved in some such form as the present volume'.[44]

The early Cornish collectors were expressing an interest in what they perceived as a fading Celtic legacy. Although the title of Hunt's book indicates that his stories came from the 'West of England', he frequently underscored the Celtic aspect of Cornwall, discussing how it was different from its Anglo-Saxon neighbour to the east.[45] Writing only two decades later, Courtney observed that 'Cornish people possess in a marked degree all the character-istics of the Celts'.[46]

As Hale suggests, Hunt, and by implication his contemporaries, was interested in cultural nationalism; that is, these early folklorists wanted to promote a distinct Cornish identity.[47] Given this, it is with some irony that publications of 'English folklore' frequently draw from Hunt and Bottrell.[48] In the same way, Dorson provides a final chapter in *The British Historians* which discusses folklorists collecting in the Celtic areas of 'the British Isles', which to his mind included Scotland, Wales, the Isle of Man and Ireland. He relegates Cornwall to the section about the counties of England.

Ultimately, the early Cornish collectors worked in the emerging context of the Pan-Celtic movement. The Cornish-Celtic revival was yet to be well defined when Hunt and Bottrell were publishing, but they anticipated that inspiration.[49] In addition, they and all the others who worked in Cornwall were the counterparts of the many dedicated people who collected in Scotland, Ireland and Wales, enthusiasts who strived to achieve much the same objective in their Celtic homelands.[50] Hunt, Bottrell and the other Cornish folklorists can be understood within this context.

Attempting to discern the motivations and perspectives of collectors is a worthwhile pursuit. Understanding the storytellers is another. Early folklorists occasionally addressed the nature and identities of those who told the tales, but this was by no means the standard. Ireland took the lead in considering the role of tradition bearers, and much of what its scholars have said about the topic can be used to cast light on the droll tellers, the Cornish counterpart of the Irish *seanchaithe*. This is the subject of the following chapter.

CHAPTER TWO

The Droll Tellers

Henry Quick of Zennor (1792–1857) offered a poignant epitaph for the world of the droll tellers, the folk raconteurs of Cornwall:

> Our Cornish drolls are dead, each one;
> The fairies from their haunts have gone:
> There's scarce a witch in all the land,
> The world has grown so learn'd and grand.[1]

Quick, depicted in an 1842 painting (see the back cover), has been called the last of the droll tellers. His poems, including a lengthy autobiographical composition, provide insight into his craft at a time when folklore was transforming. More importantly, Quick's vocation as a droll teller opens the door to consider the role and nature of these indigenous storytellers.

Cornish collectors win notoriety because their names are imprinted on their books, but this overlooks the heroic artists who preserved traditions from one generation to the next. They skilfully animated narratives to brighten the world, performing at the hearth, at a fair, or wherever the drudgery of everyday life needed to be eased. Any celebration of Cornish oral tradition must begin with the homegrown droll tellers.

Folklore is held in joint custody by everyone. Those who believe the veracity of a legend or ponder the existence of a supernatural being are participants in a culture's folklore. Everyone including non-believers share knowledge of narratives and beliefs, but it is a rare person who successfully recounts stories or tells jokes. Some simply cannot give voice to the material they have heard. Folklorists distinguish between active bearers (those who tell stories) and passive bearers of tradition (listeners who are not likely to repeat an account they have heard).[2]

Expert Storytellers

Many societies feature specialists who rise above most active bearers of tradition. These skilled narrators graduate to the next level by winning acclaim and sometimes becoming professional storytellers. In 1945, James Delargy (Séamus Ó Duilearga, 1899–1980), the founding director of the Irish Folklore Commission, presented a classic study of the *seanchaithe*, the storytellers of Ireland. His essay went a long way towards documenting the expert keepers of tradition who roamed the countryside, telling stories in exchange for room and board. Delargy was pathfinding; folklorists regard his eloquent work as the definitive early discussion about those who conveyed popular stories from one generation to the next.[3]

A subsequent encyclopaedic study by Georges Denis Zimmermann (1930–) is a twenty-first-century benchmark analysis of the Irish storyteller. He draws on evidence from early material as well as from the later period of classic folklore collection in the nineteenth and early twentieth centuries. With this information, he constructs an elaborate portrait of those who told the stories. The insights of Delargy stand, but Zimmermann adds a comprehensive review of sources.[4]

With the Irish example in mind, there is an opportunity to understand nineteenth-century Cornish storytellers. While references are limited, it is remarkable that discussing these professionals is even possible. Zimmermann suggests that most countries do not have records about full-time narrators and that Ireland is unique for the depth of its available information. Given this, it is notable that Cornish folklore collectors gave attention to the droll tellers' craft and place in society.[5]

Both Hunt and Bottrell wrote about what they called wandering droll tellers, professionals they encountered in the early days of their collecting, but who had disappeared within their lifetime. 'Droll' derives from French, appearing in English documents initially in the seventeenth century, referring to a witty person as well as to the quip that was said. The earliest documentation of 'droll teller' in the *Oxford English Dictionary* is in the 1860s, but Hunt and Bottrell attest to its use earlier in the nineteenth century when the term was part of the folk vocabulary before appearing in print.[6] While it is possible that the term 'droll teller' was late to Cornwall, documentation of professional storytellers in the peninsula extends back to Carew, writing in the early seventeenth century, regardless of the term used for them.[7] A lack of even older descriptions of these wandering artists does not preclude their still earlier existence.

Professional Cornish storytellers emerge into the written record, travelling from place to place and securing food and shelter by entertaining their hosts. The tradition is reminiscent of similar practitioners in the Scottish Highlands and in Delargy's Ireland, where they were known in English as shanachies or seanachies (in Gaelic: *seanchaí*; plural, *seanchaithe*). Evidence suggests that their Welsh counterpart, the *cyfarwydd*, was also once part of a professional class of tale-telling tradition bearers.[8]

Writing in the mid-twentieth century, British folklorist Katharine Briggs suggests that Cornish droll tellers were different from their Gaelic-speaking counterparts in that there was 'no indication of the careful accuracy of trans-mission which was so important to the Irish and Highland bards, where every deviation from strict tradition was frowned upon'. Briggs continues to observe that in Cornwall storytelling was handled differently, and audiences welcomed 'spontaneous and happy innovation'.[9] For example, Hunt describes how the droll tellers would 'modify the stories, according to the activity of their fancy', to please their audience, introducing 'the names of people remembered by the villagers; and when they knew that a man had incurred the hatred of his neighbours, they made him do duty as a demon, or placed him in no very enviable relation with the devil'.[10] Briggs concedes that a systematic study of the wandering droll teller is needed to verify her intuitive observation. Indeed, nothing exists in this regard to match the masterful treatments of the Irish storyteller tradition, and so Ireland is a good place to start when seeking to understand the subject.

The Irish Seanachies

In his 1945 essay, Delargy praised the conservatism of the Irish storyteller, suggesting that the craft,

> Attained a very high degree of perfection in medieval times to judge from the detritus of the epic literature of the manuscript tradition which has come down to us from the eighth century. But the written saga is but a pale ghost of the tale that once was told, and the personality and polished artistry of the medieval story-teller can only be guessed at by the student of the written word who has not had the privilege of hearing the living voice of the modern reciter of Irish wonder-tales, the democratic descendant of the aristocratic story-teller of a thousand years ago.[11]

He further suggested that there was 'remarkable continuity of tradition linking the living oral literature of the Gaelic West ... with that of the manuscript tradition in an unbroken chain of over 1,200 years'.[12]

5. A staged photograph captures the set for Robert Flaherty's film 'Oidhche Sheanchais' ('A Night of Storytelling'), filmed in London in 1934. Colman 'Tiger' King (standing to the right) and Maggie Dirrane (third from the right) had starred in the recently released 'Man of Aran', also directed by Flaherty (standing to the left). Both films were romantic visions of traditional Ireland. 'Oidhche Sheanchais' documented a performance of storyteller, Seáinín Tom Ó Direáin (third from the left). Consulting on the film was Irish folklorist, Séamus Ó Duilearga (seated to the left) and Robin Flower (seated far right), Irish language and literary scholar at the British Museum. Also present are cast, Micilín Ó Dioláin (with beard, seated to the right) and Paits Rua Ó Maoláin (seated on the floor). Courtesy of the National Folklore Collection, University College Dublin, acknowledging the British Film Institute.

The consequence of this point of view is that it downplays the artistry of each generation of storyteller. According to Delargy, being creative to the point of altering a story would lessen the quality of the inheritance, diminishing the narrative's virtue as a faithful remnant of a distant past. As the pre-modern professional storyteller faded from view in Ireland during the early twentieth century, Delargy found strength in his nation's traditions because he believed the centuries-long, conservative transmission of these stories made this material some of the best in the world for tracking down the 'Ur' form of a tale. Early folklorists embraced this term with a reference to a German prefix meaning 'original' or 'primitive'. In this context, 'Ur' refers to the original telling of a folktale at the point of its creation. Delargy's perception of storytelling matched his vision of Irish folklore as something with the power to reach back in time. That said, the unwavering transmission of stories over generations may have been more ideal than real.

It is also important to note that Delargy does not portray Irish storytelling as sterile. He describes the great artistry of the performance, in the phrasing of the sentence, in the pause, and in the gesture. For Delargy, the process included the audience, the importance of which cannot be underestimated. 'The story-teller reacted to their presence, to their attentive interest and their occasional plaudits and conventional phrases of approval.' Delargy goes on to point out that Irish storytellers did not tell folktales identically: 'Many story-tellers ... give full scope to their imagination and to their delight in narrative, impressing upon their tale their predilections, their shared philosophical observations, and their own strong character and individuality'.[13]

Exploring the balance these craftsmen needed to achieve, Delargy describes the Irish storyteller's enthusiasm for the tradition in his custody, 'intolerant of change, conservative as to form and order and plot'. Delargy allows for artistic variation despite the conservative nature of Irish storytelling. He suggests that the typical narrator he had come to know was a 'true artist' as he employed the spoken word, which he 'stamped with his own personality, and ... he felt at liberty ... to elaborate inside the traditional framework of the narrative the events of the story, and to clothe the commonplace of fiction with the rich garment of poetic prose'.[14]

While Delargy concedes that some storytellers varied the use of specific words, he maintains that stories had to be told as received, 'unaltered, not in regard to language, but in form and plot'.[15] His national pride is boundless as he writes:

> Irish folk-lore contains the most important single body of oral literature in the West of Europe, and its significance for the student of early and medieval Western European culture cannot be overstressed. To this vast repository, from ages long before recorded history until the present, the tenacious tradition of many generations of my people has contributed—and therein preserved—memories of long vanished civilizations and cultures, and the echoes of many voices from the limbo of the past.[16]

Delargy must be given his due. After all, he collected so much and dealt directly with the sort of travelling storytellers, the last of whom all but vanished by the mid-twentieth century. Nevertheless, there is room to question his objectivity. At times, he appears to struggle with the seeming contradiction between portraying the Irish storyteller as a conservative voice of the past and as a creative, inventive artist. Delargy's idealistic view of Irish folklore is justified, at least to a certain extent. Every indication is that its storytellers prided themselves on the preservation of the story.

On the other hand, at times it seems Delargy's romanticism leads him to overemphasize the conservatism of his nation's storytelling. He wants to see Irish folktales as remnants of a distant past, as expressions of what Jackson refers to as 'a window to the Iron Age'.[17] Any culture's storytelling probably represents a spectrum that includes conservatism on one hand and creativity on the other, and most Irish storytellers likely resided at the end that preserved more of what was heard. That said, their process may not have been as strict as Delargy maintains.

Zimmermann includes a detailed discussion of the role and limits of memorization when it comes to the transmission of longer stories. He points out that there is no good evidence that people could repeat, word for word, long stories they had heard. Instead, experienced storytellers understood the structure of the genre and could add a narrative to their repertoire by breaking the story into its essential elements. By relying on the established rules that governed the nature of oral tradition, a storyteller faced a less daunting task when it came to 'memorizing' something recently heard. The degree to which someone could or would take pride in the alleged exact repetition of a folktale depended on individual ability and interest but also on cultural preferences. Many in Ireland wanted to believe their folktales preserved an ancient inheritance, and this affected the perception of the storyteller, the audience, and the collector. The degree to which a storyteller maintained a legacy from past generations can be questioned, but clearly pre-modern Ireland idealized conservatism when it came to the telling of stories.[18]

As Zimmermann concludes, storytellers might claim that after hearing a folktale once, they could repeat it exactly as it had been told, but they 'were probably deceiving themselves.... Still, a gifted Irish storyteller was often said to repeat exactly what he had heard, and could sincerely believe that he did.'[19] The degree of fidelity in repeating a story is less important than the belief in that level of precision. It was the ambition of the *seanchaithe* to carry the tradition to the next generation as accurately as possible, and Delargy suggests that they believed they succeeded.

The Cornish Droll Tellers

As stated previously, nineteenth-century collectors describe the droll tellers, the Cornish counterpart of the Irish storyteller, as fascinated with changing stories and occasionally fitting narratives into their own invented rhymes, always striving to present something new and exciting. Both the *seanchaithe* and the droll tellers occupied the same cultural and economic niche, exploiting the market for a well-told tale, but their professed goals were different. Comparing the observations of Delargy and Zimmerman with those of Bottrell and Hunt reveals a difference that cannot be dismissed as reflecting the subjectivity of the collectors. Regardless of where the storytellers of Ireland and Cornwall are placed on the scale of preserving tradition as opposed to being inventive, it appears the two cousins of oral transmission approached their material with different ideals. The one factor they shared was that both were victims of modernization.

With the Irish context in mind, a thorough look at Cornish droll tellers is appropriate. In 1602, Carew wrote of a practice reminiscent of an older age of Irish bards: 'Sir Tristram [who] led a walking life with his harp to gentlemen's houses'.[20] The parallel between Cornwall and Ireland continued as the professional raconteurs abandoned their harps and found other ways to tell a good story. Both then witnessed the departure of this class of storyteller. Hunt notes that 'in 1829, there still existed two of these droll-tellers', but, he adds that they were not to be found by 1865, underscoring the urgency felt by early collectors.[21]

In his first volume, published in 1870, Bottrell asserts that,

> an old tinner of Lelant ... has often related to me the long giant-story with which the volume begins. It generally took him three or four winter's evenings to get through with the droll, because he would enter into very minute details, and indulge himself in glowing descriptions of the tin and other treasures found in the giant's castle; taking care, at the same time, to give the spoken parts literally as he had heard them from his ancestors.[22]

Here, then, is testimony regarding both variation and respect for tradition.

Adding to this observation, Hunt quotes 'a gentleman to whom I am under many obligations', a reference that is likely to Bottrell.[23] According to Hunt, his source described Billy Frost in St Just, 'who used to go around to the feasts in the neighbouring parishes, and be well entertained at the public houses for the sake of his drolls'.[24] Both Hunt and Bottrell also mention Uncle Anthony James of Cury, an old blind man who 'some forty years ago' travelled with a boy and a dog, playing fiddle, singing songs and telling stories. He was known as 'uncle', given the title as a means of respect. Bottrell notes that James was not a beggar, but rather, he exchanged his entertainment for room and board, seldom staying in a place more than one night. As Bottrell recalls:

> This venerable wanderer, in his youth, had been a soldier, and had then visited many foreign lands, about which he had much to tell; but his descriptions of outlandish people and places were just as much fashioned after his own imagination, as were the embellishments of the legends he related, and the airs he composed for many old ballads which he and his boy sing to the melody of the old droll-teller's crowd (fiddle). However, in all the farm houses, where this old wanderer rested on his journey, he and his companions received a hearty welcome, for the sake of his music and above all for his stories, the substance of most of which every one knew by heart, yet they liked to hear these old legends again and again, because he, or some of his audience, had always something new to add, by way of fashioning out the droll, or to display their inventive powers.[25]

Bottrell adds how people passed the evening 'and other times of rest' by telling 'traditional stories or, as they say "drolling away the time" in public-house or chimney-corner'. He maintains that by this means, 'many old legends have thus been handed down and kept alive'. At the same time, Bottrell concedes that 'no doubt the adventures in these wild tales are often embellished by the droll-teller's fanciful invention'.[26] Bottrell also notes that Uncle Anthony James 'would seldom stop in the same house more than one night, not because he had exhausted his stories, or "eaten his welcome," but because it required all his time to visit his acquaintances once in the year'.[27]

A striking aspect of the Cornish droll tellers was their inclination to use poetry. Rhyme, as opposed to conventional prose, did not necessarily dominate the droll tellers' repertoire. No doubt some relied on poems and ballads more than others, depending on personal inclination and aptitude, but many frequently employed these lyrical options. The collectors cite numerous examples of indigenous verse. Unfortunately, these almost always consist of snippets, hinting at the nature of larger compositions. Hunt's record of 'The Spriggan's Child', which he notes is 'as told by a Cornish droll', is a rare complete poem from one of the storytellers.[28] The relic, which deals with the fairy abduction of an infant, begins as follows:

6. A.K. Hamilton Jenkin wrote a series of books about Cornwall.
This old house, portrayed in his 1929 publication *Cornish Homes and Customs*,
appeared with the simple caption, 'A Cottage Home in the Mining District'.
Droll tellers visited these sorts of places in the previous century, but their world
had vanished by Jenkin's time and these relics were becoming scarce.

I'll tell you a tale, an you've patience to hear an,
'Bout the Spriggans, that swarm round Partinney still—
You knew Janey Tregeer, who lives in Brea Vean
In the village just under the Chapel Hill.

One arternoon she went out for to reap,
And left the child in the cradle asleep:
Janey took good care to cover the fire;—
Turn'd down the brandis on the baking-ire, (iron)
Swept up the ashes on the hearthstone,
And so left the child in the house all alone—

With its 144 lines, the poem tells of the abduction and eventual return
of Janey Tregeer's baby, as discussed in Chapter 6. What is important here is
the opportunity to consider the poetic craft of the droll teller. While this is

not the only example of verse from Cornish folk narrative, it is a complete poem, and it serves as an excellent example of reliance on local dialect. Hunt describes the existence of other ballads composed by droll tellers, but it was clearly a challenge to record these since they would need to be presented word for word and in the vernacular for the rhyming to make sense. Instead, it is likely that he and Bottrell summarized some of these songs and poems, presenting them in prose as the only effective way of preserving the stories in an age before recording devices. Indeed, Courtney provides a prose summary of 'The Spriggan's Child' in her *Cornish Feasts and Folk-Lore*, a book compiling articles that had appeared in the mid-1880s, and it is almost certain that her approach of transforming poetry into narrative was frequently employed by both collectors and droll tellers.[29]

Although examples of poems and songs by droll tellers are rare, a few were preserved. Hunt describes the previously mentioned droll teller Uncle Anthony James as having 'a knack of turning Scotch and Irish songs into Cornish ditties'. Hunt includes a verse that James had composed to the traditional Scottish melody, 'Barbara Allen':

> In Cornwall I was born and bred,
>   In Cornwall was my dwelling;
> And there I courted a pretty maid,
>   Her name was Ann Tremellan.[30]

While the full extent of the poetic repertoire of the droll tellers will never be known, it is clear from the few surviving examples that these artists were bards in the truest sense: they sang and recited original compositions just as they told stories in prose. As Hunt indicates, the 'wandering minstrel, story-teller, and newsmonger' reached back in time, perhaps not with their words as much as with their delivery.[31] As discussed, in the early seventeenth century Carew described one of these artists carrying a harp across the Cornish countryside, revealing a possible connection with a former era shared by the entire Celtic fringe. By the early nineteenth century when the craft was in decline and droll tellers took up the fiddle rather than the harp, some of the romance was gone.

With the use of rhyme in the telling of a story, droll tellers stand apart from many of their contemporary storytellers. Nineteenth-century collectors from elsewhere in northern Europe do not mention folk poetry to the extent described in Cornwall. Of course, folksongs were common throughout

Europe, but what was unusual in this remote south-west corner of Britain was the way its storytellers created original rhymes. [32]

Poems and songs as well as prose narratives were traditional formats, but within that context, invention was key as people expected droll tellers to deliver something new. With all this in mind, it appears that the practice of relying on verse remained an important factor for the peninsula's storytelling. Quick worked exclusively with this approach, and in that regard, he is perhaps not only the last of the droll tellers, but he is also an excellent example of what could be achieved with this medium.

Whether practising in prose or poetry, the droll tellers were ceasing to be a fixture of nineteenth-century traditional society. Sadly, their era had passed by the publication of the classic volumes of Cornish folklore. [33] Nevertheless, it is reasonable to question whether the tradition can ever die. Historian Simon Young suggests that Bottrell was in his own right 'not just a transmitter of tradition, [but that] he was also a "tradition bearer" and, in some senses, a droll himself'. [34] With the celebration of modern storytelling, perhaps Cornish droll telling need never write its final chapter.

Despite the optimistic note of what the future might hold, it is not possible to dismiss the importance of what was happening as Cornwall stepped into the modern world. The fading of the old beliefs and stories was a long process. Although folklore constantly changes, something fundamental was occurring at the beginning of the nineteenth century. Historian John Rule explores the decline of the age-old holiday feasts during this period. He notes that a '"managerial revolution" during the early industrial era began to contest traditional and customary notions of time-use'. The same was true of all aspects of folk culture. Again, as Rule points out, the decline of the former ways 'certainly did not happen quickly or uniformly; that it was happening, however, is firmly indicated in several diverse sources'. [35]

Similarly, Philip Payton addresses how Cornish folk society was transforming. In an essay comparing nineteenth-century Cornwall with the Irish case of Bridget Cleary of 1895, Payton discusses a society as it experienced modernity and industrialization and how people sought paths that allowed for the preservation of their culture during a time when change was inevitable. Bridget Cleary presents a stark example of how difficult it can be to negotiate between traditional and modern worlds. In this situation, a husband burnt his wife to death, having concluded that her listlessness indicated she was a replica left by supernatural beings who had abducted his actual wife. His drastic action was intended to encourage the return of his spouse. The husband was convicted of murder by a court which had no sympathy for beliefs grounded in the past. Transitional periods are rarely welcomed and inevitably some people are destined to suffer more than others. The challenges that both Cornwall and Ireland faced were profound. Confronted with these monumental changes, several enthusiasts sought to record the stories and ways of life that were fading.[36]

Hunt, Bottrell and other nineteenth-century collectors were capturing oral tradition as it existed just as much of it seemed to be evaporating. Many of the legends and tales in their volumes were vestiges of what had been told before, possibly for centuries, but these stories were also part of an evolving process that continued as long as people entertained one another with the spoken word. Ultimately, the old ways were extinguished and these narratives vanished, but it is important to understand that they were not fossils, frozen in form and then collected; instead the publications of the collectors capture something that was dynamic. Perhaps nowhere was this sense of folklore in constant change more valid than in Cornwall because of the creativity of its droll tellers.

If Quick was indeed part of the final episode of the droll tellers, his example points to how much the profession had transformed. Quick made a meagre living selling broadsheets of his poems, the printed content of which was a step removed from the oral tradition celebrated by Hunt and Bottrell. That said, Quick earned his way with the turn of a phrase and like many professional storytellers, he conveyed the news of the day. The fact that he relied on publications as much as on a personal recitation of his poetic compositions underscores the nature of the new world in which he lived: while professional European storytellers of previous generations earned bed and board by telling tales, reciting poems, singing songs and bringing news from distant lands, Quick sold his printed wares to an increasingly literate population. The loss of the old droll tellers who were the source of so much that Hunt and Bottrell collected was a major blow to the survival of traditions in the face of modernization.

Change and the Tradition of Storytelling

To a certain extent, the idea of Cornish droll tellers actively changing stories to suit the moment plays directly into the work of the Soviet folklorist, Vladímir Propp (1895–1970). He maintains that strict rules of composition provided the structure of the folktale which artistic storytellers employed as they created new stories. To accomplish this, the narrator drew on tens of thousands of motifs, the elements of stories shared by everyone. These could be everything from Cinderella's glass slipper to a ghost who is grateful for the burial of his remains. Propp argues that what appeared to be tale types was, in fact, an illusion caused by the repetition of traditional motifs constantly reordered into the structure of the tale. Others, including the renowned Danish folklorist, Axel Olrik (1864–1917), also write of the structure of oral tradition, but for Olrik, his 'Epic Laws' did not negate the concept of traditional tale types.[37]

Similarly, in the descriptions of Bottrell and Hunt, Cornish droll tellers were clearly passing on plots they had heard before. They used creativity to alter stories, but they were bound by the rules of composition. While the result may have introduced new variants, these nevertheless drew on traditional tales and legends. The collections of Bottrell and Hunt can be catalogued to fit them into larger regional repertoires, indicating that the stories were not the product of the random cobbling together of motifs; rather they were playful presentations of older material. These modifications in turn became traditional, for it was the creativity of the droll teller that allowed the Cornish to develop so many ecotypes, unique local versions of widespread stories, modified to suit life in a remote land.

The fact that legends (stories generally told to be believed) rather than folktales (fictional narratives) dominated Cornish folklore, certainly affected this process.[38] The nature of legends influences storytelling, enhancing creativity. Reimund Kvideland and Henning K. Sehmsdorf point out that,

> Recent fieldwork suggests that legends are more typically presented in a kind of dialogue or informal conversation. Unfortunately, there is no empirical evidence to prove that this also applies to the way stories were told in the past. But it is noteworthy that we have much more information about storytellers specializing in folktales than in legends. The two forms of storytelling are by no means the same: the legend has always been less dependent upon the specialist for its transmission.[39]

It might seem that this opened the door to even more variation in Cornwall, compounding the effect of the creative droll teller. But the observation of Kvideland and Sehmsdorf may not have applied here to the full extent; the Cornish collectors recorded extravagantly long legends that approach the formal format and artistry of the folktale. These were not casual mentions of weird things that happened locally. They were complete stories that attained the level of oral literature.

Conclusion

Cornwall has slim representation compared with the multitude of professional and semi-professional collectors who amassed hundreds of thousands
of pages of oral tradition in Ireland. Instead, only a handful of Cornish
devotees published in the nineteenth and the early twentieth centuries. These
early folklorists nevertheless preserved an important legacy. Fortunately, its
indigenous storytellers carried the torch long enough to have some of their
material recorded. As Icelandic scholar Einar Ólafur Sveinsson observes of his
homeland, 'there is no doubt that the stories owe their existence and quality
not a little to a band of exceptional story-tellers who were better than others
at remembering and making the most of them'.[40] From the Cornish droll
tellers and their collectors, it is possible to discern a great deal about the oral
tradition of the period. This includes arriving at an understanding of the droll
tellers themselves. These professional storytellers may have approached their
craft in a way that differed from their Irish counterparts, but ultimately, there
is nothing right or wrong about the choices to be conservative or creative, just
as there is nothing inherently superior to preferring rhyme to prose.

It is exhilarating to imagine an Irish folktale as faithful to its counterpart of
centuries before. That thrill may be diminished in Cornwall, but its surviving
narratives testify to considerable artistry, something that is no less delightful.
In Ireland, the goal, realized or not, to tell stories the way they were heard
certainly influenced the conservation of tradition. In Cornwall, storytellers
were encouraged to adapt to the situation, and this, too, likely affected the
way legends and folktales passed through generations.[41] Invention contributed
to the creation of what von Sydow calls ecotypes, new variants. Consideration
of this possibility provides an opportunity to shed new light on the folklore of
Cornwall.

CHAPTER THREE

Folkways and Stories

One for sorrow; two for mirth
Three for a wedding; four for a birth

This simple rhyme, often with additional verses, was common in various forms throughout Britain and Ireland, surviving in places into the twenty-first century. People used it to predict the outcome of the coming day based on the number of magpies one encountered in the morning. A reference to this snippet of folklore appears in A.L. Rowse's delightful 1942 memoir, *A Cornish Childhood*. Recalling his earliest years, Rowse (1903–1997), an Oxford historian of Elizabethan England, provides an opportunity to consider working-class Cornish folklore at the beginning of the twentieth century.

In his book, Rowse makes approximately two dozen allusions to something that can be regarded as oral tradition. For the most part, he does not offer enough information to cast any illumination on the cultural elements but reading *A Cornish Childhood* through a folklorist's lens allows for a means to appreciate how story and belief are woven into the fabric of life. Rowse's memories draw on day-to-day experiences in an unassuming way. Folklore publications are removed from the original context and placed in a library like wonderful museum artefacts, but it is worth remembering that traditions are at their best when they are integral, breathing parts of life.

Early on, Rowse recalls three traditions his parents recounted but which had died out before the author's childhood. The first notes his father's childhood participation in the harvest ceremony of 'Crying the Neck', about which the author declares, 'by my time it had quite died out'. The second was also observed by Rowse's father, but again it had vanished by the author's own youth, namely the Christmas-time folk play, known as a 'mumming', of St George and the dragon. The third was the 'shivaree', the post-wedding party that a community would convene as the newlyweds attempted to retire to a quiet bridal suite. From Rowse's point of view many traditional aspects of Cornish culture had disappeared by the early twentieth century and were thus beyond his personal reach.[1]

This, however, downplays Rowse's contact with his own time's folklore. Other references to oral tradition are numerous, and many are subtly integrated into his narrative as though the author himself did not recognize that they were something more than simple recollections. These expressions of folklore provide a backdrop for Rowse's early twentieth-century Cornwall. He recalls not only children's games but also traditional tunes. For example, Rowse remembers that 'Uncle ... had some songs of the Crimean War, all about the Russian Czar in his long league boots'. Christmas mumming may have ceased, but the season's carols remained, including one which integrated the traditional game of twelve, known to modern celebrants in another carol, 'The Twelve Days of Christmas'.

Many other references are subtle, mere hints at underlying beliefs: a clock stopping is an omen of death; white hawthorn flowers are regarded as bad luck and as previously mentioned, the ability to predict the nature of the day can be determined by the number of magpies spied in the morning. The accounts of feasts, fairs and an end-of-war floral dance allow for insight into a rich calendar filled with folk practices. The mention of the 'kissing gates', the location for young people courting, articulates another aspect of traditional life growing up in Cornwall.

Witches and supernatural beings also coloured Rowse's childhood world. He cites the phrase 'laugh like a pisky' to describe his uncle. Rowse recalls his uncle impersonating a ghost but he also refers to a woman who looked like a witch whom people believed 'had the power to ill-wish them'.

The author referred to a Cornish legend of submerged forests and the ringing of underwater bells on church steeples, sights and sounds which sailors perceived from below the waves around St Michael's Mount. Rowse says it was 'very Cornish' to regard a spider crawling across one's arm to be a 'money spider', a good omen or so he believed when young. He also records how a threepenny bit was good luck but returning home for a forgotten item after leaving on a journey could bring bad fortune. Taken together, these references hint at the everyday folklore that existed in Cornwall during the time of Rowse's turn-of-the-century youth.

Folklore permeates life and is central to culture. The process of analysis of early collections from Cornwall could fill several hefty volumes, but it is possible to consider a few selected topics as examples of insights that can be gained. Nineteenth-century Cornish folklore is at once consistent with and distinct from that of its neighbours, simultaneously illustrating cultural continuity with northern Europe and the importance of regionalism in developing diverse places.

Folktales and Legends

Pioneers in the field created an opportunity to address the recorded remnants
of Cornish folklore using a discipline that is comparative and well developed.
Pre-modern Europeans generally made a distinction between folktales—
fictional stories told for entertainment—and legends, accounts of experiences that the teller intended to be believed.[2] In deference to the work of
the Brothers Grimm and other early German scholars, folklorists frequently
use the terms *Märchen* and *Sagen* for folktales and legends, respectively. The
Cornish collections reveal examples of both, although stories to be believed
dominate.

Early on, folklorists recognized that over a thousand folktales were told
from Ireland to India and that these stories could be catalogued and studied
through a comparative, geographic method. Thanks to the work of Kaarle
Krohn (1863–1933) and Antti Aarne (1867–1925), both from Finland,
and the American, Stith Thompson (1885–1976), a tale type index provides
an inventory of folktales in this vast region. Folklorists identify each tale
type with a number preceded by the initials 'AT' to signify the work of
these two authors, but now it is more common to see a reference to ATU
to acknowledge the refined index by Hans-Jörg Uther (1944–).[3] As a matter
of context, the Department of Irish Folklore in Dublin preserves thousands
of recorded folktales, which represent more than three hundred tale types.[4]
Throughout Europe, folktales represented the core of the peasantry's popular
oral literature, lengthy stories normally told at night. Because folktales were
often violent or even sexual in nature, children were typically excluded from
the late-night storytelling sessions. In censored, abridged forms, folktales
transformed into published fairy tales or what the Brothers Grimm call
Kindermärchen, 'children's folktales'. Because of the published literary transformation, the original oral inspiration was far removed from the subsequent,
diminutive, printed mutation, which gained notoriety with modernization.

Cornish collections preserve several examples of traditional folktales. Many
will recognize a widespread cycle of stories that involves the sturdy hero who
kills a giant, which is catalogued as ATU 650A, 'Strong Hans', discussed in
Chapter 9.[5] Bottrell's story 'Tom of Chyannor, the Tin-Streamer' and Boson's
Jowan Chy-an-Horth, py, An try foynt a skyans can be regarded as examples of
an obscure folktale catalogued as ATU 910A, 'Wise through Experience'.
Hunt's 'Cornish Teeny Tiny or Gimme my Teeth' is an example of ATU 990,
'The Seemingly Dead Revives'. Both Bottrell and Hunt preserve the story of
'Duffy and the Devil', which is a Cornish variant of folktale type ATU 500,

made famous by the English story of 'Tom Tit Tot' and the Grimm's tale of 'Rumpelstilzchen'.

Bottrell also recalls the storyteller Uncle Anthony James singing a version of the 'Lenore Legend'. This describes a maiden and her dead lover who tries to persuade the young woman to accompany him to the world of shadows. Although this story appears in the folktale type index as ATU 365, 'The Dead Bridegroom Carries off his Bride (Lenore)', it was frequently told to be believed. The Cornish examples, which include material from Hunt, appear to be legends, as discussed in Chapter 8.[6] Apparently, some other Cornish variants of folktales were also believed to be true, crossing into the realm of legend. For all the rigidity of academic classification systems, people often told legends as elaborate pieces of fiction, and folktales sometimes became legends, narratives to be believed.

One of the problems in studying Cornish folklore is that the Aarne–Thompson index does not identify Cornish variants of these tale types. This is in part because Bottrell, Hunt and other Cornish sources do not appear in their bibliography. Owing to this oversight, a comprehensive index of Cornish folktales and legends is crucial for future research. Of equal significance is the fact that those who do study the folklore of Cornwall frequently regard it as part of English culture. The result is that Cornish stories are either overlooked or blurred together with those of Cornwall's eastern neighbour.

Yet another reason that Cornish folklore has been disregarded is grounded in the prevalence of legends in its collections. Folklorists were slow to study legends and to realize that many of them had diffused in the same way that folktales had travelled far distances. The study of legends is rooted to a certain extent in von Sydow's early interest in the genre. Among his numerous contributions are invented or adapted words pertaining to legends, which many now regard as excessive. Nevertheless, some of his terms are useful.

For example, von Sydow coined the term 'memorates', which are short, first-person accounts of one's own experience. Although these narratives may be enthralling, other people are not likely to repeat them and transform them into stories that migrate. There were also traditional legends, often more complex stories that diffused across regions and fell into patterns which folklorists organize by 'types'. When it comes to these sorts of accounts as mentioned earlier, it is best to look to the Norwegian folklorist Reidar Th. Christiansen (1886–1971) and his index of 'migratory legends'.[7] Many nineteenth-century Cornish stories of the supernatural tended to be elaborate, moving beyond the memorate and pointing in the direction of the migratory legend.

The idea that the supernatural exists in various forms is intimately tied to legendary material because belief is best expressed in stories. Legends define and communicate the nature of the supernatural. Numerous Cornish variants of a legend involving people who attempt to steal treasure from piskies focus on the danger of the situation. These examples entwined story and belief, serving to remind people that encounters with these entities could be perilous and that the fairy world was best avoided and accorded respect. Although the classification is not clear, the Cornish accounts seem to follow the pattern of Migratory Legend type, ML 6045, 'Drinking Cup Stolen from the Fairies', described in Christiansen's index.[8]

Cornish examples of the 'Midwife to the Fairies' can be grouped into another type of legend spread throughout Europe. Hunt published three versions of the story which include the motif of an ointment intended exclusively for the newborn fairy. The human midwife wipes her eye with the balm and as a result can see supernatural beings. When she encounters the baby fairy's father once the ointment has changed her sight, it becomes clear to him that she must have used the magical substance and has acquired the power intended only for those of the otherworld. The story frequently ends with the supernatural being taking away the sight of the woman's offending eye. Christiansen classifies the story as ML 5070, and although it was well known elsewhere, Cornish variants take on their own unique cast, as described in Chapter 6.

It is possible to identify many other stories from Hunt and Bottrell in a similar way: Briggs classifies the well-known Cornish story of 'Lutey and the Mermaid', as a variant of ML 4080, but the issue is complicated as discussed in Chapter 7.[9] There are more stories from Cornwall that match classification schemes for the larger region. For example, as described at the beginning of Chapter 1, Hunt mentions a narrative that 'is told all around the Cornish coast', in which a voice declares 'the hour is come but the man is not'. At that point, according to Hunt's text, someone is magically compelled to rush into the ocean and drown. Christiansen classifies this widely distributed legend as ML 4050. Again, variants of this story occur throughout Scandinavia, Ireland and the rest of Britain.[10]

With each of these examples, analysis begins with an examination of variants collected elsewhere to understand similarities and differences. It is then possible to consider how the traditions correspond to the Cornish belief system and how the folklore of the peninsula compares with that of neighbouring cultures. Comparative analysis dominates much of the subsequent chapters. All that need be said here is that most Cornish stories have counterparts elsewhere and that understanding them in their regional context is the best way to learn from this material.

It is also possible to conclude at the outset that Cornish oral tradition described supernatural beings which were consistent with those of the rest of northern Europe. Much of the region shares a unique idea that some supernatural beings lived in family groups in otherworldly villages that mirrored human society. People referred to them by terms including 'elves' and 'fairies' but also *sidhe* in Ireland and the Scottish Highlands, and troll, *huldrefolk* and other names in Scandinavia. The Cornish had a well-developed array of words for the fairy folk including 'piskies', 'spriggans' and 'knockers' to cite but a few examples, each allegedly with specific characteristics and roles; the problem with these distinctions is discussed in Chapter 4. The northern European tradition was different from what could typically be found among continental Europeans who generally regarded supernatural beings as acting alone or at most in small, homogeneous groups (often in pairs or threes). Cornish supernatural beings were part of a continuous tradition that spanned from Denmark and Sweden to Iceland and from all of Britain and Ireland to Brittany.[11]

This is only a limited sample of how modern folklorists can work with stories that early Cornish collectors documented. International systems of classification refer to sources and previous studies from a wide variety of nations. Legends and folktales in Cornwall belong to a larger European tradition and attempts to learn from the material should begin with the body of scholarship that has tackled the subject elsewhere. With this method, it is possible to place Cornish tradition in context, defining it along a spectrum of possibilities by demonstrating its shared and distinct characteristics.[12]

At the outset, it is important to acknowledge that the lack of extensive sources limits the analysis that can occur when investigating Cornish folktales and legends. American folklorist Alan Dundes (1934–2005) points out that the examination of oral tradition based on limited variants can provide insubstantial results:

> one can easily understand why professional folklorists are so appalled when amateurs restrict their analysis of folktales to just a single version—as often as not the German version, which it turns out is a synthetic, conflated, composite text never originally told in that form by any German nineteenth-century informant.[13]

The consequence of Dundes's observation in relation to Cornish folklore studies could be regarded as devastating. When it comes to Cornwall, there is no professionally collected material meeting the standard Dundes describes, and variants are rare. Nevertheless, it is possible to glean a great deal from the published sources that do exist.

7. An illustration by Joseph Blight for William Bottrell's 1873 volume shows a woman about to pass her infant through the famed Mên-an-Tol, a Neolithic megalith near Madron in the west of Cornwall. People believed that handing a baby through the aperture constituted a rebirth that could cure an ill child; the lithograph expresses a folk belief about disease and the effectiveness of a magical practice.

Cornwall lacks extensive archives with a multitude of variants of legend and folktale types, but the material that it does have need not be ignored. When a story is an obvious variant of a well-known, widespread legend or folktale, its mere occurrence in a Cornish publication means something. A certain amount of caution is warranted when working exclusively with nineteenth-century published variants that are either in isolation or represented with only a few examples. Nevertheless, analysis can be strengthened by drawing on examples of several types, considered together as a group and compared collectively to their international counterparts to determine how the entire body of tradition is distinguished from others in the region.

Cornish Folkways

Many early European folklorists focused on folktales and legends, but Cornwall is also graced with sources that reveal a great deal about practices referred to as 'folkways'. While Rowse recalls these sorts of traditions in his memoir, many others describe them as well; these expressions of folk culture warrant attention. Calendar customs, magical practices, and a wide variety of other cultural components including architecture, crafts, festivals, food, dances, ballads, jokes, dramas and games fall under this umbrella. These aspects of Cornish folklore can be understood as distinct examples of similar traditions, helping to define the unique character of the people west of the River Tamar.[14]

Even a cursory summary of the possibilities would exceed what is appropriate here, but a single example, well known to enthusiasts of Cornish folk culture, may suffice to demonstrate the possibilities. Hunt, Courtney, Jenkin and others document a ritual known as 'Crying the Neck'. As noted, Rowse also mentions it. The practice celebrated the end of the harvest using a phrase of unclear origin and meaning. Sources describe the ceremony in various ways. In one case, a reaper cut and plaited the last stalks and raised them up, while workers gathered into three groups. The first shouted three times, 'We have it'. The next answered three times, 'What 'av 'ee?'. The third replied, again three times, 'A neck!'. This was answered by all with a cheer. Sometimes everyone stood in a circle with the person holding the neck in the centre. Hunt describes the group starting the chant with 'The neck' followed by 'We yen!' which he translates as 'we have ended'. Thomas disputes this translation and suggests, instead, that the meaning is 'We hae 'im!'. The plaited stalks hung with honour on a wall, often near the hearth of the farmhouse.[15]

Some sources mention a second phase of the ceremony involving a young man who raced with the neck to the farmhouse. There, a female servant stood guard with a bucket of water, and if the man managed to enter the house without being drenched, he could steal a kiss from the woman who had failed at her task. 'Crying the Neck' nearly died out in the twentieth century, presumably in part because mechanized harvesting reduced the workforce and changed the dynamics of the process. Nevertheless, the tradition enjoyed a revival thanks to the Old Cornwall Society. The term 'Crying the Neck' also appears in Devon and South Wales and it is clearly part of a larger tradition that used other phrases elsewhere in Britain for similar rituals.[16]

The pioneering Scottish anthropologist James Frazer (1854–1941) incorporates the practice of 'Crying the Neck' and its other British counterparts into a larger discussion about a figure he calls 'the corn mother'. For Frazer, these practices echo imagined Neolithic rituals that involved sacrifices to ensure the bounty of the harvest. Thomas subsequently takes up the motif in his treatment of Cornish folklore, embracing Frazer's conclusion that the folk memory of ancient sacrifices surfaced in recorded Cornish folkways.[17]

8. 'Crying the Neck' near Towednack in 1928, appearing in *Cornish Homes and Customs* by A.K. Hamilton Jenkin, who could only document a remnant of the custom. By this time, the ceremony had faded from tradition and was emerging in a resuscitated form. Attendees are spectators in hats, coats and ties; gone are the exhausted workers who shouted out the responses in celebration of completing the toil of harvest.

Jacqueline Simpson and Steve Roud in *A Dictionary of English Folklore* cite the existence of numerous harvest effigies from various places in Britain, and they provide an eloquent critique of Frazer. They point out how attempts to understand these sorts of harvest ceremonies have been 'stultified by the tacit acceptance of J.G. Frazer's theories'. In addition, they describe how the failure to reconsider this folk practice is overdue since 'Frazer's ideas have long been discredited'. In a call to action, Simpson and Roud conclude that 'we still need to move on to a post-Frazer era'.[18] This raises the question then as to what can now be said about the practice of 'Crying the Neck' in south-west Britain.

Pre-industrial northern European farmers typically believed that the vitality of the whole crop remained in the field until the final stalk had been cut and workers had corralled the strength of all the grain into the last corner. Legends from Scandinavia, for example, speak of the risk presented by this concentration of the harvest's potency. Stories told of witches and supernatural beings trying to steal the last grain, because with it, they could take everything that was good about the entire field, leaving the farmer with a crop that would fail to provide nourishment.[19] In those places where farmers believed this was a threat, they often adopted rituals that would protect the last stalks, even though this quantity was insignificant compared with the entire harvest.

The Cornish practice of 'Crying the Neck' fits into wider regional practices of magically safeguarding the harvest's essence from theft at the critical moment. The tradition is at once consistent with what occurred elsewhere while also being unique in its own specific details. Examining this custom as part of wider traditions provides a means of understanding Cornish folklore as something that occupies a place within the greater region but which at the same time remains distinct. By the time the 'Crying the Neck' ceremony was recorded, most participants probably did not know about any deeper meaning in the event. It was merely a common, age-old practice.[20] Folklorists sometimes refer to this sort of holdover as a blind motif; that is, people retain a custom but have forgotten its significance. Suggesting what it meant based on contemporary or near-contemporary observations from elsewhere is problematic in its own way, but it is less extravagant than inventing a Neolithic explanation, reaching back thousands of years into the past with nothing more than speculation, as Frazer had done.[21]

Conclusion

A few observations are possible when considering the pioneering collections of Cornish oral tradition. Firstly, there needs to be caution against a widespread perception throughout Europe that what was disappearing was better than what followed. Besides drawing on the power of nostalgia, this concept was based on the idea that rural European societies were static before industrialization, inspiring people to regard folklore as something of a fixed bedrock dating back to a remote golden age. Although change sometimes seemed glacial before the twentieth century, it is understood that culture is dynamic and is in a state of constant transformation, however gradual. What is more, variation from place to place and between individuals was considerable, so collected oral tradition, no matter from what period, does not reflect the definitive expression of a culture. To some extent, early scholars sought to reconstruct the 'true' primal folklore of a bygone time, attempting to find the original or 'Ur' form of tale types, legends and cultural practices such as a harvest-time sacrifice. That goal usually proved elusive if not unattainable, but this does not diminish the value of the collections. Bottrell, Hunt, Courtney and others who documented tradition provide portraits of a Cornwall in transition.

Secondly, the study of Cornish folklore should be mindful of related traditions that extended from Scandinavia to Ireland. At the same time, whether considered in a Celtic, English, or northern European context, the Cornish legacy has a distinct stamp. Its early collectors amassed material that represents an opportunity to illuminate what is known about the oral traditions of Cornwall before modernization profoundly changed the region, and in this way, its legends and folktales have the potential to add a new dimension to the study of European oral tradition.

Finally, folklorists have developed a sophisticated, comparative means for analysis when exploring the traditions. Consequently, the door stands open to extract new insights from the publications of its early collectors. As Dundes comments,

> if one were asked to indicate the single most important character-istic of practitioners of international folkloristics, it would be their unswerving commitment to a comparative perspective. Unlike folklorists who are content to restrict themselves to local, regional, or even national traditions, the internationally-minded scholar is ever seeking to relate such traditions to a wider context.[22]

This comparative method of the folklorist dominates the subsequent chapters.

CHAPTER FOUR

Piskies, Spriggans and Buccas

Bottrell published 'The Fairy Dwelling on Selena Moor' in his second volume of *Traditions and Hearthside Stories of West Cornwall*, which appeared in 1873. The legend consists of one of the more elaborate descriptions of Cornish piskies, the fairies of the peninsula. Its details generally concur with other northern European material, and yet some motifs bear the unique stamp of Cornwall. The story tells of William Noy, a west Cornish farmer who one night decided to take a shortcut through Selena Moor on his way home. People searched for him for three days until they heard his dog howling and his horse neighing. The rescue party found the animals within a half mile of the farmer's home. The horse led them to a derelict barn where they found Noy asleep.

The people woke the farmer, who was bewildered and surprised to see that it was morning, and even more astonished to learn that three days had passed. He told of an amazing journey through a country unknown to him. He saw lights and heard distant music and hurried towards them until he reached a point where his dog and horse would go no farther, so he hitched them to a thorn tree. He proceeded through a beautiful orchard and found a house where hundreds of richly dressed revellers danced and sat drinking at tables. The people, like their benches, tables and cups, seemed small in stature. Noy found himself standing next to a young woman, dressed in white, and taller than the others, playing tambourine.

After a while, the woman drew the farmer aside to the orchard, and he recognized her to be Grace Hutchins, a former sweetheart who had died several years before. She warned him against kissing her, which was his first inclination, and she also cautioned him against eating anything served in that enchanted place. Hutchins described how the fairies had exchanged her with a changeling, a lifeless substitute, often called a stock, that people had buried in her place. She said that she, too, had taken a shortcut across Selena Moor, and that lost, had found herself in an orchard where she picked and ate a plum. She fell in a faint and when she awoke, the little people were around her, rejoicing at their human captive. Hutchins went on to explain that they too had been

9. People who stumbled into the enthralling piskie world were in mortal danger. W.H.C. Groome painted this for *North Cornwall Fairies and Legends* by Enys Tregarthen, published in 1906. Tregarthen fictionalized folk narratives, but this image encapsulates the real fear of confronting the supernatural as expressed in legends.

mortals long ago, but that they now lived as shadows of their former selves, eating bitter seeds and berries that took on the appearance of ruddy apples and other delicious fruits.

Noy said he asked if any babies had been born to the fairies, and Hutchins explained that there had been an occasional birth. She also said that they were not Christians but rather star worshippers. But she also described some satisfaction with her life since she had gained the ability to transform into a small bird and fly around him.

When Hutchins' supernatural masters called for her to return to the feast, Noy decided he would try to rescue them both. He took his gloves from his pocket, turned them inside out, and threw them among the fairies. At once, they all disappeared, but his former betrothed also vanished with them, and he was left standing alone in the derelict barn. He felt something strike his head, and he fell to the ground, where he was found by his rescuers. After returning from the enchanted place, Noy languished and never regained any interest in his life.[1]

Types of Stories

As described in Chapter 3, folklorists rely on a system of classification of a certain kind of traditional story known as migratory legends to conduct comparative studies across various cultures. This, however, is only one form of legend, a narration told to be believed. As previously mentioned, von Sydow also identified legends that he called 'memorates'.[2] These are anecdotes about individual experiences.

How someone understands an unusual experience is framed by the beliefs of that person. Strange lights in the sky in the nineteenth century could have been interpreted in many ways, but the possibilities were limited by the traditions of the time and place. A Cornish farmer in 1860 might have understood the lights as being piskies, angels, or demons, but not as extraterrestrials as might be a consideration today. Subsequently, having seen something unusual within his own time's cultural context, the same farmer might have described his experience with a short recounting, what von Sydow called a memorate.

Memorates contrast with migratory legends, also known as testimonial legends: these shared common story lines could be collected with variation across a broad geographic area often in several different countries and across linguistic boundaries, surviving over time. As described earlier, Christiansen, a Norwegian contemporary of von Sydow, began the process of analyzing and cataloguing migratory legends, focusing on Scandinavian material. With

Christiansen's work as a guide, it quickly became apparent that many variants of his Nordic stories appeared in Britain and Ireland, as well as in other northern European countries.

Some folklorists may have been inclined to pass over Bottrell's work because the nineteenth-century collector documents memorates, a form of narrative that does not lend itself to comparative study. His commitment to recording material from each community, particularly in his first volume, resulted in the compilation of many personal, first-hand recollections that were not repeated over time and consequently could not be found in other places in Cornwall or anywhere else. While the plots of isolated personal accounts cannot be studied with the comparative tools of the folklorist, the underlying beliefs revealed by the memorates are nevertheless of considerable value.

What early collectors including Bottrell and Hunt were trying to achieve was remarkable since they sought to publish a full gamut of folk narrative. In the case of Bottrell, this often appeared in print much as he probably heard it, as evidenced by the rambling nature of many of his stories; most nineteenth-century collectors would have abridged this sort of discourse into tidy tales for publication. The oral recollections in Bottrell's volumes are valuable because in addition to more traditional stories, they capture day-to-day chatter filled with assumptions about the world and its sometimes eerie nature.

For example, in his first volume, Bottrell describes a lack of 'any legendary tale connected with Newlyn worth repeating'. He was left to gather more conversational material. His source was 'in good talking humour; but all the stories she had to tell were mere anecdotes of comparatively recent occurrences'. Bottrell felt the memorates he subsequently captured were of interest nevertheless, not only because of the dialect used but also because they were, after all, the stories that he heard.[3]

In addition to memorates and migratory legends, nineteenth-century Cornish collectors recorded numerous folktales. As previously described, folktales were an elaborate form of fiction, a popular form of oral entertainment. While both legends and folktales drew on the belief system, legends often served to warn people of dangers, particularly regarding the supernatural world. Common assumptions about supernatural beings are embedded, in different ways, throughout the body of collected folktales and legends.

Types of Fairies and Related Supernatural Beings

Briggs catalogues Bottrell's story of 'The Fairy Dwelling on Selena Moor' as having elements of ML 4075, 'Visit to Fairy Dwelling', and of ML 5080,

'Food from Fairies'. In addition, her list of motifs attributed to the legend is extensive.[4] In other words, this story richly documents nineteenth-century Cornish belief while also echoing oral traditions throughout contemporary northern Europe. To arrive at how the Cornish thought of the land-based supernatural beings requires consideration of more than just this one legend. Fortunately, thanks to collectors such as Bottrell, Hunt and a variety of others, ample information on the topic is available for study.

With a nineteenth-century scientific perspective, Hunt maintained there were five distinct types of supernatural beings on land: the *Pobel Vean*, Cornish for 'small people'; spriggans; piskies; buccas, bockles or knockers; and brownies. Jenner, in his turn-of-the-century preface to the Cornish section of the treatise by Evans-Wentz, contested these categories. He suggested that the *Pobel Vean*, the spriggans and the piskies were virtually indistinguishable. He further suggested that the bucca was a separate entity and that the bockle and the brownies were probably later importations. Classifying supernatural beings is always problematic since it depends on people who might not agree with one another and whose observations can change from time to time. Since those who told these stories might disagree with the terms and designations, it is misleading to attach too much importance to these sorts of classifications.[5] Nevertheless, it is always useful to begin a discussion with an outline of belief.

The underground knockers of the mines, together with the mermaid and her maritime kin, were specialized supernatural beings linked to specific occupations and environments, and they are therefore better examined elsewhere. The other four categories are more easily grouped together under the term piskies, land-based fairies. Beliefs and stories about them help define Cornwall's place in the context of its neighbours.[6]

Characteristics

Traditions about fairy-like creatures, whether in Cornwall, Ireland, Sweden, or anywhere else in northern Europe, drew upon many shared assumptions. Having known people who believed in these supernatural beings, Christiansen was able to comment on the 'common background' of Irish and Scandinavian folklore, which consisted of the idea that the fairies were:

> a hidden race, living close to the human world, perhaps even under our very houses. As they are neighbours, contacts are inevitable, and as they are liable to be irritable, even malignant, there is always

the risk of offending them. The fact that their reactions are unpredictable increases this risk.[7]

The Cornish piskies fit easily into this pattern of the wider northern European tradition.

In addition, northern European fairies are the subject of numerous legends. Many of these are shared across the region. When examples of a specific legend type can be found, it is apparent that they have some historical relationship with one another. The analysis of these kinds of stories is the subject of the next two chapters, while the concern here is with the core nature of the piskies and related supernatural beings.

First and foremost, there is a need to discuss the term 'piskie', which appears with several spellings. Unfortunately, the source of the name is not clear. It is related to 'pixey', a widespread word with roots in the south-west of Britain. After various nineteenth-century publications appeared featuring piskies and their neighbouring counterparts, 'pixey' became more commonplace in English vocabulary. Documentation exists to place the term in the sixteenth and seventeenth centuries, but its origin is certainly much older.[8]

Many Cornish legends involving piskies are difficult to categorize because they have little more than single, generic motifs in common with other accounts. To classify 'The Fairy Dwelling on Selena Moor' as ML 4075 ('Visit to Fairy Dwelling'), for example, is to cluster it with diverse stories describing all manner of sojourns in the extraordinary world of fairies. Briggs groups several legends appearing in the collections of Bottrell and Hunt as expressions of ML 4075, but these vary and are without kinship beyond the fact that they are about people who find their way to an enchanted realm.

That said, a great deal can be learnt from 'The Fairy Dwelling on Selena Moor', particularly when considered with other stories. Cornish piskies were small, capable of invisibility, and they lived in communities similar to those in human society. Their food, which appeared to be tantalizing, was dangerous since anyone who ate even one morsel would likely be trapped in the otherworld. The creatures coveted human captives whom they enslaved as servants. Turning clothing inside out was a frequently mentioned means by which someone could avoid enchantment. In addition, the supernatural beings were the spirits of people from an ancient time. They held magical powers and could even assume animal forms. Cornish fairies enjoyed music, dancing and feasts. Even if people escaped after visiting the piskie realm, they were likely to lose interest in the mortal world.

More details, many in agreement with the legend 'The Fairy Dwelling on Selena Moor', are available from the work of Evans-Wentz. He strives to place his collected Cornish accounts of piskies into a wider Celtic world. In addition, he documents the names, ages and locations of his sources during the first decade of the twentieth century, providing valuable information that is not often presented in other publications. Evans-Wentz describes his sources as portraying piskies as 'little beings in the human form'. Miss Harriett Christopher, from the Crill Region near Falmouth, drawing on the recollections of her grandmother 'who has been dead fifty years', indicated that they were invisible by day, that they held a fair in a local field where they danced, that they abducted babies and that people would 'set out food for the piskies at night' or set a fire to keep them warm.[9]

In Constantine in west Cornwall, one source told stories about piskies living within a megalithic monument, helping a farmer and haunting the place much like ghosts. Similarly, Jane Tregurtha from Newlyn claimed that a well-disposed fairy inhabited Mên-an-Tol, a Neolithic stone monument, and worked on behalf of people to counter the ill effects of 'evil pixies [who] changed children'. From Marazion near St Michael's Mount, sources repeated the motif that piskies were tiny, one linking them to mushroom circles, which people indicated were evidence of dancing piskies. Another recalled how they led people astray and abducted children, two motifs that recurred throughout Cornwall. From Penzance, another source described two species of piskies; one living on the land and the other 'on the sea-strand between high and low water mark'.[10] The sea-strand piskies required gifts of fish to ensure a good catch for fishermen. The land-based piskies were mischievous and occasionally took people into their realm for what seemed to be a brief time, but upon returning to the human world, had clearly been for many years. Abductions such as these could be prevented by turning an article of clothing inside out.[11]

According to a Penzance source, piskies possessed a magical ointment which when applied to the human eye, made that person invisible and enabled them to join the piskies. The subject of piskie ointment is common and often linked to the well-known story of the 'Midwife to the Fairies' discussed in Chapter 6. The balm generally allows people to see piskies rather than making humans themselves invisible, so this may be a misunderstanding of the motif by the source. This discussion of the fairy ointment included the observation that the supernatural beings enjoyed 'junketing', meaning 'festivity and dancing'.[12]

Tales from Newlyn also provide details about ancient piskies. Sources maintained that these creatures were either the spirits of early inhabitants or of visitors from far-off lands, such as Phoenicians, who came to Cornwall for tin long ago. With the idea that they were the spiritual remnants of prehistoric people came the notion that they were becoming progressively smaller and would eventually disappear entirely. At the same time, some believed piskies were 'the spirits of dead-born children'. There was also the idea that male fairies 'were swarthy in complexion, and the women had a clear complexion of a peach-like bloom', all with a youthful appearance. They could be seen by a woman who accidentally picked a four-leaf clover together with straw to create a cushion for carrying a bucket of milk on her head. Piskies liked milk, but they could be stopped from stealing if a farmer 'put salt around a cow'. Another Newlyn account suggests that anyone cursed by the fairies could find a cure by means of water from a well blessed by a saint. The same source told of the regional belief that blackberries were spoiled after the evening of All Saints Day, the first day of November, because 'the pixies have then been over them'.[13]

Considering Evans-Wentz's sources, it is possible to arrive at several generalizations. Piskies were small and sometimes invisible, but they were also able to appear the size of humans. The fairies were frequently perceived to be underground, associated with megaliths, existing in the liminal space between low and high tide, or living on the moors. They were dangerous, but while they could cause harm, they could also do good. The Cornish could placate piskies with food and drink, especially milk. Piskies coveted captives. Although they focused their attention on babies, adults were also known to fall under their spell or at least to be led astray. Eating piskie food made redemption back into the human world impossible. Capture could be avoided with a coat, glove, or pocket turned inside out. Many Cornish terms were a means to approach the supernatural beings with respect, but the term 'piskie' was generic.

While people regarded piskies as being distinct from human beings, confusion arose because some believed piskies were remnants of ancient souls. The pre-industrial world did not have clear delineations or definitions, and belief and description could vary from person to person and could change over time. Nevertheless, believers generally understood that there was a difference between the ghost of someone recently departed and piskies, even if some thought piskies were the spirits of long-dead people. These were not the souls of the dead in the same sense as ghosts. Rather, this was sometimes mentioned as a way to explain how fairies, whether they were named piskies, spriggans, or any other term, came to exist. Other explanations about their origins had nothing to do with the dwindling souls of ancient people: popular perception was complex and not wedded to the idea that piskies were remnants of the deceased.

Comparison with Regional Counterparts

With this general profile, it is possible to consider how Cornwall's beliefs in piskies compared with those of its neighbouring regions. Early attempts to grapple with British and Irish belief in these kinds of supernatural beings include the efforts of Robert Kirk (1644–1692), Jane Francesca Agnes (Lady Wilde; 1821–1896), William Butler Yeats (1865–1939), Wirt Sikes (1836–1883), Sir John Rhŷs (1840–1915), and, of course, Evans-Wentz. A truly comparative analysis of beliefs dealing with similar supernatural beings must reach beyond the Celtic fringe. As others in northern Europe share common motifs and legends, it is necessary to consider their traditions as well.[14]

The pivotal work of Elisabeth Hartmann in 1936 set the stage for a comparative discussion of folklore dealing with supernatural beings. Her definitive examination of Scandinavian trolls includes a discussion of the Celtic material, in part because she studied under the direction of von Sydow and his student, Sven Liljeblad, both of whom maintained deep interest in Celtic traditions. Von Sydow fostered Scandinavian and Celtic comparative studies, and this approach persists to this day. Of note in this context is the career of Bo Almqvist (1931–2013), the long-time chairman of the Irish Department of Folklore at University College, Dublin. Almqvist was particularly important in the advancement of the analysis of Scandinavian-Celtic connections.[15]

As mentioned in the previous chapter, the shared inheritance from Sweden to Ireland and Iceland to Cornwall and Brittany included an assumption that supernatural beings, whether called piskies, elves, fairies, *sidhe*, *huldre*, trolls, or indeed something else, lived in human-like communities. By contrast, for much of the rest of the world, supernatural beings were solitary, or at most they were described in pairs or small groups. Even when found in limited numbers, they acted in a singular fashion and were not social beings living in communities. The idea of families and societies of supernatural beings is a distinct feature which sets northern Europe apart from much of the rest of the world, making it possible to consider a larger body of folklore as it was both unified and diverse.

For example, many people describe their fairy-like supernatural beings as capable of invisibility. This was so fundamental that some of the names for these creatures integrate this feature: in Norway there are *huldrefolk*, or 'hidden folk', and Iceland uses a similar term for their indigenous elves. Underpinning the idea of their size or invisibility is the notion that they have some characteristics that set them apart from humans. Many are so hideous that they are clearly perceived as different and dangerous, but not all have an obviously grotesque feature. The Swedish *skogsrå* or forest woman and the *huldra*, her Norwegian counterpart, on the other hand, are beautiful and appear normal to human eyes, and yet, legends describe men who become enticed only to realize that she has the tail of a cow or that her back is hollow and looks like a rotted-out tree trunk. Similarly, many Scottish and Northern Irish legends describe a man who happens upon a beautiful woman, only to find that she has the ability to slip in and out of the skin of a seal. Regardless of the nature of the supernatural being, people stumbled into their realm because of some unusual situation.

Yet another way that supernatural beings managed to avoid being seen was to dwell underground. Again, this characteristic inspired some of the names that were applied to them. The Irish refer to the fairies as *sidhe*, which alludes to their living inside mounds. Similarly, the Danes and some southern Swedes call them *bjergfolk*, or 'mound folk'. Throughout Scandinavia, the widespread term *bergtagning* and its various derivations denotes the abduction of people by supernatural beings who took their captives 'into the mountain'. Although this could be taken to mean to the mountains as a location, it generally meant that supernatural beings took their prisoners, literally, into the interior of a mountain. In addition, there is a widespread legend (ML 5075, 'Removing a Building Situated over the House of the Fairies') that describes fairies asking a farmer to move his cowshed because cattle dung was dropping on their table and spoiling their meals. The farmer obliges, but the importance of the legend here is that it reveals a general assumption that fairies could be living anywhere underground, not just in mounds or mountains.[16]

Another way that supernatural beings could avoid detection was by their diminutive size. This explanation for how they remained elusive only worked where people believed they were in miniature form. Besides the Cornish, many other people thought of fairies as being small. The Irish famously refer to them as the 'wee folk', and for the Danish they were once known as '*puslinger*', which also refers to their small size. At the same time, tradition typically maintained that small beings could become larger and could greet people in ways that made them appear to be normal human beings. The principal distinction between one culture and another is whether pre-industrial people thought of supernatural beings as spending most of their time in a diminutive state. In Norway, Iceland and Sweden, they were generally human-sized. While the Irish thought of the fairies as capable of being little, they did not see them as consistently small in the way that the Cornish and Danes did. Cornish legends attest to the idea that whilst fairies were generally about knee-high, they could shrink to even smaller sizes. And as Bottrell records in 'The Fairy Dwelling on

Selena Moor', there was at least some belief that each time a fairy changed into the form of an animal, it became smaller.

The petite nature of piskies inhibited stories about romance between the two worlds, but the difference in size could be overcome when the supernatural being took a larger form. There were other occasions when Cornish piskies assumed human size. For example, in the legend of a midwife or nurse summoned by a stranger, the woman realizes the stranger is unusual only when she sees him at a market. The narrative, which is widespread in northern Europe, consistently ends with the astonishing discovery that the husband of the woman giving birth is in fact invisible to everyone but her. Before that final incident, there was nothing about the father, the mother, or their baby to distinguish them as peculiar. This shows how amorphous belief and tradition could be: even in areas where indigenous fairies were generally thought to be small or hideous in some way, it was believed that they could also transform to appear like normal people. There are also Cornish legends that portray piskies growing to a gigantic stature.[17]

The image of tiny, flying fairies contributed to the Victorian misconception that they had insect wings and fluttered about flowers like butterflies, little more than charming, harmless spirits. In British pre-industrial tradition, when the fairies flew, they did so because of a supernatural ability to defy gravity not because they had wings, which are a late artistic and literary convention. Nevertheless, the motif of wings became so all-pervasive that it dominated popular culture by the twentieth century. Advocates of the spiritualist movement were convinced that the images of winged fairies captured in the Cottingley photographs taken between 1917 and 1920 were actual depictions of supernatural beings, even though the wings would have startled people only a few decades earlier.[18]

People perceived fairies as large or small, beautiful or hideous, underground or living on a mist-covered moor, but mostly they feared them because they viewed them as dangerous and best avoided. Northern European stories repeatedly tell of those who suffered after having stumbled into the otherworld. Cornish tradition concurred with this. 'The Fairy Dwelling on Selena Moor' illustrates the peril one faced when encountering that eerie otherworld. While Noy risked being ensnared, the woman he recognizes among the piskies is an example of someone trapped into permanent slavery, forever deprived of heaven's salvation, existing in miserable servitude. Even though Noy escaped his brief enchanted sojourn, he languished in a debilitated state. Encounters with supernatural beings ended horribly all too often.

Of course, the danger that the supernatural presented was not restricted to fairies and their counterparts throughout the region; there was great risk in any encounter with the otherworld. Some might object to this conclusion, citing the stereotypical 'happily ever after' ending of a folktale, but this was a form of fiction where the supernatural world was free to play a more positive role. While the protagonist of a folktale sometimes benefited from encounters with the supernatural, legends reflected actual belief in a way that was absent in the fantastic world of fiction. In the harsh reality of legend, people described encounters with fairies as generally devastating.

Although people feared encountering the supernatural, their greatest dread was of being taken. The supernatural interest in capturing people is international, and the focus is often on the loss of baby boys. In pre-industrial northern Europe, young men and women were also vulnerable and legends described them being seized. The fear of abduction by supernatural beings was so great that this motif warrants its own discussion in Chapter 6.

Often tied to the idea of being captured by the supernatural are ample international examples of the danger of eating otherworldly food. Even the smallest morsel was thought to be sufficient to prevent a person from ever returning to the human world. One of the more famous expressions of this is the ancient Greek myth of Persephone who was condemned to remain in the underworld with Hades for eating a few pomegranate seeds. The prohibition against sampling food in the supernatural realm is a prominent motif in Bottrell's 'The Fairy Dwelling on Selena Moor': eating a single plum placed Grace Hutchins in eternal servitude, and to further reinforce this point, she cautioned her former lover against consuming anything there so that he could escape.[19] Conversely, there are many tales of fairy food being delicious and harmless. Contradictory motifs often existed within pre-industrial European tradition.

While there was an elaborate tradition involving fairy food, there were also legends that discussed the need to leave something as an offering to them. Failure to provide food for the fairies, while abiding by strict rules, could be disastrous or even fatal. A modern remnant of this custom is the leaving of milk and cookies for the North American Santa Claus (Father Christmas, Saint Nicholas and other variants throughout Europe). Cornish examples include the idea that the underground knockers required a crumb from a miner's meal if they were to remain helpful.

Finally, there was the perception that fairy traditions were more vibrant in the past. While there is clear documentation of the fading of belief as industrialization and urbanization transformed northern Europe, the notion that these beliefs were in a perpetual state of decline was, perhaps, quite old. This was not only true of land-based fairies. In his third volume, which appeared in 1880, Bottrell observed that stories about mermaids were fading away because they 'so much dislike steam ships that the fair syrens have taken themselves off, with all their combs and glasses to the China seas, so as to be out of the way of the fiery monsters of the deep'.[20] He also noted that stories about knockers were told less frequently and again this is attributed to the rise of industrialization, as discussed in Chapter 10.

There is evidence that people have always thought their beliefs in the supernatural were fading and that earlier generations were more fervent in their fairy faith. Asserting that a belief in these entities was a bygone facet of English heritage features in Chaucer's fourteenth-century introduction to 'The Wife of Bath's Tale', which the character sets 'In the olden days of King Arthur [when] … all this land was filled with faerie'. The Wife of Bath adds, 'This was the old belief'.[21] It is a theme that appears to have resonated over the centuries with a repeated assertion that people regarded those from previous times to have possessed a stronger faith in the existence of a fairy world. Writing in 1997, Linda-May Ballard cites Jeremiah Curtin as describing the idea of a waning belief in the fairies in his 1895 publication on Irish folklore. Ballard then poses the question, 'Might it be that the idea that fairy belief is fading and belongs to the past, is part' of the wider tradition embracing the belief in these supernatural beings?[22]

Although not specifically from Cornwall, *Seeing Fairies: From the Lost Archives of the Fairy Investigation Society, Authentic Reports of Fairies in Modern Times*, provides evidence of British tradition enduring into at least the mid-twentieth century.[23] Modernism affected but did not extinguish fairy traditions. A Cornish example from 2017 reinforces the idea that while folklore may change, aspects of belief can defy intuition by lingering over time. *The Packet*, a newspaper serving Falmouth and Penryn in Cornwall, reported the one-hundredth birthday of Falmouth native Molly Tidmarsh. The centenarian implied that some of her good fortune in living so long may have been due to her birth under a 'piskie ball', a round lump of clay, fired together with one of the tiles used on the roof ridgeline of her family's home and business. Molly suggested that these objects were created to distract piskies who sought to come down the chimney to cause mischief for the occupants of the house. Instead, the piskie ball would entrance them, and they would dance around it until dawn, at which point they would disappear. It is unclear, and largely unimportant, if Molly Tidmarsh

10. A 'Piskie Ball' on the ridge line of a roof (centre of photograph) in Falmouth.
The object, and the tradition associated with it, came to the fore with the centenary
birthday of Molly Tidmarsh, who 'was born lucky under a piskie ball on Church
Corner'. *The Packet*, a newspaper serving Falmouth and Penryn, published an article
(22 August 2017) recognizing Molly Tidmarsh's birthday. Photograph by Paul Richards.

believed good luck was hers because she was born under the ball; what matters
here is that piskies featured in a newspaper article in 2017 without a need to
explain what they were. Molly remembered a tradition of the early twentieth
century and it still resonated with readers one hundred years later.[24]

Conclusion

Cornish folklore about supernatural beings is not unlike that of its neighbours.
Distinction can be found in what is emphasized more than in a unique set
of motifs or beliefs. Like many of their counterparts, Cornish piskies were
typically small, but differences are manifested in the degree and frequency
with which these beings embraced this attribute: they were smaller than most
of their counterparts, choosing to spend more of their time in a diminutive
form compared to other fairies. The Danish *trolde* comes closest to the Cornish
piskie regarding size, but that does not suggest a direct connection. Rather, the

different cultures of Britain, Ireland and Scandinavia shared common stories and beliefs while also expressing them in diverse ways.

While the general character of fairies serves to demonstrate similarities and differences throughout northern Europe, it is the stories that provide an opportunity to examine the unique character of Cornish folklore. The following two chapters explore legends dealing with the piskies of Cornwall. These narratives open the door to comparisons with other northern European oral traditions.

CHAPTER FIVE

Piskies and Migratory Legends

The collections of Cornish folklore include stories that are expressions of migratory legends also found elsewhere. Thanks to Christiansen it is possible to categorize some of the Cornish material as international 'types', allowing for access not only to variants from elsewhere but also to how scholars have analyzed these stories. An opportunity to observe this process unfold is provided by the Cornish subvariant of 'The Fairy Cow', ML 6055.

ML 6055, 'The Fairy Cow'

Bottrell's second series, published in 1873, recounts 'The Small People's Cow'.[1] The legend describes how the Pendars owned a cow called Rosy who 'gave twice as much milk as an ordinary one', including in the winter when others would yield little, if any at all. She always allowed her full udder to be emptied in the morning, but in the evening, she chose to give less. After milking, she would run off to 'a remote part of the field'.

Farmer Pendar's wife thought she could do a better job than her milkmaid so one evening she tried to coax more milk out of Rosy, who promptly 'smashed the wooden pail to pieces, tossed Dame Pendar over her back, and bellowing, raced away—tail on end'. Dame Pendar was so angry that she decided to sell Rosy to the butcher, even though the cow continued to produce plenty of milk. But when the farm hands tried to drive the cow to market, she would not go.

Eventually, the cow gave birth, and although the calf always had its fill of milk, Rosy continued to yield a great deal. The farm prospered until one Midsummer's Eve, the milkmaid was late in returning from a local festival. Rosy needed to be milked and met her in the field. When finished, the maid pulled some grass to form a pad beneath her hat, so that she could carry her bucket on her head to the farmhouse, but when she looked around her, she could see 'hundreds of "Small People" (fairies) around the cow, and on her back, neck, and head'. Many were under Rosy's udder, catching the flowing milk. It seems that the maid had accidentally picked a four-leaf clover when she pulled out the handful of grass to use as a cushion for her head, and this gave her the ability to see the supernatural. The milkmaid subsequently told the Pendars what she had seen.

Dame Pendar was determined to free her cow from what she regarded as the bewitchment of the 'Small People'. Her husband, however, voiced caution, suggesting that she should be willing to share the milk with their supernatural neighbours, for piskies were known to bring 'good luck when unmolested and their doings were not pried into by curious folk'. The mistress of the farm, nevertheless, was resolute. A local witch advised her to scatter salt 'over your cow [and to] wash her udder in brine or sea-water, and sprinkle it about your place'.

After Dame Pendar did so, she went to milk the cow later that evening, but the effort yielded little and Rosy kicked the bucket to pieces, knocked Dame Pendar over, and hastily left the barn. From that day on, Rosy gave no milk and seemed discontented. She and the other cows of the Pendar farm withered. The farmer, not knowing what his wife had done, consulted experts in magic, who tried various spells to remedy the situation and bring back the Pendars' former prosperity, but nothing was successful.

After a year of failed attempts to reverse his ill fortune, Farmer Pendar resolved to sell Rosy and her calf at market. Driving them there proved impossible, and finally, the cows ran off and were never seen again. Dame Pendar never recovered from being kicked, and even the milkmaid lost her youthful beauty and her many suitors as a result. The Pendars subsequently lost their land and wealth.

Bottrell then adds in his careful way: 'There are two or three versions of this story, which differ little from the above, except in locating the Small People's Cow on other farms that were dwelling-places of the Pendars in olden times'. In addition, the legend is echoed in Hunt's 'The Four-Leaved Clover'.[2] This story is much shorter than Bottrell's, but it includes the key motifs while remaining sufficiently different for it to be regarded as its own distinct version of the legend.

These narratives provide an opportunity for comparison with neighbouring folklore since they seem related to Christiansen's ML 6055. Unfortunately, Christiansen's discussion about this legend is shorter than others. While he indicates that accounts of fairy cattle are common and that 'occasionally such cows have passed into the possession of mortals', he also points out that there can be several motifs associated with the subject. He mentions that the fairy cow is typically 'superior to cows of common stock', and that they are occasionally 'offered to persons who failed to keep them because of some rite, e.g. binding them by passing steel over them'. He also describes how the cow is sometimes lost because it 'had been neglected'.[3]

Unlike Christiansen's elaborate outlines of other migratory legends, his entry for ML 6055, 'The Fairy Cow' describes a generic, single idea with an assortment of possible motifs. Longer, more developed stories with a series of motifs that consistently hang together are easier to link to one another because they share numerous traits. Despite Christiansen's brevity, it appears some narratives consistently exhibit several motifs about interaction with fairy cattle.

Scandinavian legends about the fairy cow often focus on the means of its capture, by drawing its blood or by hurling iron over the beast. If the cow belonged to supernatural sea people, there was typically a motif describing the cutting of an air-filled bladder between its nostrils.[4] An Icelandic variant features a cowman at a farm who bit an uncooperative cow on the back, which then bled. It transpired that the cow belonged to the indigenous hidden folk, and with the act of drawing blood, it became a human captive. The cow would not yield milk until the farmer's wife overheard an elfin woman who referred to the beast as 'Lappa' and described how to care for her. The story ends by saying the otherworldly animal became the mother of a line of valuable cows named 'Lappa's breed', and that the farm prospered with the new addition, 'but the cowman had little luck'.[5]

A Swedish variant describes not only how the cow was obtained but also how it lost its usefulness: in this case, a man happened to throw his scythe over a group of cows passing by, which he did not realize was being herded by one of the 'mound folk'. The iron of the scythe allowed for the capture of the cow, which was always able to fill a pail. There was, however, a rule that one 'must never empty it and start milking again'. The restriction was obeyed for some time, but once the rule was broken, the cow gave only blood, and the beast ceased to have any value.[6]

Robin Gwyndaf presents a Welsh version which describes a cow that came to an impoverished couple and was known for its wonderful milk and calves. But when the beast could not yield anymore, they decided to have her slaughtered, at which point, the cow and her calves all left and went into a lake.[7] This motif also appears in Scotland and Ireland. What is striking about Bottrell's variant is how it has been expanded into an elaborate story. Lacking the initial episode about the capture of the fairy cow which dominates Scandinavian variants, the two Cornish examples of the legend echo those found in Wales, Scotland and Ireland. Bottrell's version is an excellent expression of the artistry of the droll tellers and especially of the way they developed legends, which elsewhere, often appear as simple brief accounts. Here, Bottrell records something of near-folktale dimensions.[8]

Almqvist's 1991 survey of Irish legends includes a discussion of the fairy cow: he writes that 'the type is inadequately described [in Ireland], and whether Irish legends about fairy cows, of which there are many, should be termed migratory is doubtful'.[9] Almqvist's assertion may be influenced by Ireland's lack of the initial episode typical in Scandinavian variants. The fact that legends from the Celtic fringe celebrate a later episode dealing with the loss of the fairy cow hints at the possibility that the shared belief in fairy cattle may have found two expressions in separate traditional legends with distinct distribution patterns. Despite Almqvist's reluctance to classify any Irish legends as true variants of this legend type, Brian Earls identifies several Irish stories that he felt could be grouped with ML 6055, suggesting 'the variants ... tell how a very productive cow or other farm animal comes into someone's possession but leaves again following mistreatment'.[10]

It appears that international collections exhibit two distinct stories linked by a common core belief that people sometimes acquire and then lose a remarkable 'fairy cow'. These stories tend to fall into radically different variants that may be historically tied to one another, and yet that is not clear. The Scandinavian legend focuses on the acquisition of the fairy cow, while the narratives from Cornwall, Ireland and the rest of Britain concentrate on the exploitation and loss of the beast.[11]

11.   Piskies, in keeping with similar supernatural beings in northern Europe, enjoyed a special connection with livestock. They were known to have their way with horses, particularly at night. A farmer who found knots in a horse's mane in the morning often thought they were tied to serve as stirrups for the piskies, as depicted here. Joseph Blight drew this illustration for William Bottrell's 1873 book on Cornish folklore.

ML 7015, 'The New Suit'

'The Fairy Cow' illustrates how a widespread belief involving fairies was manifested in legends across northern Europe. Another common story that also deals with farm life, features a supernatural helper in the barn, but in this case the structure of the legend is clearer. Christiansen classifies this as ML 7015, 'The New Suit'.[12] The synopsis of this story can be illustrated with a Cornish example: Hunt's 'The Piskie Threshers' follows a pattern that Christiansen would easily recognize.[13] The legend describes how one morning a farmer discovers the grain in his barn had been threshed the previous night. That evening, he peered through a crack in the barn door and saw 'a little fellow, clad in a tattered suit of green, wielding the "dreshel" (flail) with astonishing vigour, and beating the floor with blows so rapid that the eye could not follow the motion of the implement'.

The farmer resolved to have a new suit of green made so that he could give it to his supernatural helper as a thank you. The following afternoon, he left the new clothes in the barn. When darkness fell, he crept back to look again through the crack in the door. 'He was just in time to see the elf put on the suit, which was no sooner accomplished than, looking down on himself admiringly, he sung' the following:

> Piskie fine, and piskie gay;
> Piskie now will fly away.

Aside from the use of the specifically Cornish term 'piskie', the story fits the typical pattern of what could be found in western and northern Europe.

Evans-Wentz includes two references to this migratory legend in Cornwall. The first came from Constantine on the south coast. The abbreviated account describes how 'a pisky used to come at night to thrash the farmer's corn. The farmer in payment once put down a new suit for him. When the pisky came and saw it, he put it on.' The piskie then recited the same rhyme that Hunt records and the creature then left, never to return.[14] The second reference comes from Delabole on the north-east coast of Cornwall. The source recalled how his mother and grandmother once told stories and how 'a pisky of this part ... stole a new coat, and how the family heard him talking to himself about it'. In this case, the rhyme was 'Pisky fine and pisky gay, pisky's got a bright new coat, pisky now will run away'. The legend here is mutated from its usual format since here the supernatural being steals the coat rather than receives it as a gift. This deviation can be ascribed to a source imperfectly recalling a legend heard long before. The fact that the rhyme is different from the version that both Hunt and Evans-Wentz record may again reflect the failure of memory, or it may be that the source heard the rhyme differently. Either way, it is useful to document the legend of 'The Piskie Thresher' in north-east Cornwall as well as on the south-west coast.[15]

T.Q. Couch in his 1871 *The History of Polperro* provides a different concluding verse for this legend:

> Pisky new coat, and pisky new hood,
> Pisky now will do no more good.[16]

Couch describes another variant of this legend in which a farmer looked 'through the keyhole [and] saw two elves threshing lustily, now and then interrupting their work to say to each other, in the smallest falsetto voice, "I tweat; you tweat?"'. The man then thanked them through the keyhole at which 'the spirits who love to work "unheard and unespied", instantly vanished, and never after visited the barn'.[17]

This story is echoed by several other references to Cornish supernatural beings assisting with domestic affairs. Hunt includes the piskie thresher in his list of five types of supernatural beings. Although Hunt's strict categories have been challenged, his classification system permeates discussions of Cornish folklore. Among his varieties, Hunt identifies the 'Browneys', which he describes as follows:

> This spirit was purely of the household. Kindly and good, he devoted his every care to benefit the family with whom he had taken up his abode. The Browney has fled, owing to his being brought into very close contact with the schoolmaster, and he is only summoned now upon the occasion of the swarming of bees. When this occurs, mistress or maid seizes a bell-metal, or a tin pan, and beating it, she calls 'Browney, Browney!' as loud as she can until the good Browney compels the bees to settle.[18]

This paragraph is problematic as demonstrated by Young who points out that the earlier antiquarians, Hitchins and Drew, had cobbled together unrelated references from far afield apparently inadvertently inventing the idea of a Cornish fairy named a Browney. Ultimately, this tangle of written references, literary borrowings and hints of actual folk traditions about bees in Cornwall, have little to do with folk accounts about the helpful household spirit.[19]

The idea of the household piskie also influenced Tregarthen's story 'The Curious Woman of Davidstow', which includes many traditional motifs.[20] Nevertheless, the account lacks the concluding rhyme and a large troupe of actors takes the place of the solitary supernatural helper. As is always the case with Tregarthen, no one can be certain how she obtained and modified her stories. It is possible that she drew from a literary source or if she had heard the legend told, that she changed it to suit her artistic inclinations.

In his third and final book on Cornwall published in 1880, Bottrell states that 'little is now known of the ... Browneys', using a term that occurred elsewhere in Britain to describe the supernatural household helper or thresher. Both Bottrell and Jenner regard the name as an importation into Cornish tradition.[21] While 'brownie' appears to be a reference to its dull brown clothing, there is no reason to regard the name as native to Cornwall: the fact that the rhymes preserve the name 'pisky' for the household spirit supports the conclusion that the term 'brownie' is not indigenous. Regardless, the numerous references to the idea of a household helper combined with examples of ML 7015, 'The New Suit', provide clear evidence that the legend once existed in Cornwall, but there is insufficient variation to suggest that it developed a distinct form in the south-west British peninsula.[22]

It is worth noting that while this legend was apparently common in Cornwall and other parts of Britain, it was poorly represented among the Irish: Almqvist maintains that the story was 'sporadically found in Ireland—in Antrim and Donegal' and that 'there are a few examples ... from the south-east of Ireland as well and these might very well have been introduced from England'.[23] In contrast, the examples of ML 7015 seem at home in Cornwall, the possible importation of the name 'brownie' aside.

ML 6045, 'Drinking Cup Stolen from the Fairies'

While ML 6045, 'Drinking Cup Stolen from the Fairies' may appear in the Cornish collections, the examples are problematic. In northern Europe, the story usually involves a man on a horse who interrupts a feast held by super-natural beings. They offer him a drink, but he is wise enough not to sample it. Instead he throws out the contents (which often burn the rump of his horse), and he rides away, stealing the cup. The fairies give chase, but he escapes either by riding across the furrows of a field, thereby creating a series of crosses, which stop the entities from following, or he reaches a bridge over a stream, and the running water serves as a barrier against his pursuers. Most variants then describe how the cup became an heirloom, sometimes placed in a church or elsewhere. The legend is often associated with an actual relic.[24]

There are several Cornish examples of stories that loosely follow the storyline of ML 6045. Bottrell's 'Fairies on the Eastern Green', a legend from Zennor in the far west of Cornwall, is typical of this group. It describes smugglers who came ashore, some of whom rested while others went to fetch horses. The men heard the sounds of a party, so one of them, a fellow named Tom, left to see what was happening. He spied upon a group of little men, which the account called spriggans, fairies and 'bucca-boos'. Eventually, Tom could not resist shouting out a comment about how the older supernatural beings looked comical with their long beards. His insolence angered the creatures who chased after him. They were initially small, but they grew larger as they pursued him. Tom ran and finally reached his fellow smugglers. Together they hurriedly rowed away from the shore and the spriggans could not follow because of the salt water, although they attempted to sling stones at the intruders. Eventually, the other smugglers arrived with horses, so the spriggans retreated, and the men came ashore. Tom then 'shouted to the retiring host, "We'll shave e all and cut your tails off, ef you ever show here any more." But the fairies disdained to notice his impudence and presently disappeared.'[25]

Hunt records another story that seems related to this legend. His 'Spriggans of Trencrom Hill' describes a treasure hunter who went out one moonlit night

12. The martial aspect of the Cornish piskies is not to be underestimated. Collectors, probably reflecting popular usage, sometimes referred to the more belligerent of piskies as spriggans. People would likely apply the term to the helmeted, club-wielding character on the left, from William Bottrell's 1873 book with illustrations by Joseph Blight.

to look for a trove of giant's gold he believed was buried on Trencrom Hill amongst some rocks. As he dug, a storm brewed, covering the moon with clouds. With the flash of lightning, he saw spriggans 'coming out in swarms from all the rocks. They were in countless numbers; and although they were small at first, they rapidly increased in size, until eventually they assumed an almost giant form.' The treasure seeker described them to be 'as ugly as if they would eat him'. The frightened man escaped, but the encounter left him unable 'to work for a long time'.[26]

Yet another story from Hunt employs some of the same motifs. 'The Fairy Revels on the "Gump", St Just' describes how the supernatural beings held parties on an open area below a hill. People in the area often went to watch, and if respectful and courteous, they received small but valuable presents. An old miser of St Just, near Land's End, decided he would try to take some of the treasure of the little people. He set out at night and heard their music. Wandering across the land, he stood before a hill and realized the source of the melody was directly beneath his feet. At that, it became louder and the hill opened, revealing bright lights and a procession of the supernatural beings. They came in their hundreds with their musical instruments and 'bearing vessels of silver and vessels of gold, goblets cut out of diamonds, rubies, and other precious stones. There were others laden, almost to overflowing, with the richest meats, pastry, preserves, and fruits.' He set his sights on the fairy royal table with its rich goblets and gold plates, and he slunk about, believing he was unnoticed.

Finally, the old man 'took off his hat and carefully raised it, so as to cover the prince, the princess, and their costly table'. At that, there was a shrill whistle, and the man found himself powerless to move in what had become total darkness. There was a whirring about him and he felt a multitude of pricks and pinches. He managed to roll down the hill, but he lay immobilized as his little tormentors continued to inflict their abuse. Finally, one of them shouted, 'Away, away, I smell the day!'. With dawn, the old man found that he was bound merely 'by myriads of gossamer webs, which were now covered with dew'. He rose and shook himself free, but he left the Gump with a tale of failure and without treasure.[27]

Blight recorded a related story in his 1861 *A Week at the Land's End*, four years before the publication of Hunt's legend. Blight, like Hunt, situates the narrative at the 'Gump', calling it 'a well-known haunt of the fairies'. Blight describes how the supernatural beings misled the typical traveller, played music for him, and 'beguiled his senses' with bright lights, 'leaving him alone on the dewy ground at the grey dawn, when they "hear the morning lark"'.

Blight suggests that while not many would profess to having seen the "little people," yet many tell of those who have'.[28]

These stories include one about an old man travelling across the Gump one evening, 'when there arose on the air a sound of the sweetest music—a soft, a lovely melody'. Leaving the path, he finally found the source, a group of fairies, 'holding a fair' complete with the music he had heard, but also decorated with garlands of flowers. All the while, more of the fairies arrived, and the old man was astonished by the 'gems and wonderful little articles' displayed at this diminutive festival. Blight describes how the man wished to take some of the wealth, 'so he threw his hat amongst the company, and made a dash at the coveted treasures'. Upon removing his hat, however, he saw 'but a few snails creeping over the moist grass, and the gossamer threads bespangled with dew drops'.[29] The similarity of this account to Hunt's is striking, but so too are the differences. There is a repetition of the location, the old man following the enchanting music, the effort to secure the treasure by throwing a hat over some of the articles, and the failure of the effort. Blight does not include the punishment of the would-be thief, many of the details of the wealth displayed, the fact that there was food, or that there was a royal fairy presence. Nor does Blight identify the man as coming from St Just, but rather, merely from the neighbourhood.

Hunt's brief account of another legend, 'The Fairy Revel', describes a man named Richard who came upon a fairy feast, the table set 'with the utmost profusion of gold and silver ornaments, and fruits and flowers'. He 'very foolishly interrupted the feast by some exclamation of surprise'. At that, the entire array of splendour vanished. The account maintains that had Richard touched the table, his mortal finger would have prevented the supernatural beings from taking their treasure, and the riches would have been his.[30]

Hunt records a similar legend, which he calls 'The Fairy Funeral'. In this story, a man happens upon a church, and peering inside, he sees a fairy funeral being held to bury the queen of the little people. As the first shovel of earth is thrown into her grave, the crowd let out a cry. The man involuntarily joined in, at which point the lights were extinguished. At once, the fairies swarmed past him, jabbing him with their sharp implements. Hunt concludes his tale, by saying that the man 'was compelled to save his life *by the most rapid flight*'.[31]

Finally, Hunt provides yet another legend that Briggs concludes has an affinity with ML 6045. 'The Old Woman who turned her shift' describes an elderly woman who lived alone in a house where the local spriggans of nearby Trencrom Hill liked to meet on a nightly basis 'to divide their plunder'. Each night as thanks for her hospitality, they 'placed a small coin on the table by her bedside'. The woman was not satisfied with this, however, and she decided to wait for an opportunity to take even more from her visitors. Such a night presented itself when the spriggans arrived with an especially large cache of treasure. The old woman discretely turned her shift inside out, knowing that the reversal would prevent the spriggans from attacking her. As the little men argued over the distribution of their stolen goods, the woman 'jumped from her bed, placed her hand on a gold cup, and exclaimed, "Thee shusn't hae one on 'em!"'. The supernatural beings fled, leaving everything behind. 'The last and boldest of the spriggans, however, swept his hand over the old woman's only garment as he left the house.' With her recently acquired wealth, the woman purchased a new house in St Ives, but every time she put on the shift that she had worn on that night, 'she was tortured beyond endurance'. Doctors could not explain the cause of her pains, 'but wise women knew all along that they came of the spriggans'.[32]

Couch's story, 'The Fisherman and the Piskies', combines two legends. In the first, the piskies trick John Taprail into thinking his boat was adrift, which was not the case. On his way home, he saw the piskies sitting in a half circle, holding their hats out so that the leader of the group could throw a gold coin into each one, one after the other. Taprail decided to sneak up to the gathering and hold his hat out so that he, too, could enjoy a share of the wealth. As the pile of coins diminished, he stealthily withdrew his hat. He then fled, and the piskies, realizing what he had done, pursued him. Taprail managed to reach home and shut the door just in time, but his escape was so close that the piskies were able to tear off the tails of his sea coat.[33]

In 1899, Sabine Baring-Gould recounted a story from a much earlier time. While hunting in Trewartha Marsh, a man came across an 'archdruid' who offered him a sup of wine from his golden goblet. The druid and his cup were well known, for no matter how many hunters drank from the vessel, it never emptied. On this occasion, the hunter intended to drink the cup dry, but failing with his best effort, he threw the remaining wine in the druid's face and raced away with the cup. The horse fell and the hunter broke his neck, still clutching the cup, and so was buried with it near the village of Rillaton.[34] The story has a fanciful, epic quality that is incongruous with other Cornish legends. It is of interest because it mentions a cup, unlike other variants of ML 6045 from Cornwall. By its very nature, this account is suspect and it is probably best set aside as something that is unique and unrelated to the other narratives.

These stories from various Cornish sources have motifs that come close to the plot of ML 6045. That said, versions of the legend collected elsewhere are significantly different from those originating in Cornwall. A comparison can help place the story in perspective. Folklorist Kimberly Ball describes ML 6045, 'Drinking Cup Stolen from the Fairies' as 'a legend that has been recorded in Europe from northern Norway as far south as northern France, and from Ireland in the west as far east as Finland'.[35] Drawing on the earlier work of Inger Lövkrona, Ball describes five motifs that consistently appear in variants of ML 6045:

A. A man riding a horse meets with supernatural beings.
B. They offer him a drink in a horn or a cup.
C. The man accepts the drinking vessel but casts out the drink, which falls on the horse and injures it.
D. The man flees with the drinking vessel and is followed but escapes.
E. He keeps the drinking vessel or gives it to a church, where it is used as a communion chalice.[36]

Ball points out that early scholars considered a possible pre-conversion origin for ML 6045. For example, Romantic-era authors imagined a possible connection of this legend to a cup-bearing Valkyrie. This unproven idea has an allure, but the problem here is to determine how Cornish folklore fits into the greater regional context. To begin the discussion, it is important to recognize that the account of the stolen cup is very old. It appears, for example, in William of Newburgh's (1136–1198) *History of English Affairs*, written at the end of the twelfth century. This source records a story of a Yorkshire man who was offered a drink from the supernatural beings who were feasting within a hill. He stole the cup, was pursued, and escaped. As often happens in more recent variants, the cup became the 'proof' that the incident was real. In this case, the narrative continues to describe how the hero of the story gave the stolen object to King Henry who then gave it to the King of Scotland.[37]

Whether considering a twelfth-century antecedent or dozens of examples of the legends collected throughout northern Europe, the absence of the cup removes Cornwall's narratives from the basic outline of ML 6045. Although there are outlying examples, the Cornish variants can be condensed as follows:

A. A man interrupts supernatural beings who are having a feast or are dividing treasure.
B1. The man attempts to steal some of the treasure of the supernatural beings; or
B2. The man shouts something that attracts attention.
C. The supernatural beings chase or punish the man.

This basic outline does not contradict the one provided by Ball and Lövkrona, but it lacks some of the hallmarks of ML 6045, in particular the drinking vessel, which is so central that it provides the name for the legend type. The question, then, is whether the various Cornish narratives are tied together as a unique type or if they represent a subvariant of ML 6045 to which they are historically related.

It seems likely that these Cornish legends are linked to one another. There appear to be two variants. While some feature an attempt to take the treasure, others describe the person shouting something that interrupts the fairy celebration. The story of the fairy funeral may be unrelated, and the one involving an old woman is unique because of the reversed gender role. It is difficult to address variants that stand alone, but the other stories appear to follow a pattern and to be linked.

In addition, the core of these stories is close to the basic outline of ML 6045. It is easy to imagine how an incomplete variant of the story, perhaps told without the existence of the cup, arrived in Cornwall and became the source of a local tradition. Furthermore, there is no horse, but this omission is part of a common Cornish pattern. Even if this hypothetical, mutated version of ML 6045 included a horse, it could easily have been omitted early in the history of the legend as droll tellers adapted the narrative to suit its new audience. The presence of a boat as a means of escape, employed in one of the versions, is typical of Cornish variants of other legends.

ML 5006*, 'The Flight with the Fairies'

Hunt's 'The Piskies in the Cellar', represents one of two Cornish expressions of a widespread migratory legend, ML 5006*, 'The Flight with the Fairies'. While the examples are too few to allow detailed scrutiny, these narratives demonstrate that yet another European legend type had a foothold in Cornwall. Hunt's account describes a man named John Sturtridge from Luxulyan, Churchtown, near the south coast. Sturtridge was heading home having been 'well primed with ale'. He came upon a group of piskies and heard them shout 'Ho! and away for Par Beach!'. He repeated the phrase and soon found himself on that beach. The piskies danced a while, and then they shouted 'Ho! and away for Squire Tremain's cellar'. Sturtridge again repeated the phrase and this time was transported to the cellar of Squire Tremain, 'where was beer and wine galore'. He drank a great deal, and in his inebriated state, he failed to repeat the piskies' call for another journey when they took flight back to the beach. The butler found him the next morning, and although Sturtridge attempted to explain what had happened, he was apprehended, eventually convicted, and sentenced to hang. On the morning of his execution, he stood beneath the gallows tree before a large crowd. 'A little lady of commanding mien made her way through the opening throng to the scaffold.' Sturtridge heard her cry out, 'Ho! and away for France!'. He repeated the phrase, so quitting the officers of justice 'and the multitude with wonder and disappointment'.[38]

A second tale is from T.Q. Couch's 1871 *History of Polperro*. This story follows a similar pattern. A farmer's boy from Porthallow was travelling to the neighbouring village one night. He found himself with some piskies who recited a formula, and by that means travelled to 'Portallow [sic] Green', to Seaton Beach, and then to 'the King of France's cellar'. There, he drank wine with his supernatural companions and walked through rooms prepared for a feast from where he took one of the silver goblets. After a short while, the piskies pronounced the requisite word to return to Cornwall, and the boy again did likewise, soon finding himself at his home. When he told his parents that he had travelled to Seaton Beach and then to the King of France's mansion, his father said he had been hallucinating. The boy retorted that he suspected this would be his father's response, so he showed the goblet as proof of his journey. The story concludes, highlighting the fact that the goblet remained in the family for generations.[39]

Using Christiansen's catalogue of Scandinavian migratory legends as a starting point, folklorists have incorporated other legend types into the index. ML 5006* appears in Britain and follows a pattern similar to that found in these two examples from Cornwall. The story usually ends with the man being discovered in the King of France's cellar after a night of drinking. He is then pardoned or he escapes back home with the help of one of his supernatural travelling companions.[40]

Hunt's example, 'The Piskies in the Cellar', places these escapades entirely in Cornwall, with the final scene taking place in a Cornish manor house. The escape from the gallows, however, takes the man to France, an odd twist for such a widely known legend. Little can be concluded from this one example, but it strongly resembles the sort of modification of stories that droll tellers typically made. As described earlier, droll tellers adapted existing tales so that familiar Cornish places and individuals could be featured in the narratives.

The second example, Couch's story from Porthallow, follows a pattern that is recognizable elsewhere, although it lacks the suspenseful final scene at the gallows. With so few versions of this legend, it is not possible to evaluate the differences with any real precision. All that can be said with any reliability is that it is an example of yet another legend type documented in Cornwall where it was part of the larger body of the peninsula's oral tradition.

Tale Type ATU 758, 'The Various Children of Eve'

Although a literary borrowing is conceivable, yet another possible Cornish legend is worth considering. Elizabeth Yates (1905–2001), in her introduction to a collection of piskey stories by Tregarthen, quotes from the author's notebooks:

> According to an old legend … the Almighty went to call on Adam and Eve one day after they had been driven out of the Garden of Eden. When He arrived, Mother Eve was washing her children. She had not washed them all, for she had so many, and so she brought to the Lord only those that she had washed.
>
> 'Have you no other children?' The Lord God asked.
>
> 'No,' answered Eve, for she was ashamed to present to Him her little unwashed children and had hidden them.
>
> The Lord God was angry and said, 'What man hides from God, God will hide from man.'[41]

Yates then continues, drawing on the notebook, to explain that this was the origin of the fairy folk wherever they lived, and that in Cornwall, they were known as piskeys, but also 'the Small People, and the Dinky Men and Women or the Dinkies'.[42] To this, Tregarthen added the term 'Little Invisibles'.

This story of Eve hiding her children from God is a widely distributed story, classified as Tale Type ATU 758. It appears in the German collection of the Brothers Grimm as well as in Scandinavian-speaking countries, Eastern Europe, Spain, and various other locations.[43] Although the story is classified in the folktale type index, it was commonly told to be believed and should consequently be regarded as a legend. As always, an isolated example of a story does not allow for comparison.

It has been noted that one must read Tregarthen with caution since she employed folk stories and motifs to create fictions that were removed from the original oral source of inspiration. Not knowing how much her stories deviate from traditional narratives makes serious analysis of her writings difficult. The concerns about Tregarthen aside, her description of the story of Eve and her children could not have occurred without some source. It is impossible, however, to know whether she retold the story from a published foreign source or if it was part of Cornish oral tradition.

Conclusion

The analysis of these five legend types begins the process of understanding how the narratives of Cornwall represent a unique assemblage of variants and how together they constitute a distinct cultural fingerprint. The conclusion, that legends described in this chapter appear in Cornish collections, represents a fundamental building block in the analysis of the peninsula's folklore. The fact that there are too few examples of any given type limits the enquiry, and yet the process of understanding this oral tradition rests with the consideration of as many legend and folktale types as possible, so that they may be treated as a group.

Further analysis in the following chapter adds to this process. It considers legends involving piskies and their predilection for seeking human companionship and on occasion for abducting people.

CHAPTER SIX

Seeking the Companionship of People

A publication from 1696 describes the first-hand 'account of one Ann Jefferies, now alive in the county of Cornwall, who was fed for six months by a small sort of airy people, called fairies; and the strange and wonderful cures she performed'. The text is a letter from Moses Pitt to Edward Fowler, the Bishop of Gloucester. As a child from St Teath parish near Bodmin Moor, Pitt had witnessed the events described in the booklet. He pointed out that the woman in question was still alive and regarded as a healer, having received 'salves and medicines' from the supernatural beings. Pitt tried to persuade Jefferies to recall details, but she declined, fearing if she were to discuss them, she might be re-examined by the authorities who had detained her five decades earlier. She also expressed a concern that if she provided details, Pitt would seek to profit from the story, and she said, 'that she would not have her name spread about the country in books or ballads of such things'.[1]

Nevertheless, Pitt's letter included sufficient detail to satisfy his readers. He described how the Pitt household employed Jefferies as a servant. Pitt also recalled how one day in 1645 when the young woman was nineteen years old, she was, 'knitting in an Arbour in our Garden, [when] there came over the Garden-hedge to her (as she affirmed) six Persons of small stature, all clothed in green, which she called Fairies'. She said that 'she was so frightened, that she fell into a kind of Convulsion-fit'.[2] The family took her inside to bed, and when she awoke, she asserted that the fairies had just been there and had 'gone out the Window'. Jefferies remained so sick she could not stand or work. Pitt noted that her condition was such 'that she became even as a Changeling'. She refused food during her illness and maintained that she 'was fed by these fairies'. Eventually, she recovered, prayer and church attendance being central to her cure.[3]

Pitt then described how Jefferies came to cure people beginning with his own mother when she had suffered a fall. Word travelled so 'that people of all distempers, sicknesses, sores, and ages, came not only so far off as the Land's End, but also from London, and were cured by her. She took no monies of

13. Ann Jefferies gained notoriety in the seventeenth century for her
claim that she encountered piskies and her story resonated for decades.
An 1837 illustration shows the servant dancing with fairies, from J.E. Smith,
Legends and Miracles and other Curious and Marvellous Stories of Human Nature.

them.' There were many other details provided in Pitt's letter, including
accounts of Jefferies dancing in the orchard, asserting that the fairies were
with her. Because she seemed not to be eating and she had abilities to cure
people and know their business upon their arrival, she attracted the attention
of ministers who tried to convince her that all she had experienced 'was the
delusion of the Devil'. The authorities 'sent her to Bodmin jail, and there kept
her a long time'. According to Pitt's account, they withheld food from the
young servant, but she survived the experience, adding to her remarkable
reputation.[4]

The Ann Jefferies' incident does not fall into a legend type although it
does include several recognizable motifs. It is a memorate. The fact that Pitt
witnessed the events and in turn wrote the letter gave the account a level
of veracity that caused it to gain popular attention. This example serves as a
reminder that while people told traditional stories about fairies and how they
behaved, migratory legends are distinct from descriptions of first-hand experiences. Pitt's memorate about Jefferies illustrates how belief could be part of
one's personal recollections. Those who regarded fairies as real occasionally
found evidence to strengthen their belief.

In addition, the story about Jefferies is a reminder of how much people believed that fairies sought to interact with people. Pitt described the servant in his household as being between this world and that of the supernatural. Her hold on human life was faltering so that she was becoming 'even as a Changeling'. Seventeenth-century British readers would have found it perfectly plausible that Jefferies could have had this encounter and that the fairies would have pursued her, even to the point of abducting her.

The notion that supernatural beings are attracted to people is ubiquitous. Cornish tradition includes stories that describe people crossing into the otherworld. Stories about being 'pixy-led', the Cornish versions of a Will-o'-the-wisp, feature an entity that specialized in misleading night-time travellers; this motif was common in south-west Britain. 'The Fairy Dwelling on Selena Moor', cited in Chapter 4, illustrates the interest piskies had in abducting people, but here there is not so much of a legend type as an expression of supernatural entities capturing people. Other Cornish legends fit into 'types', migratory legends from elsewhere in northern Europe, and these provide opportunities for comparative analysis.[5]

ML 5070, 'Midwife to the Fairies'

Hunt's 'Nursing a Fairy' describes how a woman was confronted one night by a man who indicated he wished to hire her to care for his baby boy. The man took her out walking and at one point blindfolded her. When he removed the blindfold, the woman found herself in a wonderful room where she was given an excellent meal. He then showed her the baby boy who would be her ward. The man placed conditions on the woman including that she should not teach him the Lord's Prayer and that she should only wash the baby in the morning using water that would appear in a white porcelain ewer. He also told her that she was never to use the water to wash her own face. She agreed to the terms and was led from the room, blindfolded again, and taken for another long walk, after which she found herself holding the baby at her own house.

The woman followed the rules and over the next few years was rewarded handsomely. The boy appeared to pretend to be playing with others, visible only to him. All the while, the woman grew curious about the water that mysteriously appeared every morning in the porcelain ewer. One day, she decided to splash some on her face and found that most of it went into one of her eyes. She immediately saw that there were many little people around her, playing with the boy. She realized that she ought not to let them know that she could see them.

Coincidentally, there had been unexplained thefts at the local market. There, the woman saw the man who had earlier procured her services. She confronted him as he stole some fruit. Realizing that she could see him, he placed his finger over her left eye and asked if she could still see him. She answered that she could, to which he recited the following verse:

> Water for elf; not water for self
> You've lost your eye, your child, and yourself.

At that, she became blind in her right eye. When she returned home, the boy was gone, and she descended into poverty.[6]

Several similar stories in the Cornish repertoire are also expressions of ML 5070, 'The Midwife to the Fairies', one of the more prevalent accounts involving these supernatural beings in northern Europe.[7] The protagonist of the Cornish examples is a woman who is asked to serve as a nurse to a boy, whether in her own house or that of her employer. In the many examples of the story, including Hunt's well-known legend of 'Cherry of Zennor' and the elaborate narrative, 'The Fairy Master' from Bottrell's collection, the nurse lives in the supernatural mansion and is told to avoid the room in which some ointment is kept. The woman usually violates the taboo and places the ointment or enchanted water in one of her eyes after which she can see her employer or his supernatural court. She confronts him, and he blinds her. Some of these motifs also appear in at least two Cornish stories involving witchcraft.[8] They are a step removed from the motif of the piskie world, but these stories follow enough of the same pattern to illustrate their association.

Evans-Wentz mentions a similar legend he collected at the beginning of the twentieth century from Penzance. This describes how a woman from Zennor went to work as a nurse, explored a forbidden room that held a pot of ointment and, after a while, used it on her eyes although the story does not tell of her applying the ointment to the child's eyes, as normally occurs in this legend type. She then saw all the pixies having a party. Her employer discovered her and sent her home with her wages. She subsequently realized she had been away twenty years even though she had not aged at all. The legend appears to include only remnants of the original story: it omits the ointment's core purpose, that of anointing the child's eyes and moreover, the woman is not blinded.[9]

Yet another legend recorded by Evans-Wentz seems to be linked to this same legend: his brief account 'Danger of seeing the "Little People"', describes a story of a woman who set water out to wash her baby, but before she could do so, the 'small people' used it for their infants. The woman splashed the water into her eyes and she could at once see the supernatural beings. They tried to blind her for the intrusion, but she escaped. This isolated motif seems loosely related to ML 5070. The fact that Evans-Wentz collected these stories in the early twentieth century illustrates the legend's durability.[10]

Finally, T.Q. Couch in his 1871 *History of Polperro* recounts a variant of ML 5070 with the midwife motif. The story follows the typical pattern found outside Cornwall of a midwife assisting with a birth and accidentally splashing the baby's wash-water into one eye. This is followed by her encounter with the baby fairy's father who was stealing at a market and by her subsequent blindness. Notably, this outlier is from Polperro near the Devonian border, hinting at a possible source of the midwife motif.[11] In addition, Tregarthen's story, 'The Nurse Who Broke Her Promise', includes the midwife motif, but as indicated, this author was at least one step removed from the spoken tradition. It is likely that she borrowed motifs from Couch or some other published source.[12] These occurrences of the midwife motif are echoed by the work of Bray in her 1838 publication, *Traditions, Legends, Superstitions, and Sketches of Devonshire on the Borders of the Tamar and the Tavy*. As with Couch and Tregarthen, her account from the Devonian side of the River Tamar captures the standard motifs of the legend of a woman summoned to help with a birth, as opposed to serving as a nurse.[13]

Besides these sources, there are other instances of this legend appearing in publications about Cornish folklore. Mabel Quiller-Couch (*c.*1866–1924), in *Cornwall's Wonderland*, recounts a story describing a woman named Joan: 'a very foolish woman, whose curiosity got the better of her, and how she was punished'. The story appears to be a reprint of Hunt, 'How Joan lost the sight in her eye'.[14]

A few generalizations are possible with the Cornish versions of ML 5070. The woman nursing the fairy child is the dominant if not the only form of the legend in Cornwall. The plot then takes two forms: one features the discovery at the market, while other legends describe the woman sent home as a punishment for her transgression which is discovered at the house of her employer. This difference in conclusion is determined in part by whether the child is cared for at the house of the employer or at the woman's home.[15]

Because international examples of 'The Midwife to the Fairies' are so common it has attracted the attention of several folklorists. Besides finding a prominent place in Christiansen's index of migratory legends, a related folktale appears as Tale Types ATU 476* and ATU 476**, the asterisks indicating distinct versions.[16] Irish folklorist Críostóir Mac Cárthaigh considers these two core stories, which emphasize the service and payment of the female helper.[17] Christiansen's migratory legend, ML 5070, focuses on the ointment and the ending, but the overlap is clear and can cause confusion. Mac Cárthaigh notes that the narrative occurs in England, Wales, France and in Cornwall.[18] Some stories feature an introduction describing a promise made to a frog or toad to be present when the little creature gives birth, an offer made in jest, taunting, or as a show of real concern for the poor animal. The woman is then summoned to act as midwife at the hour of birth. Folklorists have collected this story by itself without the ointment motif from central Europe.

According to Mac Cárthaigh, a combination of the toad story with the ointment ending occurs in Scandinavia, Scotland and Ireland. He maintains that Scandinavia became a crossroads where these two distinct narratives blended into a single legend and then, through contact with the Gaelic world, spread to Scotland and Ireland. The central European account of the pregnant toad does not apparently occur in Britain south of Scotland, and so an analysis of Cornwall's examples need only consider the version, best described in Christiansen's ML 5070, that deals with the fairy ointment.[19]

ML 5070 has two subvariants: one involves a woman called to act as midwife to help with the birth of a supernatural baby; the second describes a supernatural employer contracting with a woman to care for his child. In both cases, the legends usually follow a basic form: the woman uses the magic ointment, recognizes her former employer at the market or elsewhere and is then punished either with blindness or as occurs in many of the nursing variants, with subsequent poverty. Mac Cárthaigh points out that Ireland has examples of each of these, both of which appear in Christiansen's summary of material from Norway.

The longevity of the motif of the human nurse is demonstrated by its appearance in the thirteenth-century work of Gervase of Tilbury (1150–1228). His *Otia Imperialia* includes a story of a 'dracs', a supernatural water-being who can assume human form. This source attributes the story to an event that occurred in France's Rhône Valley, but whether the account came from that location is not known. It describes a woman who was held captive in the creature's palace. She served as a nurse for the son of the dracs. During her three years in the otherworld, she accidentally touched her eye after eating eel, and its fat caused her to be able to see the supernatural realm as it truly was. After being dismissed, the woman happened to be at a market where she saw her former employer. She greeted him. Upon finding out which eye gave her the ability to see him, he touched it, at which point she lost the capacity to see the supernatural. This early example of ML 5070 is of note not only for its age but also because it features the role of the nurse rather than the midwife.[20]

The seventeenth-century work of Kirk hints at the story's antiquity in Britain. The Scottish minister who wrote *The Secret Commonwealth*, a famed treatise on fairies, tells of a woman who was abducted after giving birth. The stock, an object left in her place having magically taken on her appearance, appeared to die, but the woman went on to live in the world of the fairies. Towards the end of her two-year sojourn, she applied an 'unction', an ointment, to one of her eyes, after which she could see what had previously been hidden aspects of a supernatural world. After realizing what she had done, the fairies caused her to be 'blind of that eye with a puff of their breath' and then sent her back to her husband. Since the woman in question spent two years in the realm of the fairies and is sent home when she violates the privacy of her hosts, the story has more in common with the variants involving the prolonged employment of a nurse rather than the single-night's work of a midwife. Unfortunately, Kirk does not mention what role the woman played among the fairies.[21]

Occurrences of the motifs present in ML5070 in Francis James Child's (1825–1896) collection of ballads provides further evidence regarding the antiquity of the story in Scotland. 'The Queen of Elfan's Nourice' describes a woman who becomes a nurse for a supernatural infant. Child uses a source that dates to the beginning of the nineteenth century.[22] As previously indicated, Bray's account of a midwife to the fairies is another early British example of this story.

Although the motif of the midwife is well known and gives the type its title, several other early published versions of ML 5070 feature the nurse variant. This is true of the legend as it appears in the collection of the Brothers Grimm. Their story, 'The Elves' (Number 39II), is an echo of ML 5070. In this case, the young woman does not help with a birth but rather assists a new mother for what seems to be three days, but when she returns, she finds that seven years have passed.[23]

Mac Cárthaigh observes that ML 5070 often leans in the direction of the folktale in its telling, both in the lack of specific time and place of the event described and in the length of the narrative. He points out that in Ireland, especially in Mayo and Kerry, the story 'is sometimes stretched to 1,500 words or more', and that a telling from Shetland was more than 2,000 words. Because many of the Cornish stories were longer than one finds elsewhere, it is not a surprise that the length of Hunt's 'Cherry of Zennor' is well over 3,000 words. Mac Cárthaigh also notes that although Scottish and Irish variants are typically close 'both in terms of content and style', the motif of anointing the eyes of the fairy child is not found in Ireland but it does occur in Scotland and Scandinavia. To this it is appropriate to add that the fairy ointment also appears in the Cornish variants of the legend.[24]

More importantly Mac Cárthaigh provides insight into the history of the legend type. He suggests that its diffusion from Scandinavia to Scotland and then to Ireland was assisted by Viking-era settlement in the northern and western parts of Scotland. In addition, he maintains that since frogs or toads were originally absent in Ireland, the island was less welcoming to the version of the story that involved one of these amphibians.[25] The fact that Irish variants do not include the motif of the ointment suggests how the tradition may have been pared down as it crossed the Irish Sea. This scenario does not address how ML 5070 found itself throughout the rest of Britain, but the evidence of Gervase of Tilbury demonstrates that the story had circulated elsewhere for centuries.

A quick overview of examples of ML 5070 in Britain provides evidence regarding the nature of the legend's distribution. Briggs documents several variants. Besides those from Cornwall, versions occur in the Shetland Islands and Scotland to Lancashire and Somerset in England with both the midwife and the nurse motifs.[26] Unfortunately, the British collections do not rise to the level of what is available in Ireland and elsewhere in northern Europe, so extracting insight with the few recorded remnants is not easy. For the purposes of comparing the material with what appears in Cornwall, it is sufficient to remark that 'The Midwife to the Fairies' was present in Britain and that both the midwife and the nurse versions appear.

Accounts from the Brittonic language areas of Wales and Brittany are particularly useful for an analysis of the Cornish material. Rhŷs for example, published a Welsh variant in 1901. 'The Midwife of Hafoddydd' describes the classic assistance of a midwife attending a fairy birth, but it is without the ointment motif and describes the woman as receiving a great reward. Similarly, Evans-Wentz records a variant from Wales that includes the traditional midwife to the fairies, together with the ointment, the market scene and blindness in one eye. In addition, Daniel Parry-Jones (1891–1981) published a collection of Welsh folklore in 1953 with a chapter devoted to 'The Midwife to the Fairies'. Although his work consists of retellings and summaries, he drew on an active tradition that featured this legend with the midwife and ointment motifs.[27]

In 1881, Paul Sébillot (1843–1918) published a version of 'The Midwife to the Fairies' from Brittany. It features many of the motifs one would expect, including the midwife, the fairy ointment and the woman recognizing the father of the baby when she saw him stealing at a market. This is followed by the fairy father removing the offending eye of the woman.[28] Another example, this one from Lewis Spence (1874–1955), *Legends and Romances of Brittany*, appeared in 1917. It describes a girl who assists with the care of a newborn and loses track of time. An additional reference by Spence to a story from Brittany involving an encounter at a market and the removal of an eye may draw on the story of Sébillot.[29] These expressions of ML 5070, together with those from Wales, point to the existence of the legend in other Brittonic areas, but it appears that the midwife variants occurred there and elsewhere in Britain and that the nursing motif was known in at least some places.

As noted earlier, Sveinsson's idea of periphery phenomena, 'when a story reaches the limit of its range of dissemination', has application to Cornish folklore. 'The Midwife to the Fairies' was popular in Cornwall, but only the nursemaid version seems to have flourished there, even though an early expression of the midwife motif existed in neighbouring Devon.[30] Further, the lack of variation suggests that the story may have been a late importation. Since Cornish droll tellers frequently modified what they told, the homogenous nature of the examples of the legend, which describe nurses who face only one of two endings, supports the conclusion that local storytellers did not have enough time to introduce new motifs or variation. That said, it is appropriate to acknowledge that the occurrence of the motifs of the ointment and the discovery at the market in association with witchcraft appears to be a variation that may have been introduced during the history of the legend in Cornwall. Perhaps this was the beginning of the kind of modifications that typified the work of the Cornish droll tellers.

In a way, it is surprising that ML 5070 could be so popular in Cornwall since it requires human-sized supernatural beings to be the actors: the ointment provides the opportunity to see just how small the piskies are, but the adjustment of this legend type, which appears to be foreign, to the Cornish point of view was not without its challenge. The story likely arrived in Cornwall with the nursing subtype but also with the internationally common final scene at the market where the use of the fairy ointment is discovered. The fact that some versions have the discovery at the employer's house was a minor adjustment for those examples taking place in that location, as opposed to the nurse caring for her young ward in her own house. It is likely that this change together with the omission of the market scene was a late modification to the legend.

Another word is warranted about the usual form of the Cornish legend of the human nurse and her piskie employer. With these stories, the focus is on the idea of a governess who cares for the child after birth, violates the order to stay away from a room in the mansion, and is then exiled from the place and often from her master whom she has come to love. This is reminiscent of Charlotte Brontë's (1816–1855) novel, *Jane Eyre*, which was published in 1847 before the Hunt and Bottrell collections appeared. The mother of the Brontë sisters was from Cornwall, and after her premature death, her sister raised the motherless children. It is possible that one of these Cornish women could have introduced young Charlotte to the story of the nurse and her ward in a strange mansion. Whether a Cornish version of ML 5070 was an inspiration for *Jane Eyre* remains to be demonstrated adequately, but the similarity is worth noting.[31]

ML 5085, 'The Changeling'

There is an international concern that supernatural beings occasionally steal infants. The anxiety is predictable since newborns are both precious and vulnerable. Christiansen describes a migratory legend that was widespread in pre-industrial northern Europe. 'The Changeling' begins with the abduction of a baby, who is replaced by a fairy magically transformed into almost the same appearance as the human child. The changeling proves to be constantly hungry and irritable, and frequently shrivels into a wizened creature that fails to thrive and mature. The mother of the household, drawing on pervasive folk wisdom, either abuses the changeling or does something peculiar in front of it: this involves such actions as using an eggshell to boil water or to brew beer. At this, the astonished changeling speaks, admitting its ancient age. An elfin woman then appears with the human infant, exchanging the two. There are many variations of the specific motifs, but the pattern remains largely the same. Examples appear from Ireland and Sweden to Iceland and Germany, including a version in the Grimm's collection.[32]

Many see these stories as a response to the universal reality of infant mortality, birth defects and developmental problems, persistent tragedies of the human condition.[33] Others have considered the role of infanticide in pre-industrial society, regarding changeling legends as justification for disposing of unwanted infants. There have been many other attempts to make sense of this large body of related accounts.[34] The important aspect of the stories in this context is to consider how Cornish changelings compare with those of neighbouring areas.

Bottrell briefly mentions how mothers, particularly 'in the high countries, … still hang from their children's necks as a charm, or kind of talisman,' a disc of polished moor stone with a hole drilled in the centre. These were intended 'to keep their precious offspring from being ill-wished, blighted by an evil eye, led astray into the bogs, or from losing themselves among the pig-sties and turf-ricks through the tricks of piskies'. Bottrell indicates that the intent was so 'that the small people may not make changelings of the young ones'. He adds that 'in spite of all their care, it often happens that the small people (fairies) steal the pretty babes and place their own wisht-looking brats in their stead'.[35] In short, Cornish mothers commonly protected their children from the supernatural with whatever means they could summon.

T.Q. Couch in *History of Polperro* confirms Bottrell's assertion that there were accounts of the theft of infants. He maintains that:

> we have a few stories of pisky changelings, the only proof of whose parentage is that 'they did'nt [sic] goodey', (thrive). It would seem that fairy children of some age are entrusted to mortal care for a time and again recalled to piskey land. People are occasionally kidnapped by the little folk.[36]

Evans-Wentz recorded stories involving changelings at the beginning of the twentieth century, documenting that the tradition survived into the modern era: Miss Harriett Christopher, from Crill, near Falmouth, provided a story about a changeling, a 'withered' girl who was left in a baby's place. It:

> lived to be twenty years old, and was no larger when it died than when the piskies brought it. It was fretful and peevish and fright-fully shrivelled. The parents believed that the piskies often used to come and look over a certain wall by the house to see the child. And I heard my grandmother say that the family once put the child out of doors at night to see if the piskies would take it back again.[37]

Stories about people addressing what they believe to be changelings appear in the collections of Bottrell and Hunt, but these often seem to be memorates, descriptions of actual events that correspond to the prevalent idea that super-natural agents did in fact abduct and replace infants. In addition, these accounts include information about ways people could address the situation when a theft seemed to have taken place. As occurs elsewhere in Europe, authors document instances of what can only be called child abuse, all in the name of attempting to lure the piskies to return the 'real', missing baby, but in general these do not include the key motif one expects of the changeling migratory legend, namely the return of the infant.

Some stories veer into the fanciful, departing from the realism of the memorates that dominate most of the descriptions. Hunt's story, 'The Lost Child', for example, features a young boy who visits fairyland and then returns. This narration has more in common with any number of other tales of adults travelling to the supernatural realm. Although it features a small boy, there is no exchange, and again, there is nothing in this story that refers to traditional changeling legends. The fact that there are other accounts which echo this story hints at the existence of an indigenous legend type of a child who went astray, was cared for by the piskies, and was then found unharmed.[38]

Young provides an exhaustive treatment of descriptions of Cornish change-lings, focusing on instances that seem both to be real and to document the implementation of widespread folk beliefs and fears.[39] His overview is extremely useful in assessing folk tradition. Clearly, the Cornish belief in supernatural beings abducting babies inspired some to ill-treat infants who exhibited developmental problems. Parents no doubt heard stories about reversing abduction, which they hoped could apply to their situation. These cases reveal belief, but they are not useful in ascertaining the content of the migratory legend lurking behind the incidents.

Despite descriptions of people acting on an assumption that fairies occasionally abducted infants, ML 5085, 'The Changeling', is rare in Cornish folklore collections, even though it was common elsewhere.[40] Hunt's publi-cation of 'The Spriggan's Child' is of interest because it is in verse form, apparently preserving a popular approach to narrative among the droll tellers, as described in Chapter 2. The story also represents the best example of ML 5085 from Cornwall.

In this case, Janey Tregeer from Brea Vean having left her sleeping infant to join the harvest, returned to find her child different in a way that 'she thought it a changeling'. She resolved to take it on each Wednesday in May to be bathed in the chapel well, after which she walked counter-clockwise three times around the hallowed source of water. As she climbed the hill on the following Wednesday, 'once more to work the holy charms … she heard the strangest voice … saying these words, quite clear and shrill: "Tredrill, Tredrill! Thy wife and children greet thee well"'. At this the infant spoke declaring that he cared little about wife or child provided he could eat his fill and be carried about by this woman. Janey Tregeer then knew that this was indeed a changeling, and she returned home and told the village women what had happened. They counselled her that 'she must beat it black, she must beat it blue, bruise its body all o'er with the heel of her shoe—Then lay it alone beneath the church stile—And keep out of hearing and sight for a while'. The mother acted on the advice, and upon returning to the church she found her own child returned to her, although the old women of the village warned, 'if it keeps its wits, we're sadly afraid the poor babe will have fits'.[41]

The changeling in 'The Spriggan's Child' reveals itself by speaking, which is usually sufficient to inspire the return of the baby, but this variant combines two motifs that typically appear in separate versions, namely the execution of some deed to cause the fairy to speak as opposed to the beating of the changeling. Because it is in verse form in local dialect, it is clear from this example that ML 5085 was part of Cornish folklore. In addition, the numerous examples of child abuse inflicted on infants that failed to thrive demonstrate that the folk belief in the supernatural abduction of babies was common throughout the peninsula. The lack of additional examples of the complete migratory legend limits the ability to analyze this specific element of local tradition.

ML 6010 'The Capture of a Fairy' and ML 6070A, 'Fairies send a Message'

Another Cornish legend alludes to the idea of exchanging people and super-natural beings, yet it does not feature an actual abduction. The story uses the term 'changeling', but it is without an exchange and is instead a narrative about the desire of the supernatural to be in the company of people, so it is included here. Hunt's reprinted 'The Piskies' Changeling', borrowed from T.Q. Couch, preserves what seems to be ML 6010 'The Capture of a Fairy' blended with a mutated version of ML 6070A, 'Fairies send a Message'. The account describes how a family found a piskie infant and took care of it. The little creature enjoyed his foster parents' hospitality until one day they all heard a voice calling out 'Coleman Gray, Coleman Gray!'. In answer to that, 'The Piskie immediately started up and with a sudden laugh, clapped its hands, exclaiming, "Aha! My daddy is come!" It was gone in a moment, never to be seen again.'[42]

Christiansen describes ML 6010 with a vague set of parameters which include the motif of people caring for a fairy child. The Cornish story described here appears to share this feature. Indeed, Christiansen mentions that some variants end with the following: 'soon afterwards somebody was heard calling from the outside' at which the supernatural being leaves its human hosts. This motif is part of the narrative of Hunt and Couch, but it cannot escape notice that the supernatural voice calling out to its kin is also central to ML 6070A, 'Fairies send a Message'. Elsewhere, this legend tells of people hearing a voice, which in one variant says that someone has died. When the household cat learns of this news, he stands up and declares that he has consequently become

14. 'Plucked from the Fairy Circle' from Wirt Sikes, *British Goblins: Welsh Folk-lore, Fairy Mythology, Legends and Traditions*, published in 1880 with illustrations by T.H. Thomas. This classic source focuses on Wales, documenting traditions that echoed in Cornwall and throughout Britain and Ireland: a widespread motif describes someone grabbing a captivated friend just as he was about to cross into the fairy circle of dance, thus saving him from an eternity lost in enchantment.

king of the cats, at which point he leaves. In another version, a man comes into a house and says that a voice told him that a nearby hill was on fire. An invisible intruder suddenly appears in their midst, usually with a bundle of stolen food, and hurries away, sometimes declaring that she is worried about the fate of her children.[43]

ML 6070A also seems to play a role in Hunt's story of 'A Fairy Caught', in which a man picks up a sleeping fairy, takes him home, and names him Bobby Griglans. The man and his wife keep Bobby a secret because he promises to show them 'where the crocks of gold were buried on the hill'. One day the couple's children allow the little man out of the barn where he is hidden. They find a fairy couple calling out for their child named 'Skillywidden'. The captive recognizes them as his parents, and with the fairy family reunited, they disappear. Briggs classifies this as ML 6010, 'The Capture of a Fairy', and indeed, it lacks a clear manifestation of the final motif found in the ML 6070A 'Fairies send a Message'.[44]

The legends of 'Coleman Gray' and 'A Fairy Caught' are akin to Tregarthen's stories of 'Skerry-Werry' and 'The Magic Pail', both telling of people who care for piskey children. As always, the works of Tregarthen require scrutiny because she created her own stories drawing on oral tradition to varying degrees. There is consequently no way to determine how much of any of her tales correspond to an actual legend. Still, the similarities shared by these two accounts and that of 'Coleman Gray' and 'A Fairy Caught' point towards a possible nineteenth-century indigenous Cornish legend that described a piskey child under the temporary care of a human, only to return to its parent. This includes the generic motif described by Christiansen with ML 6010, 'The Capture of a Fairy', but there is also evidence of the specific motif described by ML 6070A, 'Fairies send a Message'.[45]

Conclusion

The abduction of people is one of the most common themes in pre-industrial northern European legends. Cornish examples pale in comparison with those from elsewhere. The story about Coleman Gray involves a changeling in name only: no human was exchanged for the elfin child. The story of the human nurse attending a supernatural offspring describes an employee rather than an abductee.

Finally, the Cornish accounts about changelings attest to a belief that human infants were occasionally exchanged with supernatural counterparts that failed to thrive. Sources indicate that there was a general idea that ill-treating the replacement offered a chance to win the return of the human captive. The rare example of ML 5085, 'The Spriggan's Child', demonstrates the existence of this part of the international repertoire in Cornwall, but it is not possible to conclude much with this single manifestation. There are also stories involving children wandering off and being cared for by the fairies before being returned, but these do not recall the terror that supernatural abduction usually elicited.

The legend of 'The Fairy Dwelling on Selena Moor', described in Chapter 4, is a clear Cornish example of human abduction. Unfortunately, the story lacks historically related counterparts from elsewhere, and this inhibits comparative analysis. The same can be said of the account of Ann Jefferies. There can be no doubt that the Cornish believed that piskies sought the companionship of people. In addition, incidents of people being 'pixy-led' are well-known expressions of supernatural beings seeking to mislead travellers, although it is not always clear if abduction was the intent. Nevertheless, it is surprising how few Cornish legends describe abductions, a motif that provided fertile material for stories in the rest of northern Europe.

CHAPTER SEVEN

Mermaids

Piskies and other land-based entities were not the only supernatural beings that the Cornish described in stories. Nineteenth-century collectors also documented traditions involving mermaids, providing yet another means to gain insight into pre-modern beliefs. In the case of these maritime creatures, Cornwall yields a distinct body of narratives, a testament to the vitality of its folklore and its relationship to the sea. Cornish stories of mermaids tend to be elaborate, moving beyond the memorate and pointing in the direction of the migratory legend, even when they lack obvious counterparts elsewhere.

One of the more enchanting Cornish examples of belief in merfolk appears in Bottrell's first volume of tales, published in 1870. He attributes 'The Story of the Mermaid and the Man of Cury' to Uncle Anthony, the previously mentioned wandering droll teller from the Lizard peninsula, the setting of his legend.[1] According to the narrative, a family named Lutey came to be known for its white witches because of a skill 'acquired by a fortunate ancestor, who had the luck to find a mermaid ..., left high and dry on a rock by the ebbing tide'. Lutey was searching the beach at low tide for treasures and was ready to go home empty-handed 'when he heard a plaintive sound, like the wailing of a woman or the crying of a child'.

Following the sobbing, he found 'a fairer woman than he had ever beheld before', sitting in a pool of water, with golden hair 'falling over her shoulders and floating over the water, [shining] like the sunbeams on the sea ...' and with skin as 'smooth and clear as a polished shell'. At first, Lutey could only see her from the waist up, but then he noticed that a fishtail was quivering and shaking amongst the seaweed, so he recognized her to be a mermaid. 'He never had so near a view of one before, though he had often seen them, and heard them singing, on moonlight nights, at a distance, over the water.'

Lutey calmed the mermaid, assuring her that he only wished to help. She rose out of the water, her hair being 'so abundant that it fell around and covered her figure like an ample robe of glittering gold'. She explained that she was searching for something for her children to eat. She had been combing

15. Mermaids prove alluring for men, a theme explored in Bottrell's 'The Story of the Mermaid and the Man of Cury', but this motif is also shared by literature. W.H.C. Groome painted this image for *North Cornwall Fairies and Legends*, Enys Tregarthen's 1906 book of fanciful stories, loosely based on oral tradition.

her hair, looking at herself in a tidal pool, before she realized that the tide had gone too far out, leaving her stranded. The mermaid indicated that she would like to linger and talk with a man of the land and that she had often wished to have 'two tails, like you, or with a tail split into what you call your legs', so that she could walk about to see 'all the strange and beautiful creatures which we view from the waves'. But she explained that she urgently needed to return before her husband awoke and, looking for something to eat, would devour their children.

The mermaid promised to grant Lutey three wishes if he would carry her across the land to the sea. She offered her golden comb, which included a handle of pearl, 'as a token of my faith'. And she said that she would give her mirror as well, but she left it near her husband so he would believe she had not gone too far away. The creature then told Lutey that he would only need to 'pass that comb through the sea three times, calling me as often, and I'll come to ye on the next flood tide. My name is Morvena, which in the language of this part of the world, at the time I was named, meant sea-woman.'

Lutey agreed to the terms and took the mermaid in his powerful arms. As he carried her, he considered what his wishes might be, remembering stories about how people had asked for things that usually resulted in disastrous consequences. He finally said that he wanted:

> the power to do good to my neighbours—first that I may be able to break the spells of witchcraft; secondly that I may have such power over familiar spirits as to compel them to inform me of all I desire to know for the benefit of others; thirdly, that these good gifts may continue in my family forever.

As Lutey walked towards the water, the mermaid told him of the many wonderful things that existed in her place under the waves and she tried to entice him to go with her. She nearly succeeded, but just as he was knee-deep in the sea and ready to yield to her seduction:

> his dog, which had followed unnoticed, barked and howled so loud, that the charmed man looked round, and, when he saw the smoke curling up from his chimney, the cows in the fields, and everything looking so beautiful on the green land, the spell of the mermaid's song was broken.

He struggled to be free of her embrace but she clung on tightly.

Finally, Lutey called on God and pulled his knife from his girdle, threatening her. He evoked the Divinity and this together with the effect of bright steel, which the droll teller explained had 'power against enchantments over evil beings', caused the mermaid to loosen her grip. She fell into the water and swam away while still looking at Lutey and 'singing in her plaintive tone, "Farewell my sweet, for nine long years, then I'll come for thee my love"'.

Lutey told his wife about the adventure and his narrow escape, showing her the golden comb as proof of the incident. His wife let many people know what happened and the news spread. Those who thought themselves bewitched started coming to be cured by Lutey, and they found that he did indeed have the power to remove spells. Nevertheless, the ability came with a price, as the mermaid had foretold.

Nine years after his encounter, Lutey was fishing with a friend on a calm, moonlit night. Suddenly waves tossed the boat and the mermaid appeared. Lutey told his companion, 'My hour is come'. He rose, distraught, and plunged into the water, swimming away with the mermaid until both dived into the depths, never to be seen again. According to Bottrell, the family retained the gift of being able to help people. But he adds that the tradition maintained that after Lutey's disappearance, one of his descendants died at sea every nine years.

The Array of Cornish Legends and Motifs

The elaborate account of 'The Mermaid and the Man of Cury' underscores the skill of Bottrell and his source. Lacking any recording devices, nineteenth-century collectors often abridged what they heard, but much of Bottrell's work features long, complicated stories, rich in detail and the kind of digressions that exhibit the abilities of an excellent narrator. This legend was sufficiently important that a variant appears in Hunt's collection of Cornish folklore. Hunt also notes that the tradition of this narrative survived into the 1860s in the local name of a tidal rock 'known to the present time as the Mermaid's Rock'. In addition, he maintains that a local family that claimed to still possess the gift for healing also professed to have the mermaid's comb, which they showed to him as 'evidence of the truth of their being supernaturally endowed. Some people are unbelieving enough to say the comb is only a part of a shark's jaw', to which Hunt adds: 'Sceptical people are never lovable people'.[2] Hunt is known to have used Bottrell's material, so it is possible that the two occurrences are nothing more than Hunt's acquisition and modification of the story, and yet Hunt reports seeing the comb and verifying the name of the Mermaid's Rock, and so it seems that he may have collected his own variant of the legend which concludes in a more positive way.

Evidence of the popularity of the 'The Story of the Mermaid and the Man of Cury' appears as late as 1933 in Jenkin's *Cornwall and the Cornish*. The author discusses witchcraft and 'pellar' families, those supposedly imbued with the ability to practise white magic. He indicates that there were other families who also 'claimed to have inherited their powers from some ancestor who had been fortunate enough to assist a stranded mermaid back into the sea, and who had granted the faculty of magic in reward for this courteous action'.[3] Jenkin points to the existence of other variants of this legend, and hints at the motivation for keeping the tradition alive: families who wished to market skills in charming diseases or benefit through magic could attract business by associating themselves with one of these stories.

The tale of Lutey and the mermaid ends with an episode that may refer to a widespread legend. Just before his disappearance beneath the waves, Bottrell's hero says, 'My hour is come'. This recalls the story told throughout Britain, Ireland and Scandinavia and which begins Chapter 1. Christiansen classifies the account as ML 4050, 'The hour is come but the man is not'.[4] In the story, a voice is heard coming from a body of water, saying something like the words appearing in the title of Christiansen's legend. Someone then appears and plunges into the water, apparently compelled by a supernatural force to submit to drowning. Many variants of ML 4050 suggest that the body of water demands a victim ever year or every seven years, a motif echoed in Bottrell's reference to a death taking place every nine years. ML 4050 is clearly behind Hunt's 'The Voice from the Sea'. As mentioned, Hunt notes that 'in different forms this story is told all around the Cornish coast', and it appears that the migratory legend influenced the end of the Lutey story.[5]

'The Story of the Mermaid and the Man of Cury' captures many of the motifs that typify pre-modern Cornish beliefs, and it can be regarded as one of at least four legend types that appear in the peninsula's material related to these maritime supernatural beings. Besides the story of the stranded mermaid being rescued, additional legends describe a curse from a mermaid which causes the silting of a harbour or other problems; the story of 'The Mermaid's Vengeance', and an account of a mermaid coming ashore in human form, eventually seducing a man. The latter story is the focus of the famed 'Mermaid Chair', or bench, in the church at Zennor. The legend is linked with a concluding episode that involves the mermaid's front door blocked by a ship's anchor and her subsequent request to the ship's crew to move it. This final episode may have stood alone at some point, and so it might have been a fifth legend type in the Cornish repertoire related to mermaids.[6]

These stories together with additional brief references define the character-istics of the Cornish mermaid in folklore. Her appearance consists of golden hair, a fishtail and being beautiful. Her conduct includes combing her hair with a comb of gold and looking at her reflection in a mirror or in pools of water. She often sits on rocks near the shore. The mermaid sings plaintively. When interacting with people, her singing could be magically enchanting, and people believed she would drag men into the depths. The mermaid punished disrespect, warned of danger and storms, could cause catastrophe and yet could also grant favours. In addition, her golden comb was a magical treasure for those who obtained it.[7]

Sea Folk of Other Times and Cultures

With this body of folklore in mind, it is possible to look to other northern European traditions for comparison. The idea of half-animal, half-human creatures inhabiting the oceans is widespread and ancient. In many parts of northern Europe, this sort of entity is perceived to be a seal which can shed its skin to reveal the shape of a naked person. In general, the modern English-speaking world is more familiar with the merfolk possessing a human body above the waist and a scaled fishtail below.

Over the years, several scholars have examined the history of the merfolk motif.[8] Although fish-human deities appear in sources from ancient Mesopotamia, the more removed the examples are from nineteenth-century northern Europe, the less convincing the connection. In 1990, Almqvist took up the motif of the mermaid in his analysis of a legend that inspired two twentieth-century Irish poems. He begins with the acknowledgement that there were 'once all but universal' beliefs that people could transform into animals and that 'certain zoomorphic or semi-zoomorphic beings—whether explicitly stated to be enchanted humans or not—are able to remove their animal coats and take human shape'.[9]

Almqvist also discusses the 1919 thesis of Helge Holmström dealing with the 'Swan Maiden Legend', 'relating to marriages to supernatural or super-naturally transformed female beings'. Holmström made a distinction separating 'marriages to fairy women' from affairs with 'personified nightmares' and finally from human entanglements with 'aquatic beings, mermaids or seal maidens'.[10] Ubiquitous northern European stories tell of marriages between oceanic supernatural beings and men. Indeed, Almqvist suggests that one of the more widespread legends of a mermaid entrapped by a man with whom she is forced to live for several years, is found in Gaelic-speaking areas and in Scandinavia, but that it is not found in Wales or Brittany; by implication, one would not expect to find the story in Cornwall. The supernatural being and its encounters with men was nevertheless, an important part of Cornish folklore even if it did not follow the pattern of the man entrapping the woman of the sea.[11]

'The Mermaid of Zennor'

The well-known legend, 'The Mermaid of Zennor', is associated with an equally celebrated carved church bench. Her story involves a beautiful woman who periodically attended the church of St Senara in Zennor, where she sang with an exquisite voice. Although her visits spanned many years, she never seemed to age. Eventually, she encountered Mathey Trewella, a young man in the congregation who could also sing wonderfully. On her last visit, after she and Trewella left the service, they were never seen again.[12]

Later one Sunday, a ship cast anchor at nearby Pendour Cove. A mermaid emerged from the waves and said that she was returning from church. She asked the captain to raise his anchor because its fluke 'rested on the door of her dwelling, and she was anxious to get in to her children'. Bottrell provides an alternative ending, suggesting that he had heard several versions of the story. In another variant, the mermaid indicated that she was out fishing, but that it was time to take her children to church, and yet they were trapped by the anchor. In both versions, the captain hurriedly complied and sailed away, not wishing to incur the wrath of the supernatural being. According to the legend, the incident suggested to the people of Zennor that the visitor to their church was, in fact, the woman, now in the form of a mermaid, who took Trewella to her undersea abode.

'The Mermaid of Zennor' stands alone when compared with folklore from Ireland, Scandinavia and other parts of Britain. As previously discussed, the idea that the sea folk could change into human shape and would subsequently have amorous encounters with people was widespread. In Ireland, the trans-formation occurred when the mermaid took off her *cohuleen druith*, or magic cap, so she could remove her fishtail and appear to be a woman. In Scotland, to a limited degree in Northern Ireland, and in various places where Scandinavian languages are or were spoken, the supernatural being was usually a seal, which shed its skin to reveal the form of a woman.

A well-known legend involves a man who finds either the magic cap or the seal skin, which he takes and hides and without which the mermaid is unable to return to the sea but must live with the man as his wife on land. The legend describes how she lives with her husband until she discovers the location of her magic device. Often one of her children tells her about the object which their

father has hidden. At this point, she is compelled to retrieve it and return to
the ocean, abandoning her terrestrial family. Christiansen classifies this story as
ML 4080, 'The Mermaid Wife'.[13]

The motif of the transformation from animal into beautiful woman has been
entwined in art and literature for centuries, as evidenced by sources as diverse
as the *Elder Eddic* poem the 'Völundarkiða'; Friedrich de la Motte Fouqué's
1811, Romantic-era novella, 'Undine'; the 1994 film 'The Secret of Roan
Inish' and numerous ballets. The core of this story, with its love affair between
a transformed supernatural woman and a man, finds an echo in the Zennor
legend. Bottrell's telling of the story almost reaches the point of being a variant
of ML 4080 except that the mermaid is the aggressor rather than the captive.
Frequently gender roles are reversed in oral tradition, but key motifs, such as
the theft and discovery of the magic cap, are absent, making it inappropriate to
group the Cornish story with the well-known migratory legend.[14]

16.   The famed mermaid chair in the
Zennor church of St Senara has long been
a point of fascination. This is how John
Thomas Blight portrayed it for his 1861
book, *A Week at the Land's End*. The carving
has come to be associated with the legend
of the 'Mermaid of Zennor', and yet it
appears that the decoration originally
had nothing to do with the story.

'The Mermaid of Zennor' includes an odd motif in that the creature of the sea seeks to attend church. Although there are clear exceptions, most supernatural beings in northern European folklore abhor Christianity and cannot abide its institutions. In ML 4080, for example, the sea-woman usually refuses to go to services. In other legends, church bells are known to drive off land-based supernatural beings. The motif of a mermaid attending church, as occurs in the Cornish story, is unusual.

The final episode involving the request to lift the anchor is reminiscent of ML 5075. Christiansen refers to similar stories as 'Removing a Building Situated over the House of the Fairies'. The legend involves the protest of supernatural beings because the location of a cowshed has caused the entities to have meals 'spoilt by the seepage from the stable running down on the table'.[15] 'The Mermaid of Zennor' is perhaps a sea-based mutation of this widespread narrative. The terrestrial legend is distributed in Britain and Scandinavia, but it consistently involves the effect of manure on an underground home. The Cornish story appears to exhibit the same sort of change that occurs in some Cornish variants of 'The Spectre Bridegroom', the topic of the following chapter and in legends involving the theft of piskie treasure, discussed in Chapter 5. 'The Mermaid of Zennor' reinforces the idea that it is possible to define a unique ecotype for the larger body of Cornish oral tradition that is linked to but nevertheless distinct within the realm of northern European folklore. The parallel of a widespread European legend and this episode in Bottrell's collection suggests that the conclusion of the story may have also functioned as a stand-alone legend.

The carved bench depicting a sea-woman within the church is a curiosity associated with 'The Mermaid of Zennor'. Local tradition maintains that the bench was carved to commemorate the story, carrying with it the warning that young men should resist the distraction of beauty. Another possibility is that it is merely one of many carvings of mermaids that can be found in churches throughout Britain.[16] Caradoc Peters in his analysis of the artefact suggests that the Zennor story most likely became attached to the otherwise unrelated piece of art. In either case, the depiction appears to have reinforced the tradition, and that as much as anything may account for the development, popularity and survival of a distinct legend.[17]

'The Mermaid's Curse'

Hunt provides an example of another type of Cornish mermaid legend, this one situated in Padstow on Cornwall's north coast where one of the creatures inhabited a profitable harbour between Newquay and Tintagel. Someone shot at her, and in response she cursed the area so that it would be filled with sand and could no longer accommodate larger ships. Hunt identifies Seaton as the location of a similar account: this, too, was presumably an excellent harbour, ruined by sand because of 'the curse of a mermaid, who had suffered some injury from the sailors who belonged to this port'. But Hunt adds, 'Beyond this I have been unable to glean any story worth preserving'. Even without a recorded legend, the motif of an offended mermaid cursing and thereby ruining profitable harbours was clearly common in Cornwall.[18]

A few additional references to these types of legends survive. Courtney refers to this kind of story in her essays on Cornish folklore from the mid-1880s: 'Mermaids are still believed in, and it is very bad to offend them, for by their spite harbours have been filled up with sand'.[19] Without additional information, it is not possible to say anything except that this was apparently a thriving tradition in Cornwall.

Treating mermaids with disrespect, and subsequently receiving punishment, is the focus of another legend found in the collections of both Bottrell and Hunt. The story tells of Sennen Cove where the local sea-based supernatural being would cast a shroud of mist over the ocean when a storm was about to arrive and it was unsafe to sail. Hunt recounts that 'one profane old fisherman would not be warned by the bank of fog'. From the shore the weather seemed fine, so he and his crew set sail. The captain did not stop there, however. He 'blasphemously declared that he would drive the spirit away; and he vigorously beat the fog with the "threshel"—so the flail is called'. The result was that the boat passed through the fog on its way out to sea, but it was never seen again. And what is more, the mermaid abandoned the cove.[20]

'The Mermaid's Vengeance'

'The Mermaid's Vengeance' is a complicated tale from Hunt's collection. He indicates that for his narrative, he fused together three similar legends. These were from Coverack on the Lizard peninsula, Sennen Cove near Land's End, and finally at Perranzabuloe on the north coast of Cornwall, which the author suggests was best suited for the narrative.[21] The legend includes the idea of a mermaid changeling, which is unusual in its association with the merfolk. While the story might be discarded because it is an anomaly and the author's presentation is unusual, Hunt's reference to at least three versions of the legend is evidence that something at the core of his published account was a viable part of local tradition.

The story involves a rivalry between a farm labourer named Pennaluna and the jealous supervisor of the estate named Chenalls. Pennaluna had a daughter, named Selina, who was regarded as plain. Once, while playing in a pool known as a haunt of mermaids, the small child disappeared beneath the water. Her mother managed to pull her out, but from that moment, the girl was noted for her beauty and grace. The local villagers suspected she was a changeling. After that, Selina exhibited a love of the sea and a growing reluctance to attend church.

When Selina became a young woman, the squire's nephew, an unscrupulous soldier named Walter Trewoofe, came to the estate to recuperate from a wound he had sustained in battle. He was attracted to Selina, and the two began to spend time together. Chenalls recognized an opportunity to create mischief: he sent the girl's father to work another farm so that Trewoofe, with whom Chenalls had become friends, could win Selina's affection. In three months, Pennaluna returned and immediately noticed a change in his daughter, and so he welcomed the day when Trewoofe left the area. But with that, Selina became morose, and she declined in health. Soon, it became clear that she was pregnant.

At the same time Chenalls convinced the squire of the estate that Pennaluna and his wife had conspired to trap Trewoofe into a marriage with their daughter. The infuriated squire dismissed Pennaluna. The capable farmer found new employment, but his daughter deteriorated. Selina died after childbirth, and there were rumours that spirits attended her in her final days.

With the death of Selina, good fortune abandoned Chenalls, and he was dismissed. Trewoofe returned to the estate and managed to obtain a cottage near the sea for his former friend. That place became the centre of drinking and gambling. One night, as Trewoofe left Chenalls' home, he strayed from his path and found himself on the seashore. He heard the song of an enchanting voice, which he followed until he found a beautiful woman who seemed to be Selina. He took her by the arm, but she commanded him to go. He released her, and she vanished, leaving only the echo of laughter.

From that moment, Trewoofe became remorseful and the image of Selina's face haunted him. One night, he returned to the shore where he had encountered the vision of his former lover. Once again, he saw the beautiful apparition, but this time she embraced him. With a kiss to his forehead, she told him that he would be hers until his death. Trewoofe panicked and begged to be free, but the creature kissed him again, and said, 'Give me back my dead', for it appeared that this was the mermaid-mother of Selina. There was a flash of lightning, and the cottage where Chenalls lived burst into flames, killing the wicked man. The tide came in and carried Trewoofe and the mermaid out to sea where she and other mermaids tossed the dying Trewoofe about, in revenge for the misuse and death of Selina.

'The Mermaid's Vengeance' has a literary tone, and because of this, it must be treated with caution. It is included in Hunt's collection as though it was to be believed, meaning that it would have been a legend. On the other hand, parts of the story, and especially its ending, could not be recounted by a witness, so the episode would not have been told with any credibility. This story may, in fact, be based on legends that drifted towards the fictional realm of the folktale. Hunt concedes in his introduction that he altered this story, but how much is unclear. Without additional versions, it is difficult to know how the story might have appeared in oral tradition, but its core seems genuine.

The idea that supernatural beings abduct human infants and replace them with transformed members of their own group is widespread. As described in Chapter 6, northern Europeans typically describe the abductors as land-based, using such terms as elves, fairies, trolls and *huldrefolk* to identify the offending party. The idea that a mermaid would accomplish such a feat can only be at home in a maritime culture. Still, the theft requires logistics that are more easily imagined on land.

It would be possible to mistake 'The Mermaid's Vengeance' as a variant of the widespread changeling legends, but this Cornish story takes a direction that does not appear in its land-based counterparts from northern Europe. The maritime changeling of 'The Mermaid's Vengeance' is removed from the typical northern European tradition where the suspected supernatural replacement is mistreated followed by the eventual return of the human baby. In addition, the changeling is usually ugly, in contrast to Selina. Hunt remains vague about the exact nature of this character: either she is a supernatural being or she was adopted by the mermaid who gave the young girl her blessing. Either way, the story of Selina and the vengeful mermaid can be grouped only loosely with those of abducted infants.

Conclusion

A story of a possible hoax casts light on Cornish folk beliefs in mermaids. The eccentric Robert Stephen Hawker, mentioned in Chapter 1 as an antiquarian, was the alleged perpetrator. Baring-Gould reports the incident which describes Hawker as a young man in the 1820s swimming to a rock offshore from Bude on the north-east coast of Cornwall. There, he adorned himself with a plaited seaweed wig and an oilskin wrap serving as a faux fish's tail, at which point he combed his 'hair' and sang and wailed to the amazement of nearby residents. The report then maintains that Hawker repeated the display for several nights, but that he became 'very hoarse with his nightly singing, and rather tired of sitting so long in the cold'. He consequently ended his final night with a rendition of 'God save the King', after which he disappeared into the waves never to be seen again. Another report describes the nightly performances ending with a farmer's loudly voiced threat to shoot the 'mermaid' with buckshot, inspiring Hawker to retreat into the ocean once and for all.[22]

There is no way to know if the prank really took place. Regardless, the fact that it was believable that people could have been entranced by witnessing the antics of a mermaid reveals a great deal about Cornwall at the time. Belief was sufficiently vibrant that Hawker could manage the hoax, either in its telling or in its actual execution. Traditional legends provide insight into belief but encountering a primary source that hints at the vitality of that belief is another matter, and at least at that time and place, some people regarded mermaids as real.

The Cornish did not invent the concept of the mermaid, but with their narratives, they employed the motif in unusual ways. In addition, this supernatural being was the focus of a thriving oral tradition, as suggested by the Hawker hoax and as indicated by the material collected in Cornwall in the nineteenth century. At least one piece of evidence regarding mermaids reveals a lack of information, namely that the widespread story of ML 4080, 'The Mermaid Wife', does not have a clear expression in Cornwall. 'The Mermaid of Zennor' comes close to this legend type, but it stands apart: here the mermaid is not entrapped because of the theft of her magic cap; instead she seduces the man. The absence of ML 4080 in a region that did not benefit from extensive collecting cannot contribute a great deal to the discussion; it is, however, consistent with Almqvist's observation that a story so well known in Scotland and Ireland had not been collected in Wales and Brittany.

Traditions associated with mermaids in Cornwall are striking. The concluding episode of 'The Mermaid of Zennor', describing the sea creature asking a ship's captain to move his anchor, seems to be a Cornish version of a well-known story. In other places, land-based fairies ask a farmer to move his barn because cow droppings are spoiling the food placed on their underground table. This, then, is a possible ecotype of a common northern European legend, adapted to Cornish maritime culture. In a similar way, the reference to a maritime changeling in 'The Mermaid's Vengeance', is unusual, but it is less clear how the term came to be applied to a child who had come into contact with a mermaid.

In addition, the stories of 'The Mermaid and the Man of Cury', 'The Mermaid's Vengeance', 'The Mermaid of Zennor', and references to a mermaid's curse silting a harbour are examples of folklore that appear to be distinctly Cornish. In these cases, the legends thrived in Cornwall, but they may not have occurred elsewhere, suggesting they may be indigenous rather than adaptations of more widespread northern European legends. Having a distinct inventory of legend types in such a small area serves as evidence of the vitality and isolation of Cornish folklore. The examples of ML 4050, 'The hour is come but the man is not', reinforces this conclusion. The creative way that it was attached to the legend involving Lutey and the mermaid as well as the fact that the story is so well represented in Cornwall is further evidence of the strength of nineteenth-century Cornish folklore.[23]

Variations in northern European legends and folktales can be extreme, sometimes resulting from the effect of a single storyteller's inventiveness or from having a truncated variant adopted locally as the standard. In addition, each place exhibits only part of the broad swath of northern European oral tradition. Most Cornish legends and folktales can be compared with stories from elsewhere. In the case of 'The Spectre Bridegroom', discussed in the following chapter, a unique variant of a well-known story emerges, affected once again by Cornwall's maritime environment. This is to be expected. But the fact that mermaid-related oral tradition of the peninsula exhibits four distinct stories and a motif from another (ML 4050), as well as a possible ecotype of a legend (ML 5075), reaches beyond the predictable: this part of the folklore of Cornwall is a remarkable expression of the vitality of its culture and the skill of its droll tellers.

CHAPTER EIGHT

The Spectre Bridegroom

A widely distributed story, common in Europe and represented in the folklore collections from Cornwall, draws on an array of popular beliefs and motifs. In most of Europe, the tale involves a devoted young couple separated by war. The man died, but his betrothed did not receive the news. One night, his ghost visits the woman and invites her to join him on his horse. It is not apparent that he is dead, so she accepts. They charge across the landscape, and near the end of their journey as dawn approaches, the woman realizes that she is riding with the animated corpse of her lover. In most variants, she escapes, but she often dies shortly afterwards.

Gottfried August Bürger (1747–1794) made this story famous with his 1773 poem, 'Lenore'. Within a decade of its publication, the German-language masterwork appeared in English translation, becoming an immediate sensation and apparently influencing Coleridge, Wordsworth and other Romantic-era British poets. Bürger's publication was so influential when folk narrative was first being catalogued that folklorists often refer to the tale simply as the 'Lenore Legend'.[1]

'Lenore' is not, however, the only early printed example of this story. 'The Suffolk Miracle' took up the legend in an English-language broadsheet printed perhaps as early as 1689.[2] Appearing with the subtitle 'Or a Relation of a Young Man who a Month after his Death appeared to his Sweetheart', this English ballad anticipated 'Lenore' both in the printed use of oral tradition and in its popularity and influence. Other published versions from the period include the ballads 'Nancy of Yarmouth', 'Sweet William's Ghost' and 'Fair Margaret and Sweet William'.[3] The similarity of these publications to 'Lenore' was a point of curiosity among the learned of the nineteenth century.

The Cornish Legends

The early Cornish collectors published several variants of this well-known story. In fact, the ballads aside, 'English' examples are most often from Cornwall.[4] The most elaborate Cornish expression of the story appears in 1870

17. Gottfried August Bürger's poem, 'Lenore', appeared in 1773 and became an international sensation inspiring countless translations and illustrations. This lithograph is by the German engraver Johann David Schubert (1761–1822). Bürger drew on a widespread legend about a ghostly bridegroom who sought to take his living bride to his grave with him, a story found in Germany as well as elsewhere in Europe.

in Bottrell's first volume of folklore. His 'Nancy Trenoweth, The Fair Daughter of the Miller of Alsia' is extremely long and may be the most developed version of the 'Lenore Legend' recorded anywhere.[5]

Bottrell's story unfolds as follows: Hugh Lanyon, a farmer with a hereditary claim to the aristocracy, hires Nancy Trenoweth, the daughter of a prosperous miller. Frank, the farmer's son, falls in love with Nancy. When his parents tell him to marry, he declares his affection for the miller's daughter. His father objects and exiles the girl. The miller, in turn, forbids his daughter from seeing Frank, but her mother, touched by Nancy's sadness, helps her arrange meetings with the young man.

Frank eventually decides to leave Cornwall for a life at sea. He and Nancy meet for one last time at a holy well where:

> they exchanged many vows of eternal constancy, swore, by the sign of salvation that stood near the holy fount, to be ever true and constant; held a ring between them in the bubbling brook, near the source of the limpid stream, whilst they called on all the powers of heaven above and the earth beneath to witness their vows of eternal love, through life and in death. Then the ring was duly placed on the finger of the affianced bride, and a silver coin broken, of which each one kept a severed part, with many other superstitious rites then known and practised by the love-strick youths.[6]

In short, the couple use numerous magical means to bind themselves together, calling on supernatural powers in ways that exceeded church-sanctioned marriage vows.

Distraught at his son's leaving, old Hugh Lanyon asks Nancy to return to the farm, but her father refuses to allow it. Ultimately, the entire parish takes sides, divided between the cause of the miller and the farmer. To escape the situation and to remove herself during what transpires to be her pregnancy, Nancy goes to live with her grandmother, 'Old Joan of Alsia' who was a respected healer because of her knowledge of folk medicine and spells. After giving birth to a son, Nancy leaves him with her parents and travels even further away to work as a servant.

At some point during Frank's long absence, a bottle containing his name and that of his mates washes up on the Cornish coast, convincing Nancy that her lover is still alive. She repeatedly asks her grandmother to cast spells to determine his fate. The old woman divines that he will return, but specific details about how that will be are not clear.

Finally, the pining Nancy and two other 'love-sick damsels' call on the 'Powers of Darkness' on All Hallows' Eve to reveal each of their true loves. She sees Frank surrounded by waves and dripping wet, apparently angry at her. She shrieks, and the vision vanishes. The next girl asks to see her true love, and she sees a coffin: the story notes that she died soon afterwards.

Late one night in March, rough waters drive Frank's ship onto the rocks of the Cornish coast, and his crew struggles to climb to the top of the cliff overlooking the sea. He makes certain his sailors are safe before he ascends by rope battered and bleeding. He asks to see Nancy before he dies, but word fails to reach her. The night after he is buried, Nancy goes outside to look at the sea, which is calm in the moonlight.

Suddenly, Frank arrives on the horse that he had always ridden when he arranged to meet with her before sailing away. He tells her that she will be his bride before the morning, but when they touch, she says he is cold and damp. He answers that, 'We have plighted our vows and sworn to be married, alive or dead; shrink not from me in fear, sweetheart. Come, mount behind me, and let us away;—ere tomorrow night thou shalt be my bride.'

Nancy sits on the horse and puts her arm around her love, finding herself frozen in place as they rush across the landscape. At one point, the horse stops to drink and Nancy sees Frank reflected in the water by the light of the moon. His mirror image shows him wearing a burial shroud, and she realizes he is dead. As they near her home village, the sight of a blacksmith and his fire rouse Nancy. She calls out, and Frank grabs her gown. The smith uses a red-hot iron rod to slice through her dress, freeing her. But this leaves a scrap of Nancy's garment with Frank, who rides into the churchyard and plunges into his grave. People find the fabric of Nancy's dress on Frank's grave the following day. They also discover that the horse has died. The blacksmith helps Nancy return to her parent's home. There, they tell Nancy of Frank's fate, and after requesting to hold her child one last time, she directs that he be raised by Frank's parents. Finally, she asks to be buried next to Frank, and she dies in peace.

At the end, Bottrell notes 'the old story-tellers are particular in stating ... that the piece of the woman's dress burned off in the spirit's grasp was found in Lanyon's grave when it was re-opened for Nancy's burial'.[7] Bottrell then offers a sequel, lengthening the tale even more, and with this device, he explains how Frank suffered terribly when Nancy used magic to see him. This epilogue also furnishes the means for his fellow sailors to explain what had happened during their long journey: pirates had captured the men, but the Cornish adventurers overcame their captors and claimed the ship and wealth for themselves, at which point they returned to Cornwall.

The International Context

Aarne, Thompson and Uther identify this story as a folktale, listing it as Tale Type ATU 365, 'The Dead Bridegroom Carries off His Bride'. A version appears in Hunt's collection of Cornish folklore as 'The Spectre Bridegroom', a more poetic title. The classification as a folktale is problematic because storytellers conveyed most recorded cases to be believed and they end tragically, both hallmarks of legends. Briggs, for example, groups five variants of this story in her compendium of British legends, not in her collection of folktales. Perhaps because of the story's complexity and wide distribution, cataloguers have included it as a folktale, that is, part of oral tradition told as fiction with multiple episodes and typically with a happy ending. It is also likely that the story wavered between legend and folktale, serving as an example of how folklore can defy rigid categories.[8]

Regardless of the tale's place in classification schemes, 'The Dead Bridegroom Carries off His Bride' provides an opportunity to assess an aspect of the Cornish legacy that plays a disproportionate role in British folklore. Child in his important collection, *The English and Scottish Popular Ballads*, includes a useful discussion of the European variants of this story. The legend is also well documented in Ireland where it inspired an elegant 1983 overview by Ríonach Uí Ógaín and Anne O'Connor, providing a means to consider how at least some variants compare to one another. Additional examples from Iceland and even as far as eastern Europe complete the means to understand the distribution of this widespread example of oral tradition.[9]

The Cornish variants are particularly important because Child cites them as evidence of a folk tradition spanning from Britain throughout much of Europe. Bürger's 1773 masterwork, 'Lenore', was so popular that people quickly recognized British counterparts in the form of printed ballads predating Bürger's publication. But this calls into question the source of Bürger's poem: either he had seen the published English ballads or more likely, he obtained the story from the legend told in Europe. Cornish variants and the 'Lenore' poem share motifs with European oral tradition but not with the English ballads, and so it seems clear that Bürger knew of the folk narrative in Germany or elsewhere, but he did not draw inspiration from the printed ballad. Within the context of the diverse European examples of the story, it is possible to determine what is uniquely Cornish and what the variants imply about Cornwall's place in the spectrum of European folklore.

The 'Lenore' Poem and 'The Suffolk Miracle'

Examples of the story shed light on cross-fertilization between oral tradition and its printed counterparts. The poem 'Lenore' features William, a Prussian soldier who fought in one of the eighteenth-century wars of Frederick the Great, King of Prussia. With peace, others returned, but not William. Eventually, Lenore, William's sweetheart, resigns herself to the idea that he will not come back to her. She then asks for death and forsakes God. Late one night, William arrives by horse and calls for Lenore to ride with him. As he is persuading her to mount his horse behind him, William recites a rhyme: 'Look round thee, love, the moon shines clear, the dead ride swiftly, never fear, we'll reach our marriage bed'. She consents, and William repeats his rhyme, varying some of the words, causing Lenore to protest, and ask him why he names the dead.

A cock crows just as the couple reach a churchyard, and William waves it away. He points to a newly dug grave and says that this is their marriage bed, at which point, his flesh drops away, leaving only his skeleton. Lenore falls, and dancing fiends from hell tell us that this is her punishment for giving voice to her dissatisfaction with God. But they add that if Lenore were to repent and call on God, her soul could still be redeemed.[10] This poem exhibits many motifs that are consistent with European oral tradition.

The earlier English songs that appeared in popular broadsheets lacked the literary gravitas of Bürger's 'Lenore', but their wide distribution made them more well known in Britain. 'The Suffolk Miracle', for example, was a homegrown ballad situated in East Anglia that proved to be one of the more widely circulated of these early publications. It features a farmer's daughter named Nancy and her paramour, Frank, a young neighbour. Her father sought to break up their liaison and exiled his daughter to her uncle's home, 'forty miles distant'. Frank subsequently dies of a broken heart, but Nancy is not told of his death.

After 'a month or more', Frank comes to Nancy at night, riding her father's horse, and asks her to come with him. As they ride, Frank complains of a headache, and Nancy binds his head with her handkerchief. He takes her to her father's house and then stables the horse. Nancy reports to her father, who realizes that Frank, now long dead and buried, had been his daughter's escort that night. Her father goes to the stable and finds his horse covered in sweat. They subsequently unearth Frank's corpse and find Nancy's handkerchief around his head, even though his body has turned 'into mould'. When they reveal everything to Nancy, she dies of fright and grief. A final verse warns parents against trying to separate young lovers.

As with 'Lenore', many elements in 'The Suffolk Miracle' are consistent with variants from oral tradition. The motif of the handkerchief around Frank's head furnishes physical evidence within the story that the incident really occurred, a powerful device common in many legends.[11] The ballad also deviates from most oral variants in that the corpse makes no effort to take Nancy into the grave.

Understanding the Cornish Variant

Against this backdrop, it is possible to consider nineteenth-century published collections from Cornwall. Bottrell's story of 'Nancy Trenoweth', described above, uses the same names, Nancy and Frank, as they appear in 'The Suffolk Miracle'. That aside, there are significant differences. Hunt's version is an abridged adaptation of the story that Bottrell published in 1870, and so the example from Hunt can be discounted for the purposes of this analysis.[12]

Additional Cornish variants appear in the collections: Bottrell published 'A Legend of Pargwarra', which relates a story located at a place that the 'old folks also called ... the Sweethearts' Cove, from a tradition of its having been the scene of a tragical [sic] love-story ...'.[13] Hunt provides a similar story, 'The Lovers of Porthangwartha', which differs sufficiently to suggest that the two early folklorists recorded distinct recitations of the same legend. Bottrell's story tells of a rich farmer whose daughter, again named Nancy, falls in love with one of the servants, a young man named William, who goes to sea during the summers. In winter, William entertains the household with stories of distant lands. When Nancy's mother realizes that her daughter has fallen in love with William, she tells her to find a better match. Nancy's father, however, is sympathetic and suggests that if William were to take a voyage where he could acquire a great deal of wealth, he could win Nancy's hand.

Prior to William's voyage, Nancy and William vow their commitment to one another, using a variety of magical means to bind themselves together. After three years, Nancy takes to walking the cliffs, searching for the ship that would return her beloved William. 'One moonlit winter's night', Bottrell tells us, Nancy 'heard William's voice just under her window saying, "Sleepest thou, sweetheart, awaken and come hither, love; my boat awaits us in the cove, thou must come this night or never be my bride"'. Nancy's Aunt Prudence hears William's words as well as Nancy's response that she would come. Prudence looks outside to see William, 'dripping wet and deathly pale'. Nancy leaves with William, and Prudence dresses and follows, but no matter how quickly she runs, she cannot catch up with the young lovers who 'seemed to glide down the rocky pathway leading to Pargwarra as if borne on the wind'.

Finally, Prudence sees them in the cove on a large flat rock beside a boat. A fog rolls in, and although Prudence calls, there is no answer. When the mist clears for a moment, Prudence sees by the bright moonlight that 'the boat and the lovers had disappeared'. The next day, William's father goes to Nancy's parents, expecting to find his son, because the previous night, the young man appeared before him and told him he was going to collect his bride. That afternoon, a sailor comes to William's father and tells him that William had become the captain of a ship with rich cargo. He had wanted to take the ship's boat to shore at Pargwarra to visit Nancy and her parents, but he had fallen into the sea and could not be retrieved. Bottrell concludes by writing 'all knew then that William's ghost had taken Nancy to a phantom boat, and a watery grave was the lovers' bridal-bed. Thus their rash vows of constancy, even in death, were fulfilled.'

At the end of 'A Legend of Pargwarra', Bottrell makes several observations that are useful in this context. He indicates, for example, that 'there are other versions of this story, that only vary from the above in details of little interest'. While knowing the other details would have been valuable to this analysis, Bottrell is revealing that he had encountered an active tradition in which the story was repeated.

In addition, Bottrell makes two references to printed material. He recalls that the story was 'best known to me from fragments of a quaint old "copy of verses"'. He also notes that 'I have recently tried in vain to find anyone who knows the old "copy of verses", the argument of which I have for the most part followed'. Apparently, the collector is suggesting that his version of 'A Legend of Pargwarra' was adapted from his memory of a document that he had once seen but could no longer find. Complicating matters, an early printing of several versions of 'The Yarmouth Tragedy' often ends with a man named 'Jemmy' dying at sea and coming to retrieve his Nancy, who willingly succumbs to drowning. These were available from several British sources with different details. It is possible that this was the source of the Cornish variant with the death of the couple by drowning, but it is just as conceivable that someone circulated a printed Cornish version elsewhere in Britain where it inspired the watery end of the 'The Yarmouth Tragedy'.

Bottrell later reveals that:

> the fragments I recited, however, recalled to a few old folks a newer piece called the 'Strains of Lovely Nancy', that used to be printed in a broad sheet and sung and sold by wandering ballad singers of the west, forty or fifty years ago; and from what I have heard of the latter one might conclude it to have been a modernised and an imperfect version of the ancient tragedy.

With this, he is suggesting that 'A Legend of Pargwarra' inspired publications in the early part of the nineteenth century, and it is easy to imagine that while the oral tradition influenced the printed lyrics of songs, the published version, in turn, influenced the oral tradition.[14] The tradition Bottrell describes recalls Quick's career, the so-called 'last of the droll tellers' mentioned in Chapter 2; Quick committed his verses to print so he could gain payment for his story-telling. With these three observations, Bottrell provides insight into the nature of the tradition he encountered in the mid-nineteenth century.

Hunt also published this story, recording it as 'The Lovers of Porthangwartha', which he notes with the following: 'This is said to mean the Lover's Cove'. He provides less detail than Bottrell, as is usually the case, but Hunt does relay that 'a simple story, however, remains, the mere fragment, without doubt, of a longer and more ancient tale'.[15] A comparison of the two versions of the legend, attached to the same cove, is instructive. It would be easy to imagine that Hunt had simply reworked Bottrell's notes, abridging the story, but this is clearly not the case. As was typical, Hunt summarizes a great deal that a skilful droll teller would have used to craft an elaborate narrative, but not all raconteurs are created equally, and it is possible that Hunt heard his version in a shortened form. More importantly, while his story deviates significantly from Bottrell's, the two share motifs that suggest they are part of the same body of oral tradition.

For example, both versions lack the motif of the horse ride. Because the young man in these two legends is lost at sea, the ultimate destination of the night's adventure cannot be an earthly grave. And unlike more terrestrial variants, the woman dies while in his company, apparently willing to begin her eternal voyage with him. In addition, the stories share the motif of the rock where they are last seen before disappearing into the sea, and moonlight, an essential feature to allow the events to be seen, adds the same eerie quality to both tales. An older woman observes the couple as they disappear into the waves, and in each story, she reports hearing singing, which Bottrell attributes to mermaids, 'whose wild unearthly strains were wont, before tempests, to be heard resounding'.

While the shared motifs point towards the common body of oral tradition that focuses on the same location, differences indicate distinct sources. Hunt tells of finding the body of the young woman 'a day or two after in a neighbouring cove'. He also relates that people eventually heard that the young man died far away on the night of the incident. For Bottrell, William's death also happened that night, but it occurred while he was attempting to come ashore near his home. In addition, Hunt's lovers pledge their eternal devotion 'under the light of the full moon', while Bottrell offers an elaborate description of a night-time ceremony including that they joined hands 'in a living spring' and:

> broke a gold ring in two ..., each one keeping a part. And to make their vows more binding they kindled, at dead of night, a fire on the Garrack Zans (holy rock), which then stood in Roskestal townplace, and joined their hands over the flame, called on all the powers of heaven and earth to witness their common oaths to each other living or dead.

For all the detail, Bottrell does not mention a full moon, but rather refers to the ceremony occurring in the dead of night.

In addition, the witness to the final incident varies in each. In Bottrell's version, she is an aunt, and for Hunt she is 'an old crone'. Bottrell has the young man fetch his bride-to-be, coming to her window, while Hunt describes the woman descending to the cove and waiting for her bridegroom who eventually appears, after which the two seem 'to float off upon the waters'. The array of distinct details throughout suggests separate manifestations of the legend. This reinforces the idea that there were, as Bottrell describes, other versions of this story.

Hunt provides a hint of yet another variant in the introduction to his third edition of Cornish folklore. He credits Bottrell with information about a ballad from oral tradition, giving just enough details to suggest it was probably a variant of Tale Type ATU 365, 'Lenore'. Hunt includes five verses of the ballad sung by 'an old blind man', the previously described droll teller named Uncle Anthony James. The snippet establishes that two young lovers are separated by the death of the man, and 'then follows a stormy kind of duet between the maiden and her lover's ghost, who tries to persuade the maid to accompany him to the world of the shadows'.[16] This is not enough to grasp much about the specific motifs included in this version, but it is further information about how popular the story was in Cornwall.[17]

The Irish Variants

The survey of the Irish variants of the story by Uí Ógaín and O'Connor provides a useful means to examine the essential components of 'The Dead Bridegroom Carries off His Bride'. Following this approach, it is possible to have a basis for comparison. The two Irish folklorists see the story as follows:

1. *Establishing the situation with the couple.* Two young people pledge themselves to marry, but the union is deemed unacceptable because of religion or a difference in social status.

2. *The young man's death.* The Irish folklorists indicate that although there are various ways that the young man dies, 'in all versions … the boy dies without the girl's knowledge'.[18]

3. *The rendezvous.* As prearranged, the young man arrives at night with a horse to elope with the young woman; she sits behind him on the horse.

4. *The various accessories that appear.* In some versions, she carries a bundle of clothes.

5. *The journey.* The Irish folklorists point out that 'in all versions the couple rides away on horseback'.[19]

6. *The discovery of the spirit's true nature.* This part of the story shows greater variation. Three Kerry versions have the young woman asking the young man to spur the horse to ride more quickly, but he says he cannot, the reason being that he has no strength in his foot because he is dead. In one of the Kerry versions, it is not directly apparent that something is amiss until he jumps from the horse and widens the grave so they can both sleep there. Many of the versions feature the crowing

of a cock, which the young man denies hearing or he asserts that it is unimportant. In some variants, he makes no reply. The young woman usually becomes uneasy because of his strange words. In two Galway versions, she sees by the moonlight that the horse only has three legs. Some examples describe her seeing a moonlit reflection in a stream, revealing that he wears a burial shroud or a death band, the fabric tied over the top of the head to keep a corpse's jaw from falling open.

7. *The escape*. The Irish versions also exhibit considerable variation in the conclusion. The Kerry variants have the young woman throwing herself off the horse as they pass a house or a forge. In tales from Kerry and Longford, she leaves her bundle of clothes, which are discovered the next morning, shredded and scattered atop the young man's grave. In another version, she escapes into a house and bars the door. He persuades her to put her hand through the window, and he slices off the ends of her fingers, which are found in his grasp during his wake the next day. The Galway versions have a blacksmith who runs to help the young woman, driving away the revenant with a piece of red-hot iron, which the smith sometimes uses to burn through the fabric in the dead man's clutch. The blacksmith is absent in the Kerry examples. Many versions describe the young woman's subsequent ill health, and the County Longford narrative explains that she died three weeks after the incident.

The Cornish Contribution

The kinship between the Cornish and Irish variants is evident, but differences are significant as well. Bottrell's elaborate tale, 'Nancy Trenoweth, The Fair Daughter of the Miller of Alsia', compares nicely with the Irish material, including as it does, the midnight ride, the recognition of the lover's true nature as seen in his moonlit reflection in water, and the young woman's escape with the help of a blacksmith and his red-hot iron. These motifs are sufficient to demonstrate a genetic relationship between the Irish and Cornish material, and at the same time, they prove that the two bodies of similar tales could not have grown separately out of the ballad tradition, which did not employ shared motifs. Similarly, the poem 'Lenore' could not have inspired the traditions, as it also lacks the motifs that appear in both Ireland and Cornwall.

While many details tie the variants together regardless of the country of origin, the maritime career and watery death of the young Cornishman represent a significant divergence, nicely adapted to Cornwall's sea-going

18. A nineteenth-century Icelandic collection of folklore included an example of the 'Lenore Legend'. This illustration dates to 1864, accompanying 'The Deacon of Myrká'. It captures the terrifying moment when the deacon's head pitches forward, allowing his would-be bride to see his exposed skull shining in the moonlight. At that moment, she realizes that she rides with a corpse.

economy. Both Bottrell and Hunt describe the couple walking to a cove and boarding a boat that transports them to an undersea grave. Here, Cornish storytellers have modified the tradition into something that is almost entirely new, lacking the horse and the terrestrial resting place. The role, if any, of 'The Yarmouth Tragedy' in affecting the Cornish variants is unknown, but the Cornish focus on the sea sets it apart from other variants collected by folklorists in Europe.

The motif of the moonlight plays a central role in the array of international examples, but the Cornish versions featuring the flight to the sea require lunar illumination to serve another function. In most examples outside Cornwall, moonlight provides the means for the woman to discover that her companion is dead. Many of the stories describe how she sees his reflection in water, made visible by the light of the full moon, revealing that he is wrapped in a shroud or that he wears the headband used to keep a corpse's jaw from opening, a motif that appears in some Irish variants. As noted, two Galway versions have the woman seeing that the horse lacks a fourth leg. In an Icelandic legend, the man's head pitches forward as the horse takes a jump, and with that, the woman sees the back of his skull shining in the moonlight.[20] In the Cornish expressions of

Tale Type ATU 365, 'Lenore', however, the woman does not survive the night, and so she cannot provide the details of how moonlight might have helped her understand what was happening. Instead, the moon allows a third party to bear witness to the strange events.

The motifs unique to Cornwall set its narratives apart from the rest. The lost lover fits into the context of the maritime industry, which regularly sent Cornwall's sons on distant expeditions. But the implication of this deviation made the horse an awkward remnant of a foreign story. These changes, combined with the insights of Bottrell and Hunt, make it clear that a vibrant Cornish tradition modified a legend which was widespread in Europe.

One further piece of information hints at an additional, thought-provoking connection. Child writes that 'the ballads seem less original than the tales; that is, to have been made from the tales, as "The Suffolk Miracle" was'. He further notes that 'reverting now to the English tales, we perceive that the Cornish is a very well-preserved specimen of the extensive cycle'. Child also cites a version from Brittany collected by Sébillot, which the French collector indicated in 1879 was like the poem 'Lenore'. Child suggests the variant from Brittany is much like 'The Suffolk Miracle', but as he notes 'This is the English ballad over again, almost word for word, with the difference that the lover dies at sea ...'.[21] This is insufficient to demonstrate an oral tradition shared by Cornwall and Brittany, influenced and adapted to the sea, but this tantalizing clue suggests one may have existed.

Legends of the Dead

The Cornish story of 'The Spectre Bridegroom' draws on two ideas that are worldwide. The first is the belief that the dead occasionally walk among the living. The second is that sometimes supernatural beings have love affairs with people, usually with a tragic result. Both motifs are international and in turn have inspired a great deal of literature. Because the boundary between folklore and the written word is porous, each has influenced the other.[22]

Tales of ghosts permeate literature and have done so for thousands of years, with examples appearing in Homeric poetry, the Old Testament, continental medieval literature and Icelandic sagas. Counterparts in oral tradition are so widespread as to suggest that this was the case before the invention of writing. Although stories of hauntings are ubiquitous, it is generally accepted that most of the dead rest in peace. And yet, some do not. The Finnish scholar, Juha Pentikäinen, considers a belief in the dead who trouble the living because they lack an acceptable status in death. This concept applies nicely to the situation of

'The Dead Bridegroom Carries off His Bride', an observation of Uí Ógaín and O'Connor.[23] In this case, the ghost cannot rest because of the intensity of the love he and his betrothed shared in life. In addition, many stories underscore the excessive nature of their secret vows and the fact that the lovers often employ magic to bind themselves together. There is an implicit warning here that one should not use supernatural means beyond Christian prayer and ceremony to affect outcomes.

Numerous examples of ill-fated, supernatural romances come to mind in European literature. These sorts of liaisons have inspired medieval stories of sexual encounters between elves and people, ballets featuring seductive swan-women, and modern novels and films with rakish vampires. The popularity of broadsheet ballads describing the 'Spectre Bridegroom' draws on this same fascination with what happens when people cross the barrier that separates the natural from the supernatural, all in the name of love.

For what appears to be the earliest printed expression of this specific motif, one needs to reach back to eleventh-century Scandinavian literature. The medieval collection of verse, *The Poetic Edda*, includes the 'Second Lay of Helgi the Hunding-Slayer'. This describes how Helgi, a dead hero, returns from the grave on a horse to beckon his beloved Sigrún to him for one last night of conjugal bliss. The document hints at the age of the motif, but it also suggests that initially, the story may have played out differently: Sigrún willingly enters Helgi's burial mound to lie with him. The poem subsequently relates that the heroine 'lived but a short while longer, for grief and sorrow'. With this, the medieval text concurs with the conclusion of its more recent counterpart.[24] This example suggests that for pre-Christian society, crossing the line into the realm of the dead in the name of romance could be seen as heroic. Nineteenth-century expressions of the story generally assert that no living person would want to enter the grave, even if it were the last resting place of a lover.[25]

Conclusion

Bottrell, ever the intuitive folklorist, recognizes the similarities shared by the broadsheet ballads and his collection. Without the comparative tools developed only a few decades later in the early twentieth century, he could not have known how his stories would tally with a larger oral context shared with other parts of Europe.[26] A quick look at sources from other countries demonstrates that the Cornish droll tellers did not borrow their stories from the broadsheet ballads. They may have taken some motifs or names from the published sources, but the Cornish storytellers charted a new direction for the international, centuries-old tale. Bottrell's 'Nancy Trenoweth' hints at how elaborate the telling of this legend could be. His story is full of diverse motifs which define a unique Cornish contribution to the variants of the story. These versions were not the poor cousins of material from elsewhere, but instead, they were part of a fully developed, thriving Cornish oral tradition.

The Cornish focus on the maritime career of the young man was taken so far that the droll tellers eliminated the horse and replaced it with a boat. The drowning of the young woman before speaking to others required a different witness to the startling event, shifting the moonlight away from its original role of enabling the would-be bride to see the true nature of her intended; in the Cornish stories, the moonlight provides a third party the opportunity to observe what happened. As 'The Dead Bridegroom Carries off His Bride' travelled from one area to the next, Cornish storytellers modified it to suit themselves and their listeners, precisely the way von Sydow described how oral tradition adapted when it diffused.[27]

Thompson, the master of the folktale, wrote in 1946 that 'no comparative study of the relation of [Tale Type ATU 365] to the ballad has been made which would indicate whether verse or prose would seem to be the original form'. He then indicates that the Baltic States had many representations of the story, whereas 'versions hardly appear in other parts of Europe'.[28] A comprehensive monograph might confirm his suspicion that the story originated in the east, but the analysis of the Irish material and this look at Cornish variants demonstrate that the tradition thrived in western Europe as well. Because many motifs shared in the stories do not appear in the ballads, it is clear the legend was not inspired by printed broadsheets, but rather thrived in oral tradition, predating and ultimately supplying the material for the ballads themselves.

The following chapter, which examines the subject of giants, addresses yet another aspect of indigenous Cornish folklore. In this case, however, the topic is entwined with non-Cornish traditions and how people from other parts of Britain viewed Cornwall and its behemothic supernatural creatures.

CHAPTER NINE

Giants

Ancient traditions tell us that, long before monks or saints set foot in Cornwall, a mighty race of Titans dwelt in our hills, woods, and carns, who were anciently the masters of the world and the ancestors of the true Celtic race, and who, as they exceeded all other people in health and strength of body, were looked upon as giants.[1]

Thus begins Bottrell's initial book on Cornish folklore, published in 1870. For this pathfinder among folklorists, giants were so important to the Cornish oral tradition that he uses the subject for his opening words, but he finds additional significance in the topic, believing that it also sheds light on the indigenous 'Celtic race'. Abundant Cornish legends provide an opportunity to understand this colossal supernatural being.[2]

While Cornwall has a rich tradition regarding giants, stories about them have a deep legacy throughout Britain and Ireland. A problem arises, however, in that some well-known stories about these enormous creatures are said to take place in Cornwall but are not actually Cornish in origin. It is necessary, therefore, to determine whether specific examples represent authentic Cornish folklore or traditions held outside of Cornwall that were projected onto this remote peninsula.

Cornish Giants from Antiquity

Several historical documents identify Cornwall as a particularly important home for giants. Geoffrey of Monmouth, the twelfth-century British historian mentioned in Chapter 1, maintains that the mythic Trojan settler of Cornwall, Corineus, 'experienced great pleasure from wrestling with the giants, of whom there were far more there than in any districts' of Britain.[3] He proceeds to recount a tale about a contest between Corineus and Gogmagog, who was 'a particularly repulsive' indigenous behemoth, twelve feet in height. The two wrestled, and at the outset, the giant broke three of Corineus's ribs. At that, the Trojan hero became furious and:

> heaved Gogmagog up on to his shoulders, and running as fast as he could under the weight, he hurried off to the nearby coast. He clambered up to the top of a mighty cliff, shook himself free and hurled this deadly monster ... far out into the sea. The giant fell on to a sharp reef of rocks, where he was dashed into a thousand fragments and stained the waters with his blood.

The text then describes how that place was 'called Gogmagog's Leap to this day'.[4]

The fourteenth-century Cornish poet John Havillan placed giants squarely in his homeland:

> There gyants whilome dwelt, whose clothes were skins of beasts;
> Whose drink was blood; whose cups, to serve for use at feasts,
> Were made of hollow Wood; whose beds were bushie thornes;
> And lodgings rocky caves, to shelter them from storms;
> Their chambers craggie rocks; their hunting found them meat.
> To ravish and to kill, to them was pleasure great.
> Their violence was rule; with rage and fury led,
> They rusht into the fight, and fought hand over head.
> Their bodies were interr'd behind some bush or brake,
> To bear such monstrous wights, the earth did grone and quake.
> These pestred most the western tract; more fear made thee agast,
> O Cornwall, utmost doore that art to let in Zephyrus blast.[5]

In his *Survey of Cornwall*, written in 1602, Carew repeats Geoffrey of Monmouth's reference to the giant Gogmagog and provides some of the same story. Carew maintains that the giant helped shape Cornish geography.[6] Later in the seventeenth century, John Milton (1608–1674) also repeats the story in *The History of Britain*.[7] These early sources provide evidence that people long regarded Cornwall as a place where stories about giants thrived. Folklore collected in the nineteenth century echoes this. Indeed, discussions of 'English' giants invariably cite Cornish sources or feature stories set in Cornwall. Early chapbooks, pamphlets sold by pedlars and other merchants, placed the epic contests of Jack the Giant Killer in the peninsula, even though the popular publications were produced elsewhere for a larger British audience.[8] Ironically, Cornwall was both a home to piskies, some of the region's smallest fairies, and to giants.

The Northern European Giant

Cornwall was not unique in its association with giants. Traditions of enormous supernatural beings were well developed elsewhere in northern Europe including in other places in Britain as well as in Scandinavia. Legends about giants were generally etiological, meaning that they were told to explain the origins of things, typically old structures or features in the landscape. The name of the Giant's Causeway recalls an old legend that tells of one of these entities who built a path to walk from Ireland to Scotland. Wade's Causeway is a Roman road in Yorkshire, and in this case, it is a landmark credited to Wade the Giant. The etiological role of giants was paramount, but the explanation of the landscape, megaliths, or extraordinary landmarks in general could merge with stories about other supernatural beings. For example, the Devil's Dyke in Cambridgeshire is an example of a tradition which holds that Satan affected the landscape in a way normally reserved for giants.[9]

Consistent with what is found elsewhere in Britain, there are several landscape features associated with Cornish giants. For example, people look to the notorious giant, Bolster, when considering some places in Cornwall. Near Chapel Porth Cove not far from St Agnes on the north Cornish coast, indentations in a stone are seen to be the result of the fingers and foot of Bolster, imprinted as he stooped to drink. Similarly, 'Bolster Bank' is an ancient earthwork that stretches over three kilometres at the base of the hill known as St Agnes Beacon on the north-west coast of Cornwall. It was likely a defensive structure, but with original intent forgotten, folk belief introduced the idea that Bolster created the feature. This landscape is now a focus of 'St Agnes Bolster Day' celebrated on the first day of May. The event includes a re-enactment of the killing of the giant who appears as an enormous puppet, slain through the trickery of the saintly maiden as discussed below.

Other giant-related Cornish features include Dodman Point on the south coast near Mevagissey; the Iron-Age fort known as Giant's Castle at St Mary's on the Isles of Scilly; Carn Brea Castle near Camborne and Redruth in the west of Cornwall, where people refer to granite blocks as the Giant's Hand, Head, Coffin, Wheel, and Cradle. In addition, the Giant's Hedge, originally extending over ten kilometres near Lerryn, inspired a folk rhyme:

> Jack the Giant had nothing to do,
> So he made a hedge from Lerrin to Looe.

Bottrell also recounts how a cave east of Hayle had been called the Giant's Zawn (a Cornish word designating a deep narrow sea inlet), the imagined

The Giant Bolster. striding from the Beacon to Carn Brea.
— A distance of six miles —

19. The image of 'Bolster' by famed Victorian illustrator George Cruikshank for Robert Hunt's *Popular Romances*, published in 1865. The artist described in a note how he imagined the Cornish giant: 'if a Giant could stride 6 miles across a country he must be 12 miles in height, …. In order to get a sight of the *head* of such a Giant, the spectator must be distant a mile or two from the figure. This would … place the spectator about 15 miles distant from the Giant's head.'

home of a creature named Wrath, but he concedes that the place had gained
the more recent name of Ralph's Cupboard, in recognition of a smuggler.

Together these Cornish landmarks provide living links with belief, evoking
the timeless connection of ancient supernatural beings of gigantic proportion
with the landscape. Belief may fade, and legends cease to be told, but as people
recall a place that honours a giant, the supernatural being remains part of the
local cultural legacy. Specifically, the names and celebration associated with
Bolster look beyond legend, to how belief inspired people to perceive the hand
of a giant in their landscape, perpetuated over generations. In the most recent
chapter of Cornwall's heritage, people have adapted their tradition, transforming it into a modern commemoration of an old story.[10]

While Cornwall shares much with other northern European traditions
involving giants, understanding the complexity of story and belief is more difficult
outside of Cornwall. Nordic giant folklore, for example, is not easy to unravel
since the line separating giants from trolls is often blurred. In addition, an older
body of literature documents gigantic opponents who fought the gods in the
pre-conversion primordial world of Nordic mythology. Many European stories
describe giants as extraordinary adversaries, and generally the endings describe
their demise. Because legends tend to place giants in a remote time, it was easy
for legends to transform into folktales, accounts told as fiction. Of course, all
supernatural beings could appear in both legends and folktales, but giants, as
entities of a distant and fabulous past, were especially apt to appear in both.[11]

A legend about a giant may have been told to be believed, but it could not be
set in the present: while many pre-industrial people thought it possible to see a
fairy, for example, one was not likely to encounter a giant because they typically
lived 'long ago' and stories often described how they were driven to extinction.
British accounts of giant-defeating heroes were naturally set in the past but
frequently, they were also consigned to a strange, distant land. In England, these
exotic places were often Wales or Cornwall which were sufficiently remote from
a pre-modern English point of view. It is worth pointing out in this context that
as late as the mid-twentieth century, the celebrated J.R.R. Tolkien (1892–1973)
placed his giants in the 'Welsh wilderness'. In his fantasy romp, *Farmer Giles of
Ham*, he described these enormous supernatural beings in the 'Wild Hills' west
and north of an imagined medieval English village.[12]

Lotte Motz (1922–1997) observes a similar situation from an early
Scandinavian perspective which also placed giants in remote locations. She
argues that the homes of giants were often seen as being 'to the north and east
of the heartland of Germanic settlement,' and that they 'belong, in these cases
to the vast area of present-day Lapland, Finland, and northern Russia where a

non-agricultural population had wrested from the earliest time of history, its living from the forest and from the sea'.[13] Although Motz may be leaning here towards an explanation of how different archaic lifestyles became associated with the popular notion of giants, it is more likely that these were simply seen as far-flung mysterious places where many strange things occurred and existed.

Giant-related Traditions from and about Cornwall

While many in Britain perceived Cornwall and Wales as exotic locations likely to be inhabited by giants, it is important to consider the nature of giant-related folklore as it manifested in Cornwall. The first step in the process of understanding Cornish giant traditions is to separate them from stories told elsewhere but with a setting in the peninsula. Padel maintains that Geoffrey of Monmouth was from Cornwall, but the validity of his argument is irrelevant when considering the nineteenth century: the medieval writer may have been Cornish, but over time his place of birth became obscure and his historical narrative emerged as the property of all of Britain. In addition, the story of mortal combat between Corineus and Gogmagog was confined to print and was not something that nineteenth-century collectors could have gathered in Cornwall. By republishing the account, Hunt strengthened the perception that it was an example of current Cornish folklore.[14] Careful consideration is unlikely to disentangle the origin of the story of Corineus and Gogmagog but it can be set aside when considering nineteenth-century traditions.

In contrast with the legacy of Geoffrey of Monmouth, Bottrell's rambling legend, 'The Giants of Towednack' has all the appearance of a typical Cornish narrative. Embedded in the tale is additional insight as the collector reveals, 'in this portion of the droll, the old folks of Lelant and Towednack (where the story is best known) relate many uninteresting details with respect to the week of games and feasting which celebrated the arrival of the tinkard in their country'.[15] In short, Bottrell condensed a long account which he likely heard told in Cornwall.

The antiquarian Halliwell-Phillipps provides an example of how non-Cornish narratives can be confused with those actually from the Duchy. He provides a web of English stories about giants in Cornwall together with what are likely native Cornish accounts about them. His book, *Rambles in Western Cornwall by the footsteps of The Giants*, celebrates the English perception that the remote place was home to traditions about giants, but he is vague as to whether he recorded any stories and beliefs during his 'rambles'. He opens his first chapter, 'The Land of Giants', with the familiar account of Corineus and

the giant Gogmagog which is clearly borrowed from elsewhere. Other observations mention Jack the Giant Killer, which is said to be an English tradition.[16]
There are reasons to call into question the work of Halliwell-Phillipps since
he had a poor reputation for scholarship. In general, his volume can be set
aside, but his work serves as an example of how easily English traditions about
Cornwall have become blurred with those that are genuinely Cornish.

'Strong Hans' and Tale Type ATU 650A

Bottrell's 'The Giants of Towednack' features a strong young man named Tom
who fights a local giant, 'about fifteen feet in his boots'. During the struggle,
Tom mortally wounds the giant, is sorrowful for the deed, and then inherits
his estate, which includes a great deal of treasure. Tom is then challenged by
Jack the Tinkard, who is in turn victorious. The two then become fast friends,
but the story drifts away from the subject of the giant, which serves merely as
an introduction.[17]

   This story is echoed in several other Cornish narratives including Hunt's
'Tom the Giant, his Wife Jane, and Jack the Tinkeard'; 'The Lord of Pengerswick
and the Giant of St Michael's Mount'; 'Tom and the Giant Blunderbuss' and
his 'How Tom and the Tinkeard found the Tin, and how it led to the Morva
Fair'. These can be loosely classified as expressions of the folktale, ATU 650A,
'Strong Hans', although like many giant tales, folklorists define the group with
only a few motifs rather than as a complex of several plot devices that consistently appear together. The fact that these stories feature an incredibly strong
hero does not by itself suggest they are historically linked. Given the rare
examples and the limited similarities of the Cornish stories to others in the
European catalogue, these variants do little more than to express a concept of
heroism and giants that is consistent with that of northern Europe in general.

   British examples of ATU 650A are made even more problematic by the fact
that several English expressions of this story are set in Cornwall, giving the
impression that these, too, are instances of Cornish folklore. After separating
English and Cornish traditions about the strong hero and the giant, only a
marginal opportunity for analysis remains. Fortunately, these are not the only
giant stories from Cornish sources.

Giants Throwing Stones and Tools

In 'The Giants of Trecrobben and the Mount', Bottrell provides a brief account of
a giant asking another to throw him a hammer. The one obliges, but as he hurls

the tool across Mount's Bay, the wife of the other steps in the way and is killed.[18] This is echoed by Hunt's 'The Giant of St Michael's Mount loses his Wife'. These stories are expressions of a single motif: F.531.3.2.3, 'Giants throw tools back and forth', but this classification is silent on the death of the giant's wife.[19]

The motif of giants throwing stones appears elsewhere in Britain and is so prevalent that it even occurs in the writings of Tolkien and C.S. Lewis (1898–1963).[20] It is also reasonable to see this motif behind Thor flinging his hammer at giants. This is particularly true of his struggle with the giant Hrungnir who threw his enormous whetstone at Thor just as the god hurled his hammer. Pre-conversion northern European stories often linked the attributes of heroes with those of their adversaries.[21] The inclination of giants to throw things is ubiquitous, and the Cornish stories underscore how this widespread tradition appeared in the peninsula. Since the death of the giantess does not feature often in the stories, it is not possible to reach any meaningful conclusions about it.

Stones in the Landscape

The Cornish also attribute large rocks in the landscape to other escapades of the giants, a tradition that persists to the present. For example, T.C. Paris tells a story in his 1851 *A Hand-Book for Travellers in Devon and Cornwall* of the Giant's Staff in St Austell Downs which is credited to a giant walking in the hills one night when the wind blew off his hat. While chasing it, he found he was impeded by his staff which, 'he thrust … into the ground until his hat could be secured'. He did not find his hat, but when he returned he also lost track of his staff. The legend serves to explain the existence of the twelve-foot tall monolith, known as the Giant's Staff, or Longstone.[22]

An important cycle of legends provides yet another explanation of how giants left rocks in the landscape. Several Cornish narratives mention the spilling of stones from the apron of a giantess, a motif that is well known elsewhere. For example, Bottrell describes the origin of the earthworks at St Agnes. In this case, Bolster the giant ordered his wife to clear a field of stones and deposit them on the top of a hill. The story differs from other narratives of how stone features were created in that it does not include the idea of a broken apron string, which is common elsewhere in Britain, but it does demonstrate that the motif of the giantess hauling rocks in her apron occurred in Cornwall.[23]

There are other stories from the Cornish collections featuring the motif of a giantess hauling and spilling rocks. For example, Hunt's story, 'The Giants of the Mount', describes the giant Cormoran and his wife Cormelian. Cormoran

20.   Joseph Blight created this lithograph for William Bottrell's books on folklore.
It depicts early inhabitants of Cornwall watching a giant in primitive dress as he moves
enormous rocks. His sculpted landscape left remarkable features that seem beyond
the abilities of humanity, attesting to the existence of his kind from long ago.

wanted to build his home on what would become St Michael's Mount, which, at
the time was situated some six miles from the sea and was known as 'the White
Rock in the Wood'. He selected a quarry of white granite blocks and enlisted
his wife to help carry them to the site of their new home. As Hunt writes,
'it would seem that the heaviest burdens were imposed upon Cormelian, and
that she was in the habit of carrying those rocky masses in her apron'. The
narrative describes that, given there were 'large masses of greenstone rock'
nearer to the proposed site of the giants' new home, Cormelian reasoned that
those rocks would be just as good as the white ones.

> One day, when Cormoran was sleeping, she broke off a vast mass of
> the greenstone rock, and taking it in her apron, hastened towards
> the artificial hill with it, hoping to place it without being observed
> ... When, however, Cormelian was within a short distance of the

'White Rock,' the giant awoke and presently perceived that his
wife was, contrary to his wishes, carrying a green stone instead
of a white one. In great wrath he arose, followed her, and, with
a dreadful imprecation, gave her a kick. Her apron-string broke,
and the stone fell on the sand. There it has ever since remained,
no human power being sufficient to remove it. The giantess died,
and the mass of greenstone resting, as it does, on clay slate rocks,
became her monument.[24]

This motif of a giantess carrying large stones in her apron is used to explain
other features in the landscape throughout Europe, suggesting that it is part
of a larger tradition.[25] Often in these stories, the giantess spills some of her
burden or her apron string breaks causing some or all of her stones to tumble.

Although a giantess is typically at the heart of these stories, the legends can
also feature a giant as opposed to a giantess, the devil, a witch, fairies of various
sorts, the goddess Athena and even the Virgin Mary. In addition, the distribution
of this motif is extensive, appearing in England, Wales, Ireland, Scotland, the
Isle of Man, Jersey, Brittany, Scandinavia and Germany.[26] Barclodiad y Gawres,
'the apronful of the giantess', is a Megalithic burial chamber in Anglesey off
the Welsh coast that commemorates the idea of a giantess carrying large stones
in her apron.[27] Motz and von Sydow consider examples from Germany and
Scandinavia, where stories account for offshore islands or isolated boulders.[28]
Variations sometimes describe soil or sand instead of rocks. In addition, some
stories feature a glove or some other piece of clothing rather than an apron to
carry the rocks.

A poem, generally credited to Jonathan Swift (1667–1745), celebrates an
Irish legend involving a giant hag dropping stones from her apron:

> Determined now her tomb to build,
> Her ample skirt with stones she filled,
> And dropped a heap on Carnmore;
>
> Then stepped one thousand yards, to Loar,
> And dropped another goodly heap;
> Gained Carnbeg; and on its height
> Displayed the wonders of her might.[29]

This example from Irish literature underscores the antiquity and geographic
distribution of the broken apron string of the giantess. In addition, the motif

is echoed in the Mediterranean island of Malta where the enormous Sansuna is reputed to have built a megalithic temple, carrying stones on her head while cradling a baby under her arm.[30] The occurrence of this well-known motif in the collections of Cornish folklore demonstrate how the indigenous oral tradition was in keeping with that of its neighbours.

Giants Bleeding to Death

Another Cornish story features the idea of tricking a giant to bleed himself to death. Hunt and Bottrell include accounts of the giant Bolster, which describe how St Agnes convinced the enormous supernatural being that to prove his love for her, he needed to fill a chamber near the sea with his blood. Bolster complied, but he failed to see that the chamber led to the sea and he bled to death.[31] This motif also appears in Hunt's story, 'The Hack and Cast', situated in Gorran Haven near St Austell, where a troublesome giant became ill. A doctor arrived and told him that he needed to be bled by filling a hole near a cliff, which the giant did not realize fed into the sea. The giant obliged, but lost so much blood that he became weak, at which point the doctor kicked him off the cliff, killing him.[32]

These motifs are unfortunately too isolated to afford much insight. In a curious parallel, ATU 328, 'The Boy Steals the Giant's Treasure' often ends with motif G.520, 'Ogre deceived into self-injury'. The folktale type is famously expressed as 'Jack and the Beanstalk', which English tradition places in Cornwall, and yet there is no evidence of this story having been collected there.

ML 7060, 'The Disputed Site for a Church'

Spooner discusses a Cornish story about the need to relocate the construction site of a church in response to the objections of a giant. Christiansen classifies this type of narrative as ML 7060, 'The Disputed Site for a Church' which describes how the construction materials for a church are moved before the building can be completed. The man building the church recognizes that a supernatural being, often an elf-like creature or a troll, refuses to accept the planned location for the church. As a result, the people relocate the site. Sometimes the first spot selected for the construction is a pre-conversion sacred site, protected by the supernatural being. Spooner's Cornish accounts about a giant who objects to the site of a church appear to be related to this Scandinavian cycle of legends.[33]

In Scandinavia, church building more commonly features in ML 7065, 'Master Builders and their Supernatural Helpers'. Because of the need to explain how a church of some distinction, or some other imposing structure, came into being, people often looked for the agency of an extraordinary entity, such as a giant. ML 7065 is a widespread Scandinavian legendary cycle that features a giant, a troll, or sometimes even the devil who constructs a church for a price. The person who agreed to the bargain typically avoids payment by finding out the name of the mysterious builder who either dies or flees.[34] Cornwall does not have an expression of this more common legendary cycle involving the name of the supernatural helper. Nevertheless, this legend is reminiscent of narratives about the relocation of the construction site of a church, which manifests in Cornish variants.

Giant Playing with a Man

Bottrell's story of 'The Giant of Carn Galva' includes a touching narrative about a person from Choone who befriends the local giant by joining him in games. The giant 'in a good-natured way, tapped his playfellow on the head with the tips of his fingers' but not knowing his own strength, unwittingly killed him when his fingers entered the man's skull. While it is possible to perceive a generic motif in this account, namely F.531.5.1, 'Giant friendly to man', a specific parallel to this motif as expressed in Bottrell's legend is lacking, and the example from Cornwall appears to be unique.[35]

There is, however, a Scandinavian legend which tells of a giant's daughter who brings home a farmer together with his ox and plough so that she can play with them. Her father tells her to take the little creatures back to where she found them because it would not be right to abduct them in this way. Christiansen classifies this as ML 5015 'The plaything of the troll'.[36] There is no obvious reason to make a historical connection between 'The Giant of Carn Galva' and this Scandinavian legend type, but there is a shared underlying theme: although giants could be well disposed towards people and occasionally sought to engage with them, their enormous size could cause accidental harm.

Conclusion

Separating giant-related Cornish folklore from stories that non-Cornish story-tellers situate in the peninsula is a fundamental step in understanding these traditions.[37] While having its own narratives, Cornwall has also been the subject of a wider English folklore which easily conceived of the remote Duchy as a likely abode for giants. With that point clarified, it is possible to consider the body of native giant stories in greater depth.

At the core of giant legends throughout northern Europe is an association of these supernatural beings with strength, wealth, and rocks, and the Cornish examples are consistent with this idea. In the larger European body of material, narratives often describe giants throwing rocks or heavy tools, spilling stones carried in an apron and turning into rock at dawn's first light. Perhaps because rocks are primeval and are sometimes enormous in proportion, they were easily linked in the folk mind with giants, who are thought to have shaped the landscape with them. Motz underscores this observation by pointing out that one of the Old Norse names for a giant, *berg-búi*, means mountain or rock dweller.[38] The throwing of stones or tools between two giants represents a specific manifestation of this association. This is true also of a giantess hauling stones in her apron. These motifs express a general connection with stone in narrative form. Furthermore, legends about the apron string breaking under the weight of the rocks provide a specificity that goes beyond a generic link between rock and giant, suggesting a shared tradition throughout the region. Without a common body of story, diverse places were not likely to invent a motif as specific as the broken apron string.

A subject as impressive and widespread as giant folklore often attracts imaginative discussions. A modern psychotherapist, Brendan McMahon, asserts that Tom 'with his wheel and axle recalls images of the ancient Celtic sky gods, an interpretation that reaches back to the dawn of European thought'. According to McMahon, Jack in his hide coat conjures the image of the sorcerer depicted in the cave of the Trois-Frères in the south-west of France. He also employs a Freudian interpretation, drawing on the story of Oedipus, to understand the typical storyline of the hero slaying the older giant.[39] In another attempt to understand the topic, anthropologist Paul Manning writing in 2005 suggests that Cornish giants represent agricultural society while their foil, Jack the Tinkard, symbolizes the tin industry. This is part of Manning's attempt to see the 'Jewish' knockers of Cornwall as representative of the capitalistic mining economy as opposed to the consumer-based agricultural society.[40] Since these sorts of connections and interpretations cannot be proven nor refuted, they do little more than inspire speculation.

Approaching Cornish giant stories with comparative analysis opens the door to gleaning a better understanding of their role in local folklore. Unfortunately, there are insufficient accounts of Cornish giants to arrive at much in-depth analysis based on more than conjecture. Three observations are nevertheless appropriate. The first is that the popular perception of giants in Cornwall is shaped as much by English folklore as by actual Cornish texts. Source analysis can distinguish between that which constitutes indigenous tradition and that which has been set in Cornwall by storytellers from elsewhere. Secondly, it is appropriate to note that narratives about Cornish giants include motifs that are consistent with traditions found elsewhere: the generic attributes of giants are basically the same as those found throughout northern Europe. Finally, several Cornish motifs are unusual. These include the giant being tricked into bleeding himself into the sea and the giantess killed when a giant throws a tool, but there is too little information to draw indisputable conclusions about these traditions.

The way giants in folklore collections illustrate how others perceive Cornwall introduces the final two chapters. The transformation of the native knocker, the underground spirit of the mines, into the North American tommyknocker, underscores not only an indigenous aspect of folklore but also how others perceived that tradition.

CHAPTER TEN

Knockers in the Mines

Hunt records a story about 'an old man and his son named Trenwith' who had experience with knockers near Bosprennis on the south coast of Cornwall. These mining spirits are reminiscent of piskies and similar supernatural beings aboveground, dangerous but nevertheless capable of generosity towards people of good character. Unlike the piskies, the knockers commanded the subterranean world of the mine, a treacherous and eerie place.

In Hunt's story, the father and son saw the knockers bringing rich ore to the surface of a mine they were known to haunt. The miners promised the knockers a tenth of the profits in exchange for permission to excavate the vein of tin. They struck an agreement, and the men set to work. Everything proceeded well as long as the miners kept to the bargain, but when the father died, young Trenwith, who 'was avaricious and selfish, ... sought to cheat the Knockers' by hoarding all the wealth. His luck turned. 'He took to drink, squandered all the money his father had made, and died a beggar.'[1] This is typical of legends told about Cornish knockers: the creatures took the form of diminutive old men who played pranks and either warned miners of danger and led them to treasure or, conversely, punished transgressions.

Perhaps wherever miners went underground during pre-industrial times, they imagined the eerie environment populated with supernatural beings. Germans referred to their own similar spirits as *Kobolde* or *Wichtlein*; for the Welsh, they were *Coblynau*; in Bohemia they were known as *Haus-Schmiedlein*; in Malaya as *Chong Fus* and in the Andes as *Muquis*. For the English, the mine spirits were goblins or dwarfs. Although the Cornish called them knockers or knackers, sometimes they used indigenous terms for supernatural beings: Bucca, Bogle or Spriggan. 'Knocker', after all, was something of a generic word. According to an 1896 article in *Folklore*, Burne describes evidence that the miners of Staffordshire had a tradition of 'mining dwarfs' that behaved much like the Cornish entities and were, in fact, called 'knockers'. Indeed, it seems that the name 'knocker' was widespread.[2] This is not surprising since the word refers to noises often associated with underground supernatural

21. Pre-Raphaelite artist Arthur Hughes (1832–1915) illustrated George MacDonald's influential fantasy novel, *The Princess and the Goblin* (1872), which includes this depiction of menacing supernatural miners. Because nineteenth-century images of Cornish knockers are rare, this often appears in that context.

beings: that is, they 'knocked' as timbers creaked and groaned and as the forces of nature made themselves known in other audible ways. Although miners elsewhere in Britain commonly used the name 'knocker' for underground spirits, the word quickly became linked in the popular mind with the Cornish who were prominent in mining and consequently came to shape much of the industry's folklore.[3]

Early publications assist in outlining historical forms of belief in these underground spirits. Georgius Agricola (1494–1555) describes supernatural beings in German mines. His *De Animantibus Subterraneis Liber* identifies a spirit he called *Cobalos*. He claims the Greeks shared these sorts of entities, which were gentle, full of laughter and eager to appear to be working. Agricola goes on to say,

> They are called little miners, because of their dwarfish stature, which is about two feet. They are venerable looking and are clothed like miners in a filleted garment with a leather apron about their loins. This kind does not often trouble the miners, but they idle about in the shafts and tunnels and really do nothing, although they pretend to be busy in all kinds of labor, sometimes digging ore, and sometimes putting into buckets that which has been dug. Sometimes they throw pebbles at the workmen, but they rarely injure them unless the workmen first ridicule or curse them .... The mining gnomes are especially active in the workings where metal has already been found, or where there are hopes of discovering them and cause them to labor more vigorously.[4]

Throughout Europe, these mining spirits usually assumed something of the form that Agricola describes. Early on, the motif had a place in literature, occurring in the eighteenth-century surrealistic writings of E.T.A. Hoffmann (1776–1822). His Elis Frobom in 'The Mines of Falun' is an expert miner and uncanny personification of the underground world.[5]

Cornish Knockers and Knackers

In 1851, Devon-born Charles Kingsley (1819–1875) published *Yeast: A Problem*, in which his character, Tregarva, answers Sir Lancelot's question, 'What are the Knockers?'. Tregarva, which British readers would recognize as a Cornish name, replies that,

> They are the ghosts, the miners hold, of the old Jews, sir, that crucified our Lord, and were sent for slaves by the Roman Emperors to work the mines, and we find their old smelting-houses, which we call Jews' houses and their blocks of tin, at the bottom of the great bogs, which we call Jews' tin.[6]

Although mining spirits were ubiquitous, the Cornish knocker became widespread as a result of immigration; how that occurred is discussed in the following chapter. The focus here is on the tradition in Cornwall, famous for its mineral wealth. For centuries the Cornish earned a reputation for skill in working rich deposits of tin and copper. Besides the literary account by Kingsley, Cornish mining spirits are documented in numerous sources, most of which were written by collectors of the nineteenth or early twentieth centuries.

Cornish legends about knockers typically tell how they punish greed and reward good behaviour, as indicated in Hunt's story of the Trenwiths described at the beginning of this chapter. Numerous other stories reinforce the idea that miners who neglect to show appropriate courtesy suffer ill fortune at the hands of the knockers. For example, Bottrell's collection includes the account of Tom Trevorrow, a miner from St Just, Cornwall, who ordered the knockers to be quiet, telling them to 'Go to blazes, you cussed old Jews' sperrats [spirits]; or I'll scat [knock] your brains out'. Trevorrow later refused to share his supper with them. Bottrell describes the knockers reciting a rhyme to the miner:

Tom Trevorrow! Tom Trevorrow!
Leave some of thy fuggan for Bucca,
Or bad luck to thee, to-morrow!

When the miner failed to leave some food for the spirits, they threatened him again:

Tommy Trevorrow, Tommy Trevorrow!
We'll send thee bad luck to-morrow,
Thou old curmudgeon, to eat all they fuggan
And not leave a didjan for Bucca![7]

The knockers ruined Trevorrow's luck. In desperation, he took up farming, an unwelcome occupation for a Cornish miner.

Hunt records a story of a lazy man named Barker of Towednack parish who found an old mine, called a 'fairy well', where he could observe the knockers. He watched, he presumed in secret, as they worked and engaged in conversation. One day as the knockers were quitting their labour, they each explained where they were going to place their tools, and the last among them declared, 'I'll put mine on Barker's knee'. The man felt a terrible pain in his leg and was subsequently lamed for life. The knockers punished his impertinent curiosity. According to Hunt, Cornish sufferers from rheumatism often said, 'I be as stiff as Barker's knee'. The existence of such a colloquialism together with the fact that Deane and Shaw were able to record the legend in Cornwall as late as the 1970s suggest that this story was once widespread.[8]

Bottrell and Hunt both have additional references to knockers in their collections, but these do not include information that adds to the understanding of the tradition. Evans-Wentz augments this material with his early twentieth-century survey of Celtic supernatural beings. His broad approach allows for only brief mentions of such specialized forms as the knocker. Jenner, in his introduction to Evans-Wentz's section on Cornwall, mentions the knockers, saying that 'the story, as I have always heard it, is that they are the spirits of Jews who were sent by the Romans to work in the tin mines, some say for being concerned in the Crucifixion of our Lord.... They are benevolent spirits, and warn miners of danger.'[9]

Evans-Wentz also provides an overview of knockers from a Penzance source, who said the underground spirits,

> would accept a portion of a miner's *croust* (lunch) on good faith, and by knocking lead him to a rich mother-lode, or warn him by knocking if there was danger ahead or a cavern full of water; but if the miner begrudged them the *croust*, he would be left to his own resources to find the lode, and, moreover, the 'knockers' would do all they could to lead him away from a good lode. These mine pixies, too, were supposed to be spirits, sometimes spirits of the miners of ancient times.[10]

Evans-Wentz adds with a footnote that when he suggested the noises were due to natural causes, another Penzance source, an old miner who believed in the knockers, 'became quite annoyed, and said, "Well, I guess I have ears to hear"'.[11]

Several other twentieth-century authors also mention Cornish knockers, but their publications are for the most part problematic, lacking clear identification of sources. In most cases, it appears that they may have borrowed from Bottrell, Hunt and Evans-Wentz. Elizabeth Mary Wright (1863–1958) includes some largely repetitive information on Cornish mining spirits in a 1913 publication that focuses on dialects. Jenkin in his 1927 book *The Cornish Miner: An Account of his Life Above and Underground from Early Times* cites Bottrell as the source of at least some of his material on knockers.[12]

Deane and Shaw in their original version of *The Folklore of Cornwall*, published in 1975, include material first appearing in Bottrell and Hunt. They also apparently added their own observations, presumably collected in the early 1970s. By that time, however, it seems the tradition had faded, and it is possible that their sources had, by that time, been influenced by the many publications on Cornish folklore available for more than a century.[13]

The Nature of the Knockers

With these sources and their limitations in mind, it is possible to arrive at generalizations regarding the Cornish belief in knockers. Typically, the miners regarded them as dwarf-like men with wrinkled faces and long grey beards. These mischievous creatures took their name from the background noise of rapping and tapping in old mines. If treated kindly, they could be helpful.

Most Cornish sources suggest that knockers were believed to be spirits of Jews who laboured underground long ago. Oral tradition maintains that Jews worked in Cornish mines during the medieval period, but there is no historical basis for this. Bottrell, Hunt, Jenner, Evans-Wentz and Wright all suggest that the prominent folk belief was that Jews were exiled to the mines presumably for their alleged part in the Crucifixion.[14]

In keeping with the idea that knockers were spirits of Jewish miners, the Cornish maintain that the creatures did not work on Saturdays, which was their Sabbath. Contrary to this belief, however, nineteenth-century sources also pointed out that the knockers did not work at Easter, All Saints' Day, or Christmas, at which time they sang carols and held a Christmas Mass deep within the mines. Additional motifs include the observation that 'Jews' bowels' referred to small pieces of tin in old smelting works; 'Jews' houses' meant archaic smelting works; 'Jews' leavings' were mine refuse; and 'Jews' pieces' were ancient blocks of tin. There is little variation in the traditions surrounding the Jewish origin of the knockers, which seems to be the predominant folk

22. A small lithograph by Joseph Blight for William Bottrell's 1873 book on folklore is a unique nineteenth-century depiction of Cornish knockers. The image includes little bearded miners with pickaxes and other tools and dressed like their human counterparts. Two stand in the foreground, while others lurk in the forbidding shadows of the tunnel, its timbers framing the scene.

explanation. Jenkin asserts that some Cornish miners may have also believed that knockers were the spirits of pre-Celtic miners, but he is the only one to mention this idea. The fact that people long believed in a Jewish origin of the knockers is shown in the fiction of Kingsley as early as 1851.[15]

In addition, Tregarthen's whimsical story, 'The Thunder Axe', takes the notion of a Jewish-knocker connection to an extreme. She conceives of one elderly supernatural miner as a gem cutter dressed 'in long robes with a black skullcap', but everyday people apparently never described the knockers in this exaggerated way. Because Tregarthen often changed the stories she heard, this outlier is likely a literary, fanciful adaptation rather than an accurate depiction of folk belief and narrative.[16]

Anthropologist Manning puts forward a thought-provoking treatment of knocker folklore, focusing on their asserted Jewish origin. He maintains that 'the Jews became by turns ghosts, fairies and then nothing at all'.[17] The intent here is not to diminish Manning's work, which contributes an enormous amount with his consideration of this Jewish motif. Nevertheless, examining the knockers in the context of other northern and western European beliefs places the idea of a Jewish origin in a different context.

Throughout the region, people infused their world with supernatural beings ranging from ghosts, angels, demons, saints and to what can generally be termed fairy-like creatures. Pre-modern traditions were often vague regarding the boundaries separating these entities. As described previously, when discussing possible origins of supernatural beings, people typically expressed belief in the form of migratory legends. Naturally, they sometimes perceived fairies through a Christian lens. Thus, many saw the creatures as angels who refused to take sides in the cosmic battle between Satan and God, not good enough for heaven but not bad enough for hell; or they were the children Eve hid, having failed to clean them before God came to visit, and so the Deity ordered that those who were hidden from Him would be hidden from humanity.

The fairies of northern Europe were also sometimes considered to be the ghosts of people long dead, a forgotten race too ancient to walk the world as ghosts and so they were now diminutive spirits that could only be regarded as fairies of some sort. Thus, the *sidhe*, the fairies of Ireland, are often associated with ancient tribes displaced by the Celts. Many thought of these distant people as living before the time of Christ and therefore ineligible for admission into heaven but not bad enough to be exiled into hell. This last explanation serves as an example of how people sometimes looked to spirits of the dead to explain fairies. This does not mean, however, that the tradition evolved from beliefs in ghosts into legends about fairies, any more than these entities began as angels and devolved into the supernatural neighbours of humans. Instead, people considered the fairies as living in their world and sought to explain them with whatever traditions seemed appropriate to apply.

Briggs in her article 'The Fairies and the Realms of the Dead' discusses how the line between fairies and ghosts was sometimes blurred. It was not uncommon for fairies to drift along the spectrum and be regarded as ghosts, and this especially occurred as fairy lore faded. Although people sometimes thought of fairies as the spirits of ancient people they did not generally see ghosts drifting along the spectrum and becoming fairies. Bottrell asserts in his third and final volume that knockers 'seem rather to be a hybrid race between ordinary ghosts and elves', but this is in keeping with much of folk belief in a wider variety of supernatural beings. Bottrell also quotes one of his sources as saying, 'I know that strangers ... and grand learned folks like our passen [parson], don't believe in the sperats [spirits] we cale knackers workan in the bals [mines], and say that the noise, made by these ghosts of tinners, is caused by water oazan out of a load and drippen into a pit....'. Clearly, here the knackers are equated with the 'old ghosts of tinners'. Attributing some fairies with an ancient human origin was an after-the-fact explanation rather than evidence that ghosts became supernatural beings such as the knockers.[18]

The Cornish belief that a specialized type of supernatural being inhabited the eerie environment of the mine almost certainly came first; they then pondered on the origin of these creatures. It is highly unlikely that they considered a belief in an ancient Jewish population associated with mining that somehow devolved into elf-like entities. Manning is correct to ask why Cornish knockers became so closely associated with Jews. His consideration of this link in the context of the development of capitalism is an interesting exercise, but that is a leap too great for the methodology of comparative folklore studies. The Jewish association of the knockers is yet another distinct Cornish fingerprint in the realm of European folklore. That said, it is important to place this motif in perspective: the Jewish origin of the knockers was conjecture applied at a later date. The knockers began as underground fairies, and people, as they did throughout Europe, blended these sorts of supernatural beings with ghosts and other traditions as they tried to make sense of what they regarded as the extraordinary in their everyday lives.

The Jewish folk explanation for knockers should not mask the fact that these entities act like, and were assumed to be, a kind of fairy attached to a specific occupation. The knockers can be understood as underground supernatural beings who attracted an array of legends and beliefs including the mistaken idea that there were once ancient Jewish miners in Cornwall. Like many other European traditions about fairies, the knockers illustrate a blurring of the line which separates the ghosts of the long dead from the elves.

Comparison and Interpretation

The Cornish knocker tradition was one of the most elaborate of its kind in Europe. Unfortunately, stories associated with these supernatural beings do not fall into 'types' that folklorists have indexed from other places. This inhibits the ability to conduct comparative analysis. Despite this, it is possible to consider various aspects of the tradition in Cornwall. Firstly, many stories involve rewarding good behaviour and punishing bad, in keeping with fairy lore throughout northern Europe, if not elsewhere. Legends describe how miners of worthy character could profit from their underground excavations while those less honourable failed and were reduced to destitution. Secondly, anecdotes refer to the idea that knockers warned miners about the possibility of danger, often involving the imminent collapse of support timbers in the mines.

The miners of Cornwall faced profound changes in their lives in the eighteenth and nineteenth centuries. The growth of the industrial economy caused a greater market for mineral resources. The Cornish had mined their land for thousands of years, depleting the immediately accessible tin, much of which was on or near the surface. Increased demand quickly consumed easily reached, shallow underground 'lodes', the tin and copper ore bodies that made Cornwall famous. This caused a fundamental shift in Cornish mining strategies.

Cornish mining was originally a limited, collective endeavour. A family or a group of friends would bid on an ore lode owned by someone else. Securing an agreement to work, they would proceed with the excavation and reimburse the owner according to the agreed amount. If these 'tribute' miners were lucky and found the resources richer than they had hoped, profit would increase. Extraneous excavation and safety precautions were kept to a minimum to maximize profit. One major impact of the industrial revolution was to force shafts to greater depths in pursuit of unexploited minerals. In addition, the dynamics of an emerging modern world witnessed increased consumption of copper, which tended to be deeper than tin.[19]

The changes in the industry caused Cornish miners to shift from independent, self-employed craftsmen to wage earners. Property owners interested in the efficiency of their operations formed management hierarchies to supervise labourers. At the same time, technology became more sophisticated, replacing traditional methods. Unfortunately, there is no way to be certain how this change affected the belief in knockers because of inadequate documentation of pre-industrial folklore. Nevertheless, it is possible to surmise what early tradition might have been like and to understand how it changed.

Noted British historian Keith Thomas suggests that folk traditions such as the knocker originated with the rise of industrialization:

> In the early industrial period the mining industry generated a host of semi-magical practices, ranging from the belief in the existence of subterranean spirits or 'knockers', to a taboo on such actions as whistling underground or working on Good Friday. It also propagated a magical method of finding ore: the diving rod, cut and used in a highly ritual manner, was introduced from Germany in the mid sixteenth century and became popular a hundred years or more later.[20]

Thomas has little basis to assert that these practices and beliefs originated during the early industrial era or that they were introduced from Germany, but his point is well taken, namely that as industry demystified the world, it also contributed to the creation of new traditional practices, or at least the promotion and adaptation of old ones. In the case of the Cornish knocker, nineteenth-century legends clearly point to the existence of folklore linked to the old tribute miners, part of the earlier economy. The fact that the tradition survived and could thrive in the industrialized mines highlights the strength of the belief system but also the fact that it included aspects that allowed it to become a practical part of the emerging world.

Stories of knockers leading miners to rich lodes of ore would have been relatively meaningless to an underground labourer paid by the day. Clearly this motif dates to a time before the transformation of Cornish mining into a capitalist-industrial endeavour. Since miners, regardless of the era, were concerned with their own safety, the part of the knocker tradition about their role in warning of the mine's imminent collapse continued to thrive. Indeed, it was probably pragmatically useful. Miners could not necessarily distinguish between diverse and subtle sounds in the mine, and they might have failed to realize consciously that as the timbers moaned one way, it was safe, but when the mines echoed with other sounds, it meant danger. Much of nineteenth-century mining expertise was based on experience, not science. The belief that a supernatural creature might be causing the noises could have served to focus the attention of the miners to these subtle signals.

As late as the 1930s, George Orwell (1903–1950) observed that English miners relied on the 'feel' of the mine:

> An experienced miner claims to know by a sort of instinct when the roof is unsafe; the way he puts it is that he 'can feel the weight on him.' He can, for instance, hear the faint creaking of the props. The reason why wooden props are still generally preferred to iron girders is that a wooden prop which is about to collapse gives a warning by creaking, whereas a girder flies out unexpectedly. The devastating noise of the machines makes it impossible to hear anything else, and thus the danger is increasing.[21]

Whether miners called it instinct, intuition, or the warning of knockers, they were, in fact, giving expression to their interpretations of the underground environment.

Mermaids and Knockers

An additional commentary is appropriate regarding the parallels and differences in the traditions about knockers and mermaids in Cornish folklore. The peninsula's maritime folklore resonates somewhat with its mining traditions. Both occupations were well developed in Cornwall before industrialization, and sailors and underground miners were usually all male. There were even beliefs that it was bad luck to have a woman on board a ship as well as belowground in a mine. In addition, both the sea and the mine were extremely dangerous and potentially eerie environments. These professions bore distinct similarities when compared with the different, aboveground world of the farmer, for example.[22]

Not surprisingly, there are Cornish legends involving both the mines and the sea that feature supernatural beings either punishing disrespect or warning good men of danger, thereby saving their lives. The knocker played this role belowground for the miner and of course the mermaid did the same for the sailor at sea. Predictably, both types of creatures were regarded as potentially dangerous and terrifying. The similarities between the two cease at a certain point, most obviously when it comes to their respective gender: the knockers are always described as male, while the mermaid is female.

In addition, both were expressions of the fundamental idea common throughout much of northern Europe that many supernatural beings existed in societies and communities that reflected those of humans. Since underground miners were traditionally all male, it is not surprising that knockers reflected the mines' male workforce. The significance of the mermaid, however, is more complex. Although sailors traditionally worked in an exclusively male environment, mermaids were not the equivalent of sailors. They existed in the sea, and so that was also where their entire community was and naturally mermen were part of that group. A complete merfolk society existed.

The Cornish mermaid legends are also distinct from those of the knockers in that most of the stories about them involve people on land coming into contact with them near the shore. With a few exceptions, these are not stories about sailors on the open sea. Instead, the traditions are about people pursuing a variety of occupations who happen to encounter mermaids near the shore. These narratives emerge from the proximity of the sea, tied to the fact that no part of Cornwall is far from water. The knockers were part of an occupational tradition and belonged to the world of mining, while the mermaid was an aspect of everyone's folklore.

Conclusion

As described in Chapter 2, Payton points out that Cornish folklore underwent a shift with the development of industrialization. He also suggests that people found ways to reconcile their now sophisticated industry and the traditional culture that many continued to value.[23] Beliefs and legends about knockers serve as evidence of this. Many of these legends were better suited for pre-industrial times when miners worked in self-employed teams that would benefit from finding more valuable ore. Nevertheless, belief survived industrialization as well as the transformation of Cornish miners into wage earners less concerned with profit than with safety. Because folklore also included the idea that supernatural beings could warn of mine collapses, that part of the pre-industrial tradition continued to thrive: it honed the senses and had real value for miners themselves, irrespective of any transformation of the economy that they faced.

Besides his discussion of industrialization, Payton cites Alan Kent in the context of Cornish miners adapting to change. Kent suggests that modernism, and especially the reality that miners needed to seek work throughout a worldwide network, helped foster a new form of oral tradition, the 'Cousin Jack' stories. These were suited to the emerging environment of emigration and an international community. It is within this context that the knocker tradition must now be considered. This is the subject of the final chapter.[24]

CHAPTER ELEVEN

Tommyknockers, Immigration and the Modern World

F.D. Calhoon, in his remembrance of ethnic groups in the mining region of Grass Valley, California, refers to a late example of tommyknockers, the underground supernatural companions of North American miners. Published in 1986 but recalling a time earlier in the twentieth century, his first-hand account tells how Cornish immigrants milled 'high-graded' gold ore in cellars below their kitchens. Some workers were known to steal these valuable samples from mines and then to hammer the rock apart to retrieve the precious metal.[1] The subterranean pounding of their hammers raised questions among the children, but parents dismissed the noise caused by the illegal high-grading by drawing on the belief in tommyknockers. As Calhoon recounts,

> Supposedly, the 'little miners' gathered under the house where children were especially good. If they listened, and were real quiet after they had gone to bed, and were supposed to be going to sleep, they just might hear their little friends hammering away with their tiny single jacks. It is surprising how many residents of the mining towns still tell of being lulled to sleep by the rhythmical pounding from deep below. If the rock was especially hard, and the pounding unusually loud, the children were told that the tommyknockers must have been using double jacks the evening before.[2]

Whilst Calhoon is not a folklorist, and his publication is problematic because it lacks sources, dates and other details, he nevertheless documents a stage in the evolution of stories associated with the Cornish knocker and its American descendant, the tommyknocker. Clearly at this point, the tradition had evolved into a fictitious saying or 'fict' as von Sydow calls it: a story that adults told for children to believe.[3] By drawing on the memory of the tommy-knocker, parents turned aside enquiries from youngsters who might otherwise have discovered the unlawful activity. Reinforcement of a belief was not the intention. The tommyknocker had drifted far from the original inspiration, but it remained part of local tradition.

While giving a presentation about these supernatural beings in 2007, I received a testimonial from a retired miner who had encountered tommy-knockers in the late 1950s. He explained that after drinking, he went into one of the older, abandoned levels of a mine near Golconda, Nevada, to sleep off his intoxication. He was alone in that part of the excavation and awoke to rapping and groaning. He immediately thought the sounds were from tommyknockers, which his father, also a miner, had told him about, and after half a century, he still related the story with animation. He recalled that his father had said they were Cornish mining spirits, and although he told his narrative with some humour, the miner also stressed the terror he experienced at the time, for fear that the spirits were real even after five decades. When I asked if his father was from Cornwall, he explained that he was a Portuguese immigrant. Whether the young miner of the 1950s believed the noise was caused by supernatural beings is not of primary importance here. The significance of this episode is that an element of an older tradition persisted, in that the sounds of the mine evoked the existence of tommyknockers, such that even someone completely unconnected with Cornwall could tell the story.

These late manifestations of mining spirits together with their earlier counterparts provide an opportunity to examine how the processes of immigration affected one of the better-known aspects of Cornish folklore. The contrast between older and later expressions of belief and stories reveals differences in cultures and mining techniques as they transformed over time and space. Remarkably, documentation of tommyknockers in the New World is far more common than sources about the original knocker in Cornwall.

Cornish Emigration to America

When the Cornish went to North America, they took their beliefs. Of all the groups from Britain, perhaps none was as important to the mining American West as the underground experts from Cornwall. Their significance was disproportionate to their numbers. Approximately 250,000 Cornish emigrated during the 'long nineteenth century' as it came to be known (c. 1789–1914). This was a significant number from the Cornish viewpoint: the 1861 census records only 369,390 people living there. It is possible that between 1871 and 1881 up to a third of the mining population of Cornwall (that is, people from the mining districts, all occupations and ages and both genders) had departed.[4]

For the New World, during a century when millions arrived, these numbers were hardly astounding. In addition, spread over the course of nearly a century, the potential effect of the Cornish was further decreased numerically in any given place as they scattered across the globe to Australia, Mexico, South America, South Africa, Canada and the Western United States. That said, their consequence to the mines of the American West was considerable.

The Cornish left their homeland out of economic necessity. After 1815, with the end of the Napoleonic Wars, Cornwall suffered from volatility in the value of tin and copper, its two principal minerals. In addition, the Cornish had mined for thousands of years, and the most accessible ores had been depleted. The increased cost of mining and the lower value of the product created depressions beginning in 1825. Hard times during the following decades continued to inspire emigration: Cornwall experienced food shortages in the 'Hungry Forties' and a crash of copper prices in 1866 and of tin in the following decade proved crippling to the Cornish industry. These factors, combined with higher wages in international mining, enticed many to leave home.[5]

For centuries, Cornish miners had been accustomed to migration. Unlike farming, mining depends on a non-renewable resource in specific locations. There was, consequently, a long-standing Cornish tradition of moving as ore in one area was depleted and other deposits were discovered. Lead mining opened in Wisconsin and Illinois early in the nineteenth century and the discovery of copper in Michigan in the 1840s attracted attention in Cornwall. The move to the North American frontier was a natural one for the Cornish, and America acquired the whimsical name of 'the next parish over'.[6] The Cornish subsequently participated in mining throughout the North American continent. The 1850s found the 'Cousin Jacks', as Cornish miners were known, in California, and the 1860s took them to Colorado and Nevada. By the end of the nineteenth century, Cornish miners had become a standard part of the Western mining town.

Early California surface mining in the wake of the 1849 Gold Rush, however, did not require the Cornish expertise in deep, hard rock mining. This meant that they were not initially guaranteed premier status there. The Cornish were consequently slow to go to a mining district until it had abandoned surface extraction in favour of underground excavations. Indeed, the Cornish often waited to make certain a hard rock mining district had a secure future before relocating since they could command the job market with sufficient authority to arrive late and still find employment. The development of subsurface gold deposits in Grass Valley, California, beginning in the 1850s demanded specialists such as the Cornish, and this provides a significant benchmark in the history of Cornish immigration to the Far West of the North American continent.[7]

During the 1850s, surface excavations dominated what would become the Comstock Mining District in the Nevada Territory. In 1859, workers began open-pit mining to exploit ore near the surface. Following the industry's pattern in early California, inexperienced miners could supply most of the labour. Workers quickly exhausted easily accessible deposits, leaving deeper resources that demanded trained hard rock miners. New, elaborate excavations also called for a permanent labour force. The mining district subsequently attracted Cornish miners who became one of the more important ethnic groups contributing to the development of the Comstock Lode. This was a typical pattern throughout the mining West.[8]

Due to the prestige of the Cornish miners, their influence eventually came to be felt aboveground as well as in the mines underground. They introduced the Cornish pasty, for example, which was part of the mining community's staple diet. Cornish wrestling became popular and the Cornish gave the West a new vocabulary. The emigrants imported their term 'lode', meaning ore body, but many other mining words also trace their origin to Cornwall. In the mines, the Cornish used their special type of pump to drain water. There are dozens of examples of Cornish influence in the mining West, but perhaps their most colourful contribution was the knocker, who transformed into the tommy-knocker, the popularity of which exceeded the limited numbers of Cornish emigrants themselves.[9]

The American Tommyknocker and Associated Mine Spirits

Throughout the American West, miners of the nineteenth and early twentieth centuries often asserted that there were spirits in their workplace. Although people typically attributed this tradition to the Cornish, it was not theirs in exclusivity. Miners of diverse backgrounds were known to share in the belief. By comparing American stories about mining spirits with the original tradition in Cornwall, it is possible to arrive at some sense of the changes that occurred during the process of diffusion.

Several authors have written about American tommyknockers since the mid-nineteenth century. Wayland Hand published articles in part about this subject in the 1940s. Caroline Bancroft followed with analysis of the belief in Colorado. In 1971, James Baker addressed the topic of tommyknockers in Oregon. These folklorists drew on their own collecting and on one another for information about this tradition.[10]

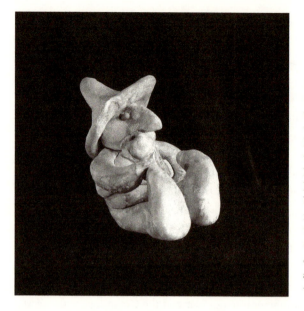

23. Wayland Hand
(1907–1986) described
miners making clay effigies
with matchstick eyes,
leaving morsels of food
to win the favour of the
North American tommy-
knockers. This replica,
based on the description, is
in the Historic Fourth Ward
School Museum in Virginia
City, Nevada, where the
entity stands guard over
an exhibit dealing in part
with Cornish immigrants.

Hand, the eminent Western folklorist, describes miners leaving morsels of food before clay effigies of the mining spirits in the hope that the spirits would look kindly on their human counterparts. He suggests the tommyknockers occasionally guided miners to ore bodies and that their tapping was an ominous sign of a mine collapse. Hand also records a belief that the person who heard the noise would die. He portrays tommyknockers as mischievous and apt to hiding tools. He writes that when miners experienced unusual occurrences, they were prone to say that 'a damned bloody Tommy Knocker is around', or that 'the spirits are working again'.[11] He records that the term 'tommyknocker' was associated with a miner's pick, a miner's signalling or testing the ground and with dripping water or other similar natural sounds.[12]

Hand describes the belief in tommyknockers as being common in Utah around 1910 but almost extinct by the publication of his 1941 article. He portrays the tommyknockers of Utah as dwarf-like and as the spirits of dead miners, but also as a sinister force in the mine. For his sources, knocking was usually interpreted as a sign of trouble, but it could also lead to riches. Hand suggests that the tommyknocker tradition eventually manifested in the context of pranks between miners and tapping signals that miners used to communicate with one another.[13]

Hand's work in Butte, Montana, resulted in a portrait of the tommyknocker as spirits of the dead. He suggests that 'there was a division of opinion in favour of their friendly, or neutral, character as over against one of hostility'.[14] Hand was not able to find evidence of clay effigies in Montana, but he did record the use of the term, as he had found in California and Utah, to mean tapping signals between miners.[15]

Bancroft published her folklore research in Colorado in 1945. She observes that the belief in the tommyknocker was extinct among the young miners by that time but that the entity 'survives [as a] fragmentary belief among older miners'. It had evidently been replaced by the 'Guy in the red shirt', who became the source of falling rocks in the mine.[16]

Baker's 1971 article describes how the tommyknocker tradition had circulated among non-Cornish miners in Bohemia, Oregon. He also characterizes the tommyknockers 'as the noisy spirits who act benignly and maliciously. The "devil Tommy Knockers" cause cave-ins, falling rock, and timbers.'[17] In addition, crackling noises from a cook's stove and the noise of scurrying animals, 'farts, and other cracks and taps around the camp and in the shafts', are referred to as the noise of a tommyknocker, although these uses of the term are clearly removed from the actual belief. In the same way, when a miner taps the walls of a mine with a prospecting hammer, he is 'Tommy Knockin".[18]

Nineteenth-century stories about underground spirits also found their way into newspapers and have been employed in discussions about tommyknockers. These sorts of accounts require a critical eye, but they can be useful in identifying early examples of motifs. Most consist of descriptions of spirits that are more ghost-like than elfin. Sources of this type attract attention because subsequent authors attribute them to the tradition of the tommyknocker. Although the stories may have been intended to refer to the Cornish supernatural being, without the use of the specific term 'tommyknocker', they are best not used here.[19]

More recent authors describe anecdotes of varying quality. For example, references to tommyknockers appear in a 1937 article by Fisher Vane in The Mining Journal. The son of a mine manager, Vane grew up in the late nineteenth-century mining West. He spent much of his boyhood in Granite, Montana, and later worked on the Comstock in Nevada, eventually moving to the Gold Country of California. His article recounts stories of tommyknockers that he had heard as a child. He attributes derailed mine cars, missing tools, falling pebbles, jamming drill bits and strange sounds including laughter and footfalls to them. He also suggests that tommyknockers were protective of mine rats and frightened of women. Vane's account is whimsical, and he indicates that the spirits were real, having slowly adapted to mechanization. Vane even claims to have heard them in the Little Giant Mine of Battle Mountain, which was '*absolutely lousy* with tommyknockers'. In addition, Vane suggests that tommy-knockers are related to ghosts in the mine.[20]

The *Arizona State Guide*, a Depression-era, US Federal Works Project Administration publication, also describes the Western tommyknocker tradition. Its brief account suggests that the spirits were 'inclined to mischief rather than malice, [and that they] often carried off small tools and played pranks'. The *Guide* goes on to claim that the belief in tommyknockers was extinct but that 'long ago it was the custom to keep them in good humor with offerings of food'.[21]

A 1912 interview with Billie Williams, from Olinghouse in northern Nevada, was published in *Nevada: Official Bicentennial Book* in 1976. Williams had discovered gold at Olinghouse in 1860 and Marguerite Humphrey, a professional doll maker, interviewed him over half a century later. Yet another fifty years passed between the interview and publication, making this a problematic source, but a few motifs appear to have been faithfully recorded. Williams, who was likely of Cornish birth, maintained that the tommyknockers helped him find rich ore veins, offered protection from dangers in the mine, knocked on walls to warn of dangers and were 'the ethereal bodies of the departed miners'.[22] Miners left crumpets, pastries and other things as a reward. Williams also suggested that if no food were left, the tommyknockers became angry, blew out candles, tampered with dynamite fuses, hid tools, stole pipes and tobacco and dropped rocks on miners' heads. Williams described them as having 'large heads, big ears and noses, very wrinkled faces with long whiskers, and [as being] dressed in gay colored clothes'. Humphrey illustrates her article with a photograph of some tommyknocker dolls she had made.

In an article published in a popular magazine in 1990, George S. Baker, a miner from California, recounts an incident from the 1930s when he worked with a 'Cousin Jack miner' named 'old Jimmy'. They were underground preparing to blast when 'there was a sharp pop and the sound of pebbles dropping. "What was that?" I exclaimed with a start. "Er's Tommyknockers, I s'pose", said Jimmy. And [a slab of rock from above] ..., about the size of a pickup truck, came down with a swoosh that almost blew out our carbide lamps.'[23] Like the previous account, there is a time lag between the incident and its documentation, but this clearly includes the motif of warning and serves as evidence of the belief surviving into the 1930s. That, however, was hardly the end of the tradition.

A 1992 newspaper article from Carson City, Nevada, profiling a sculptor named Greg Melton who lived in one of the old communities associated with the Comstock Mining District, explores the artist's beliefs in mining spirits.

The reporter quotes Melton describing a tommyknocker, which he also identified as a ghost.

> Melton says he was showing a babbling tourist the [Sutro] tunnel and his dog was barking when 'I looked back in there where it gets dark and I saw him. I wasn't quite sure what I saw but he came out of one side of the tunnel. He was kinda tall and he was gray. He wore baggy clothes and had a lantern on his head. His hands swung down next to his side kind of limp-like.'[24]

Melton said that the apparition stopped, looked him in the eye, and then disappeared into the wall on the other side, at which point, the artist said, 'God, that was a ghost!'. The reporter went on to describe what Melton thought was the basis of his experience: 'About 30 miners lost their lives in the late 1800s in the Sutro mine. An old legend in the Comstock says miners who died in the mine come as tommyknockers to warn people of impending doom.'[25] Whether Melton actually believed this anecdote, or he was telling the reporter something he thought he wanted to hear is of less interest than is the fact that the tommyknocker remained as an active part of the vocabulary and spectrum of possible beliefs shared by Melton and the readers of the newspaper as recently as the 1990s.

In addition, testimony gathered on the internet in 2013 provides the following:

> My great-great grandfather was a Cornish miner and came to the US West as a miner. I remember my father telling me that his grandfather who grew up as a kid in mining camps told him about tommyknockers and that they'd knock on the walls to warn of cave ins and that they also stole tools. He also said that they'd try to steal the boots of men who fell down mine shafts—he said that when a miner took a bad fall, that often the poor guy would be found with his boots half pulled off and it was attributed to tommyknockers trying to steal them.[26]

In 2017, the same person provided additional evidence after finding her school project that had inspired her to document this tradition: 'I had forgotten that tommyknockers were very, very flat (so they could hide in cracks in the walls) and they always left behind the boots they tried to steal because boots wouldn't fit in the cracks in the walls'.[27]

This recollection was originally from a miner born in 1858 who worked near Perranporth on the north coast of Cornwall. He emigrated with his father and brother, and they all found employment at the Horn Silver Mine in Frisco, Beaver County, Utah, between 1883 and 1888. Although the internet must be treated with caution, this account is of interest because it provides a glimpse at immigrant family folklore: the source maintains that she heard the stories from her father when she was fourteen or fifteen years old. Some of the motifs are recognizable, including the theft of tools and the warning of danger, but the motifs of flat tommyknockers who sought, unsuccessfully, to steal the boots of the dead seem to be unique. This account serves as evidence of how the idea of the tommyknocker continues to reverberate into the twenty-first century in at least one family tradition in the American West.

Finally, the two examples that open this chapter, Calhoon's account and my own experience, reinforce the idea that belief in the tommyknocker survives well into the twenty-first century in the American West. Stories and belief have certainly transformed, but the fact that they lingered for decades cannot be contested. Understanding how they changed and responded to the new environment is critical to the history of this famous expression of Cornish folklore.

Comparison and Interpretation

Discussions about knockers and their North American counterpart consistently settle on the relationship between these supernatural beings and ghosts. In general, the connection between the two types of entities is ambiguous, but many people on both sides of the Atlantic assumed the underground spirits were somehow related to ghosts of dead miners. Of course, some non-Cornish underground ghosts might have been confused with, and recorded as, tommyknockers in the American West. It does seem, however, that for most accounts, Cornish immigrant tradition served as the bedrock for this aspect of North American folklore.

Perhaps because belief in the tommyknocker lasted so long in the New World, it came to reflect the influence of its new home. The variations between American tommyknockers and their Cornish ancestors were due to both geography and history. The Cornish saw knockers as the spirits of Jewish miners from long ago, reduced in stature until they became elf-like, even though this reversed the actual evolution: knockers have the appearance of Cornish piskies adapted to an eerie work environment; the Jewish-ghost connection was certainly a subsequent folk explanation for how these entities came to be working in mines. Stories in America, however, had to take a different approach. The idea of exiled Roman-era Jews was historically impossible in North America, where people have seldom welcomed the belief in elves. Most elf-like qualities of the tommyknockers did not survive the passage across the Atlantic. Nevertheless, in both Cornwall and the American West, miners left morsels of food and tallow as votive offerings to win favour from their supernatural neighbours.[28] In addition, clay statues representing tommyknockers were not meant to be likenesses of dead miners; instead, these practices refer to the fairy-like aspect of the underground spirits.

Belief in ghosts, however, has thrived in America, and so the notion of the knockers as shadows of dead miners influenced tradition in the West. The principal difference between the European and American expressions of this folklore lies in what the knockers did to, or for, the miners. In Cornwall, most legends tell of the spirits rewarding good and punishing evil. Their warnings of impending danger appear to be less common in Cornwall than in America where stories which refer to rewards and punishments are almost non-existent. The underlying message of the Cornish tradition is that a miner who is willing to accept a moderate income and who is not too ambitious or inquisitive is worthy of reward. American culture reinforces ambition, creativity and curiosity, and so the Cornish type of legend which focuses on miners benefiting from following sounds without question and then taking only a portion of the wealth were not likely to take root in the New World. The bedrock of American culture, that is, ambition and self-advancement, made its miners less comfortable with the idea of condemning a desire to take everything.

George Foster, writing in 1973 about traditional societies and change, discusses the idea of limited good. His work can shed light on the transformation from Cornish knockers to North American tommyknockers. He suggests that five points tend to dictate the peasant world view and frame of reference:

1. Peasants believe that they live in a closed system;
2. They regard the system's resources as finite, static, and limited (the idea of limited good);
3. They assume that more resources, that is more 'good' things, are available outside their closed system;
4. They believe that 'one person's gain with respect to any good must be another's loss'; and finally,

5. They seek to develop 'an egalitarian, shared-property equilibrium,
    status-quo style of life, in which by means of overt behavior and
    symbolic action people are discouraged from attempting major change
    in their economic and other statuses'.[29]

Foster goes on to point out that this peasant world view breaks down in the
face of change: 'Once the threshold to modernity is crossed by a few innovative
souls, an increasing flow of followers crosses over, and in time the limited
good premise will lose most or all of its inhibiting power'.[30] Foster's work
helps explain the transformation of the Cornish knocker into its American
counterpart.

The Cornish knocker discouraged greed, encouraging a balance in the
relative prosperity among independent mining families in a community.
Industrialization and then emigration challenged this traditional prescription
for equality, what Foster suggests is the idea of limited good and the effort to
seek equilibrium. As Cornish miners became wage earners, the capitalist institution removed the threat that one miner would gather far more than another.
Emigration further disrupted traditional society with the departure of part of
the workforce. What is more, the American ideal of the acquisition of wealth
left no room for the sort of balance that Foster suggests pre-industrial people
sought.

Nevertheless, whether in Cornwall or in a New World mine, circumstance
encouraged the preservation of the more practical aspects of the tradition. As
indicated in the previous chapter, knockers offered a means to focus intuitive
interpretations of subtle signs of mine collapse. Tommyknockers prevailed
in America because miners could select those parts of the diverse tradition
that suited them. Some motifs did not survive while others adapted. Western
mining communities retained the belief that some noises were messages from
tommyknockers, inspiring underground workers to focus on signs of danger
that might otherwise remain subliminal.

On both sides of the Atlantic, stories of spirits in the mine also represent
people's creative expression. The practical nature of the belief does not
diminish the artistic quality of its corresponding stories. Like other elements
of folklore, knockers survived for various reasons: they did not conflict with
the regional culture and environment; they had a functional role in mining
safety and they provided material for a good story. Folklore is most likely to
persist when it is both practical and entertaining.

Over time, the tradition of the Cornish mining spirit changed. Belief
eventually faded in America and Cornwall. As electric lights made mines less

gloomy and steel supports replaced wood, the environment was no longer as conducive to traditions about ghosts and underground elves. Heavy machines made subtle underground noises harder to hear so that only after-hours sightings occurred. The knockers and tommyknockers alike fled into dark corners.[31] The growing body of professionally trained mining engineers may also have weakened traditions associated with supernatural entities.

The fate of the knockers aside, it is important to recognize that they survived the crossing of the Atlantic, and they prospered in their new home. Belief in the spirits in Cornwall apparently faded shortly after the beginning of the twentieth century,[32] but the tradition seems to have remained active in America for another fifty years. At the same time and irrespective of the knocker in Cornwall or the tommyknocker in the New World, the entities continued as a vestige, part of the shared vocabulary of the people who live amongst the remnants of industry. In both places, the supernatural being became part of the way people viewed their own culture, a talisman of places with deep mining roots. The tradition includes the way people viewed the Cornish miners as much as what these immigrants, themselves, believed: the supernatural miners were not unlike the giants who provided a means with which outsiders could perceive Cornwall while also serving as a motif for so many of the indigenous Cornish stories.

Tommyknockers flourished because the accompanying folklore included messages that reinforced American culture. In the New World, tommy-knockers were more tied to the idea that they were the ghosts of dead miners, a motif less outrageous to American tastes than the belief in underground piskies. In both Cornwall and the American West, the spirits had a practical purpose: the miners believed that they warned of dangers. The adoption of the tommyknockers by non-Cornish miners illustrates that this was not exclusively the oral tradition of immigrants, destined to vanish with the passing of the first generation of the Cornish in the New World. The belief in tommyknockers became genuine American folklore, conforming to its new environment.

The story of the tommyknocker in America, however, is not simply one of survival and adaptation. The motif became part of a dynamic process of creativity and response to change. The initial anecdote that opened this chapter involving high-graders of Grass Valley, California, is pertinent at this point. These twentieth-century miners attributed the sounds of late-night milling of stolen ore to tommyknockers, not because they believed the supernatural entities were the cause of the sound but because they were a convenient means to answer the curiosity of children.

24.   The logo for Tommyknockers Brewery in Idaho Springs, Colorado features an elfin miner with pointed ears and a miner's cap and lamp. Courtesy of Tommyknockers Brewery.

In the American West, the role of the tommyknocker as a spirit who could lead prospectors to wealth gained new life for a short time. In the nineteenth century, it was still possible for independent agents to strike it rich outside the more structured wage-earning industrial system. Eventually, even in the West, mineral resources became increasingly tied up by claims, private ownership and public land management. In an ironic turn of folklore, the tommyknockers of Grass Valley once again led the way to wealth, but this time by turning aside the questions of children who wondered about the late-night hammering in the cellar. Calhoon's description of this use of the tommyknocker motif provides valuable information concerning a later stage in the development of this motif in the West.

In fact, tommyknockers have continued to play a role in profitmaking in the American mining West. From Eureka, Nevada to Park City, Utah, store owners have named businesses after these supernatural beings, hoping to attract tourists and local customers by exploiting the heritage of the area. As previously mentioned, Humphrey, the professional doll maker from Nevada, fashioned images of tommyknockers in the 1970s for sale. In addition, descendants of Cornish miners sold pasties in a restaurant named 'Tommyknockers' in the 1990s in Carson City, Nevada. Of no less importance, nowadays the Tommyknocker Brew Pub in Idaho Springs, Colorado, offers a wide assortment of beverages under the company logo of a bearded miner, complete with head lamp and pointed ears, an elfin knocker of the twenty-first century. Furthermore, as a nod to their own local folklore, the menu of Skinner's Brewing Company of Truro, Cornwall, includes 'Cornish Knocker', a golden ale, and 'Davey Jones Knocker', credited with being a 'premium pale ale'.[33]

Conclusion

Von Sydow describes a migration bottleneck that allowed only certain portions of folklore to survive when diffusing from one place to another. He cites the example of Iceland, settled in the medieval period, a subject Sveinsson also discusses with his idea of 'periphery phenomena'. Pre-modern Icelandic folklore included only parts of traditions found in Scandinavia, Britain and Ireland, the sources of much of its oral tradition. Some stories were not at home on the island, some were abandoned and others did not survive for other unknown reasons. Christiansen describes a similar bottleneck in his seminal 1962 publication, *European Folklore in America*.[34]

Subsequent publications add to this scholarship. Robert Klymasz sees the development of immigrant folklore in three stages: new arrivals attempt to preserve their folklore; the folklore necessarily changes and ultimately, people create innovative forms of folklore.[35] Similarly, Stephen Stern suggests that immigrant oral tradition tends to shift 'from longer to shorter, from complex to simple, from sacred to secular, from supernatural to realistic, from communal to individualistic' all of which is corroborated here to a certain extent.[36]

Many of these generalizations apply to the transmission of the Cornish knocker to America, but limited evidence hints at a similar transition from the pre-industrial to the industrial periods of Cornish mining. The effect of this first change on knocker-related folklore was as profound as that which occurred when the tradition crossed the ocean. With the industrial revolution, stories were forced through a 'historical' bottleneck as accounts and beliefs associated with knockers punishing greed or dishonourable character tended to wane. Similarly, legends about miners of virtue being led to profitable ore lodes were less applicable in an industrial age with its corporate ownership of mines.

With emigration, motifs such as the Jewish origin and legends associated with 'Barker's Knee' did not survive the new 'geographic' bottleneck. In addition, American stories tended to be shorter and simpler than their Cornish counterparts, but they retained the eerie supernatural as the primary focus. It is possible to see in the tommyknocker the dynamic quality of the American immigrant tradition, as suggested by Klymasz. The knocker survived, assumed new forms and was eventually adopted by some non-Cornish miners. As belief faded, miners changed the term and the motif in a variety of ways, using the name for signals in the mine and adapting the elfin image to explain their illicit milling of high-graded ore. Others used the tradition, recalling endearing references to the much-loved spirit of the mines, to market dolls, food and beer.

The example of the knocker serves as testimony to the importance of studying not only ethnic folklore but also labour-lore as Archie Green calls it.[37] Tommyknockers are etched into the folklore of the nineteenth-century

American West thanks to the countless Cornish who carried their beliefs and stories with them and to the many others who embraced the tradition in this new environment. While the stories may have become rare in folk tradition, the underground mining spirits have enjoyed a resurgence in Cornwall and the New World as part of marketing and with the celebration of local culture. Numerous publications preserve narratives of earlier times, and these in turn inspired expressions in literature and poetry. In 1910, poet Anthony Fitch evokes the spirits in his work called 'Tommy Knockers':

> An we leave the 'aunted place,
> For we won't work w'ere they be,
> An w'erever we 'ear them knocking
> We sure will always flee
>
> For it means w'oever 'ears it
> Will be the next in line,
> For the pick-pick of the Tommy Knockers
> Is the last an' awful sign[38]

Similarly, the tommyknocker features in the traditional ballad of 'Hardrock Hank':

> I'm a hardrock miner an' I ain't afeard o' ghosts
> But my neck-hair bristles like porcupine's quills
> An' I knock my knuckles on the drift set posts
> When the tommyknockers hammer on the caps an' sills
> An' raise hallelujah with my picks an' drills![39]

From Kingsley's *Yeast* to 'Hardrock Hank' and from William Bottrell to Wayland Hand, the knocker and its American counterpart have appeared in ballads, literature and collections of legends. Somewhere between the artistry of the tradition and the opportunity for interpretation rests the importance of this aspect of international, ethnic, occupational folklore.

Conclusion

The purpose of this book is to consider nineteenth-century Cornish folklore in a regional context. The position taken here is that the oral tradition of the period gave Cornwall a unique cultural fingerprint. This conclusion runs counter to the intuition of Robert Morton Nance in the early twentieth century. A luminary who promoted Cornish identity, he asserted that 'in leaving its own Celtic language and taking to English, Cornwall made a break with tradition that must inevitably have meant the loss of much of the older Cornish folklore'.[1]

More recently, Merv Davey responded to widely held assumptions about Cornish folklore. In his study of folk music and dance, he argues 'that failure to recognise Cornwall's folk tradition as a distinctive and creative art form is due to hegemonic power relations not the intrinsic nature of Cornish material'. Davey further states, 'that folk tradition has an important place in contemporary Cornish studies'.[2]

Ultimately, the prejudice against Cornish folklore draws energy from three sources. The first, following Nance, is that with the waning of the indigenous Celtic language, so too its oral tradition declined or became principally English in nature. Ireland's National Folklore Collection demonstrates the flaw in this thinking. That archive includes thousands of pages in English, but the recorded material does not represent English folklore; it is, in fact, still very Irish. Linguistic conversion did not obliterate indigenous folklore in nineteenth-century Ireland or Cornwall; collections from both places exhibit oral traditions different from that which was found in England.

The second reinforcement of prejudice against Cornish folklore is that Cornish droll tellers boasted about changing the stories they heard. Much of the Romantic-era inspiration for looking at oral tradition was the perception that it was a window on a distant past; consequently, a narrator who changed stories seemed disqualified from consideration. This idea, discussed in Chapter 2, is revisited here at a later point.

A third issue is that legends, long the poor cousins in folklore studies, dominate the Cornish collections. Although folklorists were slow to study legends, many have considered the subject. Bo Almqvist raises several points after comparing the vast scope of Irish legends with Reidar Th. Christiansen's Scandinavian catalogue. Much of what Almqvist observes is useful here. His first point, however, is of less interest in a Cornish context: Almqvist notes that many of Christiansen's types 'are totally lacking in Ireland and some others are rare there'. Scarcity of legend types cannot be considered in a Cornish context since its collections were not systematic and one cannot comment on what is missing. It is unclear whether an absence is because of an omission by people such as Robert Hunt and William Bottrell or if it represents an actual gap in oral tradition.[3]

More appropriately for Cornwall, Almqvist notes that 'many legend types are common to Ireland and Norway'. Similarly, the peninsula beyond the River Tamar exhibits a cross section of legends known elsewhere in northern Europe. Besides the fifteen examples of narrative types analyzed here, at least three other stories are also present in the Cornish catalogue of oral tradition.[4] Bottrell's account of 'Tom of Chyannor, the Tin-Streamer: A West-Country Droll' and Nicholas Boson's *Jowan Chy-an-Horth, py, An try foynt a skyans* can be regarded as expressions of Folktale Type ATU 910A, 'Wise through Experience'. It is also possible to recognize Folktale Type ATU 990 in Hunt's story 'Cornish Teeny Tiny or Gimme my Teeth'. In addition, Hunt and Bottrell both published versions of 'Duffy and the Devil', a variant of Type ATU 500, the folktale made famous by 'Rumpelstilzchen' of the Brothers Grimm. While the Cornish collection may be modest, it includes at least eighteen legend and folktale types found elsewhere. Had more folklorists worked in Cornwall, that number would likely be larger, and further research will certainly augment the inventory.

In addition, Almqvist concludes that many Irish 'types' do not appear in Christiansen's list, meaning that they did not travel to Norway or that Christiansen had not catalogued them. This is also the case with the Cornish material. For example, some legends associated with the mermaids of Cornwall do not appear in Christiansen's catalogue. The same is true of Cornish stories about giants and knockers, which are not found in regional indexes.

Almqvist observes that Irish oral tradition includes 'some of the longest variants of certain legends types that I have come across in any language'. The scope of Almqvist's knowledge was considerable, and his assertions carry weight, but Cornish material includes some remarkably long narratives that cannot be dismissed as Romantic-era embellishment. These seem to reflect the droll teller's art, and they rival the length of Irish examples.[5]

Along this vein, folklorists have observed that the neat categories of 'folktale' and 'legend' do not always fit stories people told, and Almqvist has a specific observation useful here. He suggests that many narratives regarded as migratory legends elsewhere were collected in Ireland, exhibiting a 'length and ... multi-episodical construction more akin to folktales'.[6] Many Cornish legends warrant the same comment. Indeed, it is not clear if some Cornish legends were being told to be believed. At least a few may have crossed over into the elaborate genre of the fictional folktale.

The Creativity of the Cornish Droll Teller

The observation mentioned above, that droll tellers modified their stories, invites a discussion about something that has long been controversial in folklore studies. A debate has dominated the field, pitting those who sought the historical roots of tales that diffused from some remote past against those who looked at the processes that governed and changed narratives. By emphasizing the rules and structure that is inherent in stories, some folklorists have considered contemporary and geographic factors more than historical ones. The most ardent proponents of the historical camp maintain that the goal should be to identify the oldest variants of a story by looking at geographic and historical distribution to determine where and when it originated and how it changed over time and place. Folklorists at the other end of the spectrum suggest that legend and folktale types were not traditional in any significant way and that the romantic image of conservative storytellers repeating ancient tales was an illusion. These scholars argue that rules govern how stories were created and told; this underlying structure was so important that it forced a broad spectrum of motifs into what appeared to be repeated types. For this line of thought, types are illusions, by-products of possibilities limited by rules and structure.

The observations of both camps have merit. Many storytellers clearly attempted to repeat what they heard as accurately as possible, and this demonstrates that types existed for at least a while. In the same way, the importance of underlying rules and structure is undeniable. At the heart of this debate is whether specific stories were invented once, only to be diffused through time and space, modified along the way and producing distinct variants; or if they were continually reinvented with variation to suit local cultures and environments.

When many specific motifs occur in a story repeated together as a group in diverse places and appearing in historical sources, many have concluded that these narratives are part of a single legacy. In general, European folklorists have tended to embrace the idea that folktale and legend types are part of an older inheritance. Millennia of literacy providing ancient examples of stories serve as evidence of their longevity. As late as 1964, Kenneth H. Jackson eloquently described the time-honoured ambition to look at the best-preserved examples of storytelling as a 'window on the Iron Age'. For many decades, folklorists who sought opportunities to peer into this distant past found little reason to tarry over Cornish collections. Here was a body of material that nineteenth-century collectors admitted was affected by the creativity of the droll tellers, entertainers who revelled in changing narratives rather than faithfully preserving content. When one considers the additional effects of early industrialization and of English dominance, many found even less reason to consider the oral tradition of Cornwall.

It is a challenge to explain why Irish storytellers, for example, celebrated the conservative transmission of tales while Cornish droll tellers valued change. Describing the two approaches to storytelling is a first step but digging deeper to understand differences is likely to be no more satisfactory than attempting to resolve the debate between traditionalists and structuralists. Both sides provide thought-provoking insights, but they are weakest when they assert how folklore originates.

Alan Dundes embraced a radically new way to consider the fabric of a large group of stories in 1964, coincidentally the same year that Jackson gave voice to more conservative ambitions. Dundes's *The Morphology of North American Indian Folktales* appeared at a time when many American folklorists were drawn to the structuralism of Soviet scholar Vladímir Propp. By advancing Propp's approach, Dundes was at the cutting edge of his field at the time, embracing the idea that narratives were inherently fluid.

Dundes observed that the American Southwest featured storytellers who continually changed narratives. Nevertheless, he also compared this degree of flexibility with the Arctic Inuit and the Tillamook from the Pacific Northwest, who repeated stories as they had heard them.[7] In short, while Dundes made his case that some cultures freely changed their stories, he conceded that others were conservative, something he was perhaps less interested in emphasizing in 1964. When attempting to understand Cornish folklore, it is instructive to consider his comparison of creativity as opposed to conservatism.

In addition, Dundes noted that similar stories from different ecosystems naturally reflected the animals in that location. While pursuing this line of discourse, he dismissed the idea that he was observing 'ecotypes', the concept described nearly four decades earlier by the Swedes, Carl Wilhelm von Sydow and Sven Liljeblad. Dundes emphasized that structural similarities dominated oral tradition and that as storytellers employed this structure in different places, they naturally drew on local material, making narratives appear to be expressions of an ecotype.[8]

Von Sydow and Dundes both describe the same phenomenon while insisting it was the result of their own postulated processes, neither of which can be observed or proven to exist. For Dundes, rules are the core of Native American folklore; storytellers decorate the structure with local motifs. For von Sydow, diffusing narratives adapt to local environments as storytellers replace foreign details with local motifs. The importance of structure and rules was not lost on von Sydow: Axel Olrik's laws of oral tradition restrict the effect of any overly creative narrator who sought to change a story in a radical way. The central difference separating Dundes from von Sydow is the role of the 'type'. The question is whether there are traditional story types found across the centuries as each legend or folktale diffuses from one place to another, changing to suit local situations and changing times. Dundes used his North American evidence to argue against this, but he conceded that some cultures valued the repetition of stories more than others.

The importance of Dundes in a Cornish context is in understanding how local storytellers modified legends and folktales they heard. This discussion yields a few conclusions. The first of these is that some cultures emphasized passing on tradition while others celebrated creativity and change. Secondly, an underlying structure or set of rules helps conserve tradition, restricting creative impulses. A third point is not so certain: while some have seen the existence of a structure underpinning narratives as evidence that traditional types are illusions, such a conclusion needs to rest on evidence. In fact, there are numerous examples of storytellers taking pride in being able to identify the sources of stories told. In addition, many early collectors described asking gifted storytellers to invent a new story, something that tradition bearers consistently indicated was impossible.

All that said, Dundes, Propp and Olrik each provide a means to understand Cornish folklore and the droll teller. The creative process was exaggerated in Cornwall in a way that would have been alien in Ireland, for example, but variation was nevertheless confined by rules and structure. While the artist could change the colours, it was still necessary to paint within the lines.

The Nature of Cornish Folklore

This, then, is a means to understand how traditional Cornish stories resemble those found elsewhere while also remaining distinct. Limited evidence does not permit insight as to when specific legends and folktales first appeared in Cornwall. It is easy to imagine that indigenous belief in supernatural beings had deep local roots, but ultimately all that can be certain concerns the nature of the narratives when nineteenth-century collectors were active. Folklore changes constantly, and while it would be fascinating to know how stories arrived and mutated, the situation remains clouded. That said, the opportunity to cast light on Cornish traditions is excellent, and the peninsula need not be overlooked by those who conduct comparative research in northern Europe.

Fortunately, oral traditions from elsewhere provide insight. Almqvist addresses a question in British Studies, looking to those who conclude that Anglo-Saxon invaders gave as much as they took, creating a hybridized society. Almqvist applies this to assist in his life-long study of the interaction of Celtic and Scandinavian folklore. In his essay, 'Scandinavian and Celtic Folklore Contacts in the Earldom of Orkney', he attempts to determine which traditions were borrowed and which may represent common inheritance. It is no mean task, but Almqvist wrote with authority, having spent decades pondering the question, reading sources in multiple languages to consider possible origins of parallel texts.

Cornwall presents a similar situation since it encountered not only Anglo-Saxons but also Scandinavians. Cornwall cannot be regarded as the 'Venice of the North', as Almqvist characterizes the medieval earldom of Orkney. Nevertheless, the Cornish nation was also something of a crossroads. While it resisted medieval Anglo-Saxon advances, Cornwall was not as secluded as the hinterland of Wales or mountainous Caledonia. One would expect that the Cornish had their own oral tradition before the many forces of history had their way. Irrespective of how factors affecting lives and culture played out, the folklore of Cornwall certainly exhibits the same common inheritance that Almqvist suggests 'is part of the explanation of the unity that exists today among the peoples of the British Isles'.[9]

Almqvist further writes that Christiansen,

> has pointed to a series of close parallels between certain Scandinavian and Scottish-Gaelic and Irish legends, and has introduced the term North Sea legends. It is not easy to account satisfactorily for these similarities. It may be that some of the motifs and legends are part of a common stock, but there can be little doubt either that the Norse and Gaelic speaking communities influenced one another, and that certain types and sub-types spread in either direction.[10]

25.   John Thomas Blight's portrait of a quaint mill at Pendour Cove near
Zennor dates from 1861. Cornwall was early to industrialize but stepped into
the modern world more slowly. From Blight's book, *A Week at the Land's End*.

The same approach to Cornwall's folklore seems reasonable: if more information were available, it might be possible to demonstrate that some of the
shared stories represent a common regional bedrock while others appeared in
the south-west of Britain because of later diffusion. It is easy to imagine that
this was the case even if proof is lacking.

Cornish Folklore and a Unique Cultural Fingerprint

Kaarle Krohn in his preface to *Folklore Methodology*, cites a letter from his
father, Julius Krohn (1835–1888), which describes disappointment in realizing
that the Finnish epic, the *Kalevala*, was not purely indigenous in its origin. The
elder Krohn realized that this would be a painful conclusion for those who
embraced the masterwork as evidence of the unique character of Finland, and

by implication, of its right to national autonomy. He correctly understood, however, that folktales and legends are not told in isolation; stories by their nature diffuse from one group of people to the next. Julius Krohn recognized that the *Kalevala*, like Finnish folklore in general, drew on a heritage that shared a great deal with its neighbours while also boasting a distinct adaptation that spoke of Finland's character and national genius.[11]

Because of Cornwall's Celtic roots and remote location, one might hope to find an unusual body of folklore, different from that of its English neighbours. In fact, Cornish narratives include examples of the broad swath of material documented from Ireland to Sweden and beyond. That does not imply that Cornish oral tradition must be taken as just another expression of European culture, offering nothing remarkable and only adding another brick in the wall. Instead, just as Julius Krohn celebrated the *Kalevala* of his beloved Finland, the material from Cornwall is imbued with the character of the place and its people. Few of its stories were peculiar to the peninsula, but the way the Cornish and their remarkable droll tellers dealt with this body of folklore resulted in a legacy that is, in a word, unique.

Appendix: Type Index for Cornish Narrative

This list can and should be augmented by additional research.

Abbreviations

Bottrell TH1870: William Bottrell, *Traditions and Hearthside Stories of West Cornwall* (Penzance: W. Cornish, 1870, first series).

Bottrell TH1873: William Bottrell, *Traditions and Hearthside Stories of West Cornwall* (Penzance: Beare and Son, 1873, second series).

Bottrell SF: William Bottrell, *Stories and Folk-Lore of West Cornwall* (Penzance: F. Rodda, 1880).

Briggs Legends: Katharine Briggs, *Folktales of Britain: Legends* (London: Folio Society, 2011 [1971]).

Briggs Narratives: Katharine Briggs, *Folktales of Britain: Narratives* (London: Folio Society, 2011 [1971]).

Evans-Wentz FF: Walter Yeeling Evans-Wentz, *The Fairy Faith in Celtic Countries* (New York: Citadel, 1990 [1911]).

Hunt PR: Robert Hunt, *Popular Romances of the West of England or the Drolls, Traditions, and Superstitions of Old Cornwall* (London: Chatto and Windus, 1903, combined first and second series [1865]).

Migratory Legend Index

ML 4050, 'The hour is come but the man is not', pp. 8, 40, 97, 106, 203 n.6.

1. 'The Voice from the Sea', Hunt PR, p. 366.
2. 'The Pirate-Wrecker and the Death Ship', Hunt PR, pp. 359–62.
3. Sabine Baring-Gould, *Book of Folk-Lore*, pp. 114–15.

4. 'The Story of the Mermaid and the Man of Cury', Bottrell TH1870, pp. 63–70.

ML 4075, 'Visit to the Blessed Islands', pp. 50–51, 52. (As discussed in Chapter 4, this legend type is too vague to consider in a Cornish context for actual historical connections as opposed to broad affinities. Briggs suggests that the Cornish variant, 'The Fairy Dwelling on Selena Moor', is blended with ML 5080, 'Food from Fairies'.)

1. 'The Fairy Dwelling on Selena Moor', Bottrell TH1873, pp. 94–102. Briggs Legends, classification of this as ML 4075 and ML 5080 is problematic.

2. Bottrell TH1873, p. 102; Bottrell compares this to his story, 'The Fairy Dwelling on Selena Moor'; the fact that there was a second story with a similar plot (man wanders into supernatural realm and is warned to avoid capture by his former fiancée) suggests that there may have been a legend type in Cornwall, regardless of whether it should be classified as ML 4075.

3. 'The Fairy Widower', Hunt PR, pp. 114–18. Briggs Legends, sees this as ML 4075, but that is not useful; best classified as ML 5070, 'Midwife to the Fairies'.

4. 'Cherry of Zennor', Hunt PR, pp. 120–26; Briggs Legends, p. 320, sees this as ML 4075, but that is not useful; best classified as ML 5070, 'Midwife to the Fairies'.

ML 5006*, 'The Flight with the Fairies', pp. 74–76.

1. 'The Piskies in the Cellar', Hunt PR, pp. 88–90; Briggs Legends, p. 484, sees this as ML 5006*. Motifs: F.282.2(b), Fairies say 'Ho! And away for Par Beach!'. They fly away (Baughman); F.282.4*(b), Mortal travels with fairies. He drinks too much in wine-cellar where they revel. He is about to be hanged by owner when a fairy appears and tells him to use the formula he had used the night before. He escapes (Baughman). Briggs Legends, notes that 'similar tales are told of witches'.

2. Couch and Couch, *History of Polperro*, pp. 135–36, as cited by M.A. Courtney, *The Folk-Lore Journal*, 5 (1887), pp. 180–81.

ML 5070, 'Midwife to the Fairies', pp. 40, 53, 57, 80–87.

1. 'Nursing a Fairy', Hunt PR, pp. 83–85 (nursing redaction); Briggs Legends, p. 476, does not identify a legend type; Motif: F.235.4.4(a),

Mortal nurse of fairy child gets fairy water in her eye, is able to see fairies as they are, at any time. She meets one pilfering at fair, she speaks to him; he puts out her eye (Baughman).

2. 'The Fairy Ointment', Hunt PR, pp. 109–11; witches rather than a midwife or nurse.

3. 'How Joan lost the sight in her eye', Hunt PR, pp. 111–13; witches rather than a midwife or nurse; Briggs Legends, p. 407, identifies this as ML 5070. Motifs F.235.4.1, Fairies made visible through use of ointment; F.378.6, Tabu: using fairy bathwater, soap, or ointment on oneself; F.235.4.1(a), Mortal midwife or nurse to fairy child gets some of the ointment in her eye, betrays her vision of the fairies. The seeing eye is blinded (Baughman).

4. 'The Fairy Widower', Hunt PR, pp. 114–18, ointment motif with nurse. Briggs Legends, p. 375, sees this as ML 4075 'Visit to the Blessed Islands'. Motifs: D.965, Magic plant; D.965.14, Magic fern-seed; F.211.3, Fairies live under the earth; F.376, Mortal as servant in Fairyland; F.372, Fairies take human nurse to wait on fairy child. Briggs Legends also compares this with 'The Fairy Dwelling on Selena Moor', p. 348, and 'The Fairy Master', p. 359.

5. 'The Fairy Master', Bottrell TH1873, pp. 173–95; Briggs Legends, p. 359, compares this with 'Cherry of Zennor'.

6. 'Cherry of Zennor', Hunt PR, pp. 120–26; Briggs Legends, p. 320, sees this as ML 4075 'Visit to the Blessed Islands'. Motifs: F.376, Mortal as servant in Fairyland; F.372, Fairies take human nurse to wait on fairy child; F.235.4.1, Fairies made visible through use of ointment.

7. 'The Nurse and the Ointment' (Penzance), Evans-Wentz FF, pp. 175–76.

8. 'Danger of Seeing the "Little People"', Evans-Wentz FF, p. 182; the motif of having sudden vision of supernatural beings followed by attempted blindness is not associated with the story of the midwife/nurse, but rather stands alone in this variant, associated with a human baby's bathwater.

9. Couch and Couch, *History of Polperro*, pp. 138–39.

ML 5075, 'Removing a Building Situated over the House of the Fairies', pp. 56, 101, 105, 106.

1. This story may have influenced 'The Mermaid of Zennor', which includes a similar motif: a captain is asked to move his anchor because

it is blocking the door of the mermaid's house. See Bottrell TH1873, pp. 288–89.

ML 5080, 'Food from Fairies', pp. 50–51: see ML 4075.

ML 5085, 'The Changeling', pp. 29–31, 87–90, 92, 102–3, 104. (Many of the following are not expressions of this migratory legend, per se, but rather they include a reference to the core motif of the legend.) For an excellent summary of the changeling motif in Cornwall, see Young, 'Five Notes on Nineteenth-Century Cornish Changelings'.

1. 'The Spriggan's Child', a poem as recorded by 'A Cornish Droll', Hunt PR, pp. 91–94. This is the clearest expression of ML 5085 in the Cornish collections. It is summarized in prose by Margaret Ann Courtney in her *Cornish Feasts and Folk-Lore*, pp. 126–28. See also Bottrell TH1873, pp. 200–6.
2. Brief reference Bottrell SF, p. 193.
3. Hunt PR, pp. 85–87, 'Changelings' and 'The Lost Child'.
4. 'The Piskies Changeling', Hunt PR, pp. 95–96; this is unusual because the people find a piskie infant and take care of it; it leaves in a way that is reminiscent of ML 6070A 'Fairies send a Message'.
5. 'The Fairy Fair in Germoe', Hunt PR, p. 97.
6. 'Betty Stogs and Jan the Mounster', Hunt PR, pp. 103–7; abducted infant who needs care; returned cleaned and fed; Briggs Legends, p. 293: F.310, Fairies and human children; F.361.1.16(b), Fairies warn careless mother to take better care of children (Baughman). Briggs further comments: 'The fairies' love of cleanliness and order is well displayed in this story. It plays a large part of fairy tradition, though it is not mentioned in the Motif Index.' See also Bottrell TH1873, pp. 205–6
7. 'A Pisky Changeling', Evans-Wentz FF, p. 171.
8. 'Nature of Pixies', Evans-Wentz FF, pp. 176–77.
9. 'Fairy Guardian of the Men-an-Tol', Evans-Wentz FF, p. 179.
10. 'A St. Just Pisky', Evans-Wentz FF, p. 181; two attempted abductions of a boy.
11. 'Small People', Evans-Wentz FF, p. 182.

ML 6010, 'The Capture of a Fairy', pp. 90–92: see ML 6070A.

ML 6045, 'Drinking Cup Stolen from the Fairies', pp. 40, 68–74.

1. 'Fairies on the Eastern Green', Bottrell SF, pp. 92–94. A man interrupts fairy party and is pursued by angry supernatural beings. No cup stolen.

2. 'Spriggans of Trencrom Hill', Hunt PR, p. 90. Man who is treasure hunting is attacked by Spriggans; no cup stolen; limited affinity.

3. 'The Fairy Revels on the "Gump", St Just', Hunt PR, pp. 98–101; no cup stolen; limited affinity; Briggs Narratives, p. 757, identifies this as Folktale AT Type 503, 'The Gifts of the Little People': Motifs F.340, Gifts from fairies; F.211 9, Fairyland under hollow knoll; F.239.4.3, Fairy is tiny; F.262.3.6, Fairy music causes joy; F.456.1, Spriggans; F.350, Theft from fairies; F.361.2.3, Fairies bind man fast to ground after he has attempted to capture fairy prince and princess.

4. Blight, *A Week at the Land's End*, pp. 195–97; related to Hunt's 'The Fairy Revels on the "Gump", St Just'.

5. 'The Fairy Funeral', Hunt PR, pp. 102–3; no cup stolen; limited affinity; Briggs Legends, p. 357, notes Motifs F.268.1, Burial service for Fairy Queen is held at night in Christian church; F.361.3, Fairies take revenge on mortal who spies on them.

6. 'The Fairy Revel', Hunt PR, p. 103; no cup stolen; limited affinity.

7. 'The Old Woman who turned her shift', Hunt PR, pp. 113–14; Briggs Legends, p. 479, classifies this as ML 6045 with motifs: F.385.1, Fairy spell averted by turning coat; F.351.2, Theft of money from fairies by frightening them away from it; F.361.2, Fairy takes revenge for theft.

ML 6055, 'Fairy Cows', pp. 62–65.

1. 'The Four-Leaved Clover', Hunt PR, pp. 107–9; Cornish variant focuses on how cows were lost; Scandinavian versions deal with how they are obtained. Briggs Legends, 381: Motifs: F.235.4.6(a), Milkmaid wearing four-leaved clover sees pixies climbing over and milking cow (Baughman); F.384.1, Salt powerful against fairies.

2. 'The Small People's Cow', Bottrell TH1873, pp. 73–76.

ML 6070A, 'Fairies send a Message', pp. 90–92. This also appears as Folktale Type ATU 113, 'Pan is dead'; previously 'King of the Cats is Dead'. Cornish variants are blended with ML 6010, 'The Capture of a Fairy'.

1. 'The Piskies' Changeling', Hunt PR, pp. 95–96; unusual because these are people who find a piskie infant and take care of it; it leaves when it hears the voice of its father.

2. 'A Fairy Caught', Hunt PR, pp. 450–51.

3. 'Skerry-Werry', Enys Tregarthen, *Pixie Folklore and Legends*, pp. 37–57.

4. 'The Magic Pail', Enys Tregarthen, *The Piskey-Purse: Legends and Tales of North Cornwall*, pp. 59–110.

ML 7015, 'The New Suit', pp. 66–68.

1. 'The Piskie Threshers', Hunt PR, pp. 129–30: 'Piskie fine, and piskie gay; Piskie now will fly away'. Briggs Legends, pp. 482–83, classifies this as ML 7015: Motifs: F.346(c), Fairy helps mortal with threshing (Baughman); F.381.3(a), Tabu: mortal for whom fairy works must not give fairy gifts, especially clothing (Baughman).

2. 'The Pisky Thresher', Evans-Wentz FF, pp. 172: 'Pisky fine, and pisky gay, Pisky now will fly away'.

3. 'Piskies in General', Evans-Wentz FF, p. 184; odd reference from north-east coast of Cornwall of a pisky who stole a new coat. The family heard him say, 'Pisky fine and pisky gay, Pisky's got a bright new coat, Pisky now will run away'.

4. Hunt PR, p. 82.

5. Bottrell SF, pp. 193–94.

6. Couch and Couch, *History of Polperro*, pp. 136–37.

ML 7060, 'The Disputed Site for a Church', pp. 132–33.

1. Spooner, 'Cornwall and the Church that was shifted', pp. 270–75. Spooner includes several Cornish examples of this legend type.

Folktale Type Index

ATU 113, 'Pan is dead'; previously 'King of the Cats is Dead': see ML 6070A.

ATU 328, 'The Boy Steals the Giant's Treasure' ('Jack and the Beanstalk'), pp. 132, 191 n.5. The folktale lacks clear Cornish variants, but it is often discussed in the context of Cornish folklore because English versions are frequently placed in Cornwall.

ATU 365, 'Lenore', pp. 39, 107–21.

1. 'Nancy Trenoweth, The Fair Daughter of the Miller of Alsia', Bottrell TH1870, pp. 468–527.

2. 'A Legend of Pargwarra', Bottrell TH1873, pp. 149–53.

3. 'The Lovers of Porthangwartha', Hunt PR, pp. 247–48.

4. 'The Spectre Bridegroom', Hunt PR, pp. 233–39.

ATU 476*, 'In the Frog's House' and **476****, 'Midwife in the Underworld': see ML 5070.

ATU 500, 'The Name of the Supernatural Helper' (Tom Tit Tot, Rumpelstilzchen, Trillevip), pp. 38, 164.

1. 'Duffy and the Devil', Bottrell TH1873, pp. 1–26.
2. 'Duffy and the Devil', Hunt PR, pp. 239–47; Briggs Narratives, p. 519, includes the following motifs: H.915, Tasks assigned because of girl's own boast; G.303.9.8.1, Devil spins and knits; H.521, Guessing unknown propounder's name; H.512, Guessing with life as wager; N.475, Secret name overheard by eavesdropper; C.4.32.1, Guessing name of supernatural creature gives power over him.

ATU 650A, 'Strong Hans', pp. 38, 128. Briggs Narratives lists two of Hunt's giant stories as associated with ATU 650A, but the link is tenuous (by implication, the classification would apply to at least one of Bottrell's stories). These stories in the Cornish collections are extremely close to etiological legends, set in an obvious Cornish setting in a remote time.

1. 'Tom and the Giant Blunderbuss', Hunt PR, pp. 55–59; Briggs Narratives, uses the term 'Type 650A (variant)': Motifs: F.610, Remarkably strong man; F.624, Mighty lifter; F.628.2.3, Strong man kills giant. Hunt offers an excellent note describing the circumstance of collection and its geographic distribution as well as its similarity to the well-known story, 'Tom Hickathrift' from the Isle of Ely, which Briggs Narratives also lists as ATU 650A (variant).
2. 'How Tom and the Tinkeard found the Tin and how it led to the Morva Fair', Hunt PR, pp. 66–72; Briggs Narratives, links this to 'Tom and the Giant Blunderbuss', but she does not identify this story as ATU 650A. Motifs F.531.6.8.3.3, Giants wrestle with each other; F.531.6.7, Giant's treasure; F.531.6.8.5, Giant's social relations.
3. 'Tom the Giant, His Wife Jane, and Jack the Tinkeard', Hunt PR, pp. 60–65; this is another story that fits in with this complex, although this was not part of the Briggs' collection.
4. 'The Lord of Pengerswick and the Giant of St Michael's Mount', Hunt PR, pp. 53–54.
5. 'The Giants of Towednack', Bottrell TH1870, pp. 9–46, is related to Hunt's 'The Lord of Pengerswick and the Giant of St Michael's Mount'; it is not part of the Briggs' collection, but by implication, it is grouped with these stories, and by her assertion it would be regarded as a variant of ATU 650A.

ATU 758, 'The Various Children of Eve', pp. 76, 142.

1. Enys Tregarthen notebook, described in *Pixie Folklore and Legends*.

ATU 910A, 'Wise Through Experience', pp. 10, 38, 164.

1. 'Tom of Chyannor, The Tin Streamer: A West-Country Droll', Bottrell TH1873, pp. 77–93.
2. 'The Tinner of Chyannor', Hunt PR, pp. 344–46.
3. 'Jowan Chy-an-Horth, py, An try foynt a skyans' ('John of Chyannor, or, The three points of wisdom'), written by Nicholas Boson, published in 1707 by Edward Lhwyd.

ATU 990, 'The Seemingly Dead Revives', pp. 38, 164.

1. 'Cornish Teeny Tiny', Hunt PR, pp. 452–53.

Folktales/Legends Classified with Isolated Motifs

A.977.1.2(cb), Giant carrying apron load of stones drops them when apron string breaks.

1. Bottrell TH1870, p. 51.
2. Hunt PR, pp. 46–47. See also Briggs Legends, p. 815.

F.531.3.2.3, Giants throw tools back and forth.

1. 'The Giant of St Michael's Mount loses his Wife', Hunt PR, p. 55.
2. 'The Giants of the Mount', Hunt PR, pp. 46–47. This does not involve throwing tools or stones, but it is related because the giant kills his wife who is carrying stones.
3. 'The Giants of Trecrobben and the Mount', Bottrell TH1870, pp. 49–50.

F.531.5.1, Giant friendly to man.

1. 'The Giant of Carn Galva', Bottrell TH1870, pp. 47–48.

Unclassified Legends and Texts

Generic Overviews of Supernatural Beings and Related Legends

1. 'The Pixies of Dartmoor', Hunt PR, p. 96.
2. 'Ann Jefferies and the Fairies', Moses Pitt, *An Account of one Ann Jefferies* (London: Richard Cumberland, 1696); Hunt PR, pp. 127–29; Briggs

Legends, p. 290, does not classify this as a migratory legend: Motifs: F.236.1.6, Fairies in green clothes; F.235.3, Fairies visible to only one person; F.239.4.3, Fairy is tiny; F.343.19, Fairies give mortals fairy bread; F.301, Fairy lover; F.282, Fairies travel through air; F.320, Fairies carry people away to fairyland; F.329.2, Fairies abduct young woman: return her when fight starts over her.

3. 'St Margery and the Piskies', Hunt PR, pp. 97–98.

Will-o'-the-wisp

1. Bottrell SF, p. 193.
2. 'The Pixies of Dartmoor', Hunt PR, p. 96.

Fairy Dance and the Abduction of a Man

1. 'St Levan Fairies', Hunt PR, pp. 118–19; see Briggs Legends, p. 498; Motifs: F.258.1, Fairies hold a fair; F.361.4, Fairies take revenge on trespassers on ground they claim as theirs; F.369.7(a), Persons who are led astray by fairies break spell by reversing an article of clothing, coat, glove, etc. (Baughman); F.369.7, Fairies lead travellers astray.
2. 'The Fairy Dwelling on Selena Moor', Bottrell TH1873, pp. 94–102; extensive story with many motifs; see Briggs Legends, p. 350; Briggs sees this as ML 4075 'Visit to the Blessed Islands', but that is questionable.

Knockers

1. Hunt PR, p. 82, p. 349, and p. 352.
2. Bottrell TH1873, p. 185.
2. 'Tom Trevorrow' and other references, Bottrell SF, pp. 186–94.
3. 'Barker's Knee', Hunt PR, p. 88; Briggs Legends, p. 370: Motif: F.361.3, Fairies take revenge on person who spies on them.
4. 'The Fairy Miners—The Knockers', Hunt PR, pp. 90–91; bargain kept by father is violated by son and then the mine failed. Briggs Legends, p. 362: Motif: F.456.1.2.2.1, 'Knockers' lead men to the richest lodes in the mines by knocking in those areas; M.242, Bargaining between mortals and supernatural beings.

Notes

Introduction

1. Alan Dundes, *International Folkloristics: Classic Contributions by the Founders of Folklore* (New York: Rowan and Littlefield, 1999), pp. 9–14, discusses the definition of 'folklore' and presents the original text of the 1846 article by William Thoms which first used the term, reprinting the text from *The Athenaeum*, 982 (22 August 1846), pp. 862–63. This is the Thoms, also known as Ambrose Merton, to whom the Cornish collector Robert Hunt refers: Robert Hunt, *Popular Romances of the West of England or the Drolls, Traditions, and Superstitions of Old Cornwall* (London: Chatto and Windus, originally in two separate volumes in 1865; a second edition in 1871 united the two, and there was a third edition in 1881; it was then reprinted together in 1903, the source of page citations here), p. 102.

2. Kenneth Hurlstone Jackson, *The Oldest Irish Tradition: A Window on the Iron Age* (Cambridge: Cambridge University Press, 2011). Jacqueline Simpson describes how this earlier inspiration inhibited the study of Sussex folklore; see her 'Fairy Queens and Pharisees' from Simon Young and Ceri Houlbrook, editors, *Magical Folk: British and Irish Fairies 500 AD to the Present* (London: Gibson Square, 2018), p. 23.

3. The idea that tradition is not necessarily 'traditional' dominates the essays in Eric Hobsbawm and Terrence Ranger, *The Invention of Tradition* (Cambridge: Cambridge University Press, 1983).

4. Katharine Briggs, *Folktales of Britain* (London: Folio Society, 2011 [1971]).

5. Von Sydow used the term 'oicotype' (it also appears as 'oikotype'), but this text employs the English spelling. See Nils-Arvid Bringéus, *Carl Wilhelm von Sydow: A Swedish Pioneer in Folklore* (Helsinki: FF Communications 298, 2009). See also Carl Wilhelm von Sydow, 'Geography and Folk-Tale Oicotypes', *Béaloideas*, 4:3 (1934), pp. 344–55, reprinted in von Sydow's *Selected Papers on Folklore*, edited by Laurits Bødker (Copenhagen: Rosenkilde and Bagger, 1948), pp. 44–59. For critiques, see Emma Emily Kiefer, *Albert Wesselski and Recent Folklore Theories* (New York: Haskell House, 1973), pp. 23–29; David Hopkin, 'The Ecotype, Or a Modest Proposal to Reconnect Cultural and Social History', from Melissa Calaresu, Filippo de Vivo, and Joan-Pau Rubiés, editors, *Exploring Cultural History:*

Essays in Honour of Peter Burke (Burlington, Vermont: Ashgate, 2012), pp. 31–54; Timothy Cochrane, 'The Concept of Ecotypes in American Folklore', *Journal of Folklore Research*, 24:1 (Jan–Apr 1987), pp. 33–55; Stith Thompson, *The Folktale* (Berkeley: University of California Press, 1977), pp. 440–41, p. 443. Sven S. Liljeblad's dissertation, *Die Tobiageschichte und andere Märchen mit Toten Helfern* (Lund: Lindstedts, 1927) was an important early vehicle for the concept of the ecotype; see Ronald M. James, 'Sven S. Liljeblad', *Halcyon*, 2 (1980).

6. Einar Ólafur Sveinsson, *The Folk-Stories of Iceland*, revised by Einar G. Pétursson, translated by Benedikt Benedikz, edited by Anthony Faulkes (London: University College London, 2003 [1940]), p. 240. For Cornish history see Philip Payton, *Cornwall: A History* (Fowey: Cornwall Editions Limited, 2004). For other discussions of this phenomenon, see von Sydow, *Selected Papers on Folklore*, pp. 11–43; Reidar Th. Christiansen, 'European Folklore in America', *Studia Norvegica*, 12 (Oslo, Norway: Universitetsforlaget, 1962), and Linda Dégh, 'Approaches to Folklore Research among Immigrant Groups', *Journal of American Folklore*, 79 (1966), pp. 551–56. See also, Dundes in his editorial note for von Sydow's article in *International Folkloristics*, pp. 240–41; Dundes discusses the 'concept of marginal survival or peripheral distribution' and the idea that the survivors on the periphery can preserve the oldest examples. He points out that Kaarle Krohn developed this idea in his *Folklore Methodology*, Roger L. Welsch, translator (Austin: University of Texas Press, 1971 [1926]; as *Die folkloristische Arbeitsmethode*), p. 93, pp. 115–16.

7. Philip Payton, 'Industrial Celts?: Cornish Identity in the Age of Technological Prowess', *Cornish Studies: Second Series*, 10, Philip Payton, editor (Exeter: University of Exeter Press, 2002), pp. 116–35. As a testament to Payton's comprehensive understanding of Cornwall, in the same article where he discusses the idea of the industrial Celt, he also suggests considering its maritime environment, which had, perhaps, even greater influence on the peninsula's oral tradition.

8. Ronald M. James, 'Cornish Folklore: Context and Opportunity', *Cornish Studies: Second Series*, 18, Philip Payton, editor (Exeter: University of Exeter Press, 2011), pp. 121–40.

9. Ronald M. James, 'Curses, Vengeance, and Fishtails: The Cornish Mermaid in Perspective', *Cornish Studies: Third Series*, 1, Garry Tregidga, editor (Exeter: University of Exeter Press, 2015), pp. 42–61.

10. Ronald M. James, '"The Spectral Bridegroom": A Study in Cornish Folklore', *Cornish Studies: Second Series*, 20, Philip Payton, editor (Exeter: University of Exeter Press, 2013), pp. 131–47.

11. Ronald M. James, 'Knockers, Knackers, and Ghosts: Immigrant Folklore in the Western Mines', *Western Folklore*, 51:2 (April 1992), pp. 153–76.

12. Antti Aarne and Stith Thompson, *The Types of the Folktale: A Classification and Bibliography* (Helsinki: FF Communications, 184, 1961; second revision, fourth printing, 1987); Reidar Th. Christiansen, *The Migratory Legends: A Proposed List of Types with a Systematic Catalogue of the Norwegian Variants* (Helsinki: FF

Communications, 175, 1958). This study also uses the refinement of Aarne–Thompson: Hans-Jörg Uther, *The Types of International Folktales (Parts I–III)* (Helsinki: FF Communications, 284, 285, and 286, 2011). In addition, the work of Ernest W. Baughman is valuable in this context: *Type and Motif-Index of the Folktales of England and North America* (Bloomington: Indiana University Folklore Series, 20, 1966).

13. Charles Thomas, *Studies in the Folk-Lore of Cornwall: I. The Taboo* (Lowenac, Camborne, UK: self-published, 1951); *II. The Sacrifice* (Lowenac, Camborne, UK: self-published, 1952). His article 'Present-day Charmers in Cornwall', *Folklore*, 64 (1953), pp. 304–5, is reprinted in Charles Thomas, *Gathering the Fragments: The Selected Essays of a Groundbreaking Historian*, edited by Chris Bond (Waterthorpe, Sheffield: Cornovia, 2012), pp. 5–6. This is not to diminish subsequent research; see, for example, the work of Amy Hale: 'Gathering the Fragments: Performing Contemporary Celtic Identities in Cornwall' (Los Angeles: University of California Los Angeles, dissertation in Folklore and Mythology, 1998); Hale, 'Whose Celtic Cornwall?: The Ethnic Cornish Meets Celtic Spirituality', from David Harvey, et al., *Celtic Geographies: Old Culture, New Times* (London: Routledge, 2002), pp. 157–72; Hale, 'Rethinking Celtic Cornwall: An Ethnographic Approach', *Cornish Studies: Second Series*, 5, Philip Payton, editor (Exeter: University of Exeter Press, 1997), pp. 85–99; and Amy Hale and Philip Payton, editors, *New Directions in Celtic Studies* (Exeter: University of Exeter Press, 2000), especially Amy Hale and Shannon Thornton, 'Pagans, Pipers and Politicos: Constructing "Celtic" in a Festival Context', pp. 97–107. See also the approach from outside the discipline of folklore by Paul Manning, 'Jewish Ghosts, Knackers, Tommyknockers, and other Sprites of Capitalism in the Cornish Mines', *Cornish Studies: Second Series*, 13, Philip Payton, editor (Exeter: University of Exeter Press, 2005), pp. 216–55. Jason Semmens has published on Cornish witches; see, for example, his 'Bucca Redivivus: History, Folklore and the Construction of Ethnic Identity within Modern Pagan Witchcraft in Cornwall', *Cornish Studies: Second Series*, 18, Philip Payton, editor (Exeter: University of Exeter Press, 2011), pp. 141–61; and Simon Young has published extensively on Cornish and other British fairies: see publications listed in the bibliography. In addition, Merv Davey has explored folk performance with his dissertation and an article: 'The Celto-Cornish Movement and Folk Revival: Competing Speech Communities', *Cornish Studies: Second Series*, 20, Philip Payton, editor (Exeter: University of Exeter Press, 2013), pp. 108–30.

Chapter 1: The Collectors

1. Hunt, *Popular Romances of the West of England*, p. 366.
2. For Migratory Legend 4050, 'The hour is come but the man is not', see Christiansen, *The Migratory Legends*.

3. O.J. Padel, 'The Cornish background of the Tristan stories', *Cambridge Medieval Celtic Studies*, 1 (Summer 1981), pp. 53–81.

4. O.J. Padel, 'Geoffrey of Monmouth and Cornwall,' *Cambridge Medieval Celtic Studies*, 8 (Winter 1984), pp. 1–28; Neil Thomas, *Diu Crône and the Medieval Arthurian Cycle* (Cambridge, UK: D.S. Brewer, 2002; Arthurian Studies I), p. 24. For the primary source in question, see Geoffrey of Monmouth, *The History of the Kings of Britain*, translated by Lewis Thorpe (London: Folio Society, 2010).

5. Some later publications spell Jefferies' name as Anne. Hunt, *Popular Romances of the West of England*, pp. 127–29; Katharine Briggs, *An Encyclopedia of Fairies, Hobgoblins, Brownies, Bogies, and Other Supernatural Creatures* (New York: Pantheon Books, 1976), pp. 239–42.

6. Richard Carew, *Survey of Cornwall* (London: B. Law, 1769 [1602]). For additional information, see Carew's book edited by F.E. Halliday (Bath, UK: Adams and Dart, 1970; Documents of Social History).

7. *Jowan Chy-an-Horth, py An try foynt a skyans* is available with facing page translation: Nicholas Boson, *John of Chyannor, or The three points of wisdom*, revised and translated by R. Morton Nance (Truro, UK: Cornish Language Board, 1969); it can be classified as folktale type ATU 910A, 'Wise Through Experience'. The concept of tale types is discussed in Chapter 3. See William Bottrell, *Traditions and Hearthside Stories of West Cornwall* (Penzance: W. Cornish, 1873, second series), pp. 77–93, for a later Cornish variant of the story. See also Brian Murdoch, *Cornish Literature* (Woodbridge, Suffolk, UK: D.S. Brewer, 1993), pp. 131–36; Matthew Spriggs, 'Who was the Duchess of Cornwall in Nicholas Boson's (*c*.1660–70) "The Duchesse of Cornwall's Progresse to see the Land's End …"?', Philip Payton, editor, *Cornish Studies: Second Series*, 14 (Exeter: University of Exeter Press, 2006), pp. 56–69; see also Brynley F. Roberts, 'Edward Lhwyd (*c*.1660–1709): Folklorist', *Folklore,* 120:1 (March 2009) pp. 36–56.

8. William Borlase, *Observations on the Antiquities of Cornwall* (Oxford: W. Jackson, 1754), p. 295 and see pp. 294–95 and pp. 313–16. Borlase discussed this in his *Natural History of Cornwall* (Oxford: W. Jackson, 1758), pp. 130–31. His birth year also appears as 1695.

9. Borlase, *Observations on the Antiquities of Cornwall*, p. 299.

10. Fortescue Hitchins and Samuel Drew, editors, *The History of Cornwall, From the earliest of Records and Traditions to the Present Time* (Helston, UK: W. Penaluna, 1824).

11. Anna Eliza Bray, *Traditions, Legends, Superstitions, and Sketches of Devonshire on the Borders of the Tamar and the Tavy* (London: John Murray, 1838); *A Peep at the Pixies, or Legends of the West* (London: Grant and Griffith, 1854). Bray's birth year also appears as 1789; an earlier collection of her letters was published in 1836. These letters were reissued two years later in the volume cited here. Leslie Stephen, editor, *Dictionary of National Biography* (London: Smith, Elder, and Co., 1885–1900), p. 6, pp. 234–35.

12. Robert Stephen Hawker, *Echoes from Old Cornwall* (London: Joseph Masters, 1846); *Cornish Ballads with other Poems* (Oxford: Parker and Company, 1884); *Footprints of Former Men in Far Cornwall* (London: J. Lane, 1903).

13. John Thomas Blight, *Ancient Crosses and other Antiquities in the West of Cornwall* (London: Simpkin, 1858, second edition; [1856]); *A Week at the Land's End* (London: Longman, Green, Longman, and Roberts, 1861). And see Maurice Smelt, *101 Cornish Lives* (Penzance: Alison Hodge, 2006), pp. 30–33.

14. Stephen, editor, *Dictionary of National Biography*, p. 12, p. 324; Jonathan Couch with additions by Thomas Quiller Couch, *The History of Polperro: A Fishing Village on the South Coast of Cornwall* (Truro, UK: Simpkin, Marshall and Company, 1871). Often publishing under the pseudonym 'Q', Sir Arthur Thomas Quiller-Couch (1863–1944), novelist and literary critic, was the son of Thomas Quiller Couch (1826–1884).

15. For Jacob and Wilhelm Grimm, see James M. McGlathery, editor, *The Brothers Grimm and Folktale* (Urbana: University of Illinois Press, 1988). Dundes, *International Folkloristics*, pp. 1–5.

16. Jacob Grimm acknowledged the importance of French and Italian collecting before he and his brother began their work. French and Italian efforts drew on different roots and played less of a role in the development of international folklore studies. See Jacob Grimm, *Teutonic Mythology*, translated from the fourth edition by James Stern Stallybrass (New York: Dover Publications, 1966), p. 15. See Charles Perrault, *Contes* (Paris: Editions Garnier Frères, 1967) for comparative material.

17. Ruth Michaelis-Jena, *The Brothers Grimm* (London: Routledge and Kegan Paul, 1970), pp. 47–48; and see Jacob and Wilhelm Grimm, *The Complete Grimm's Fairy Tales*, translated by James Stern with introduction by Padriac Colum and commentary by Josef Scharl (New York: Pantheon Books, 1944).

18. Jack Zipes, *The Brothers Grimm: From Enchanted Forests to the Modern World* (New York: Routledge, 1988). For additional material, see Zipes, *Breaking the Magic Spell: Radical Theories of Folk and Fairy Tales* (Austin: University of Texas Press, 1979) and Murry B. Peppard, *Paths through the Forest: A Biography of the Brothers Grimm* (New York: Holt, Rinehart and Winston, 1971). A translation of the initial collection of the Brothers Grimm provides an opportunity to see how their famed publication evolved during various editions: see Jack Zipes, translator and editor, *The Original Folk and Fairy Tales of the Brothers Grimm: The Complete First Edition* (Princeton: Princeton University Press, 2014).

19. On the association of folklore studies and nationalism see Koppel S. Pinson, *Modern Germany: Its History and Civilization* (New York: Macmillan, 1966), p. 43, p. 46, p. 52; Hans Kohn, *The Mind of Germany: The Education of a Nation* (New York: Harper and Row, 1960), pp. 56–57; and Agatha Ramm, *Germany, 1789–1919: A Political History* (London: Methuen and Company, 1967), p. 160. Kaarle Krohn in his preface to *Folklore Methodology*, pp. 3–17, published a brief biography of

his pathfinding father Julius Krohn (1835–1888). In this discussion, the younger Krohn made it clear that his father's interest in linguistics and folklore was tied to and inspired by his fervent support of Finnish nationalism. The relationship of nationalism and folklore in Cornwall is addressed by Hale, 'Rethinking Celtic Cornwall', p. 87.

20. Brendan McMahon, 'Folklore, Loss, and Social Change in Nineteenth Century Cornwall', *Tradition Today*, 2 (September 2012), pp. 33–49: http://centre-for-english-traditional-heritage.org/TraditionToday2/TT2_McMahon.pdf (accessed 22 November 2015); see especially page 34: McMahon observed that while folklore collecting had begun throughout Europe, from Ireland to Russia, 'in England the first in the field was a Cornishman'. Despite this, American folklorist Richard M. Dorson, *The British Folklorists: A History* (Chicago: University of Chicago Press, 1968), provides only brief mention of Robert Hunt and no reference to William Bottrell.

21. Bottrell, *Traditions and Hearthside Stories of West Cornwall* (1870). Amy Hale and Philip Payton use a Cornish point of view to address the term 'Celtic', but others have also entered the fray; see Hale and Payton, *New Directions in Celtic Studies*. Hale provides an excellent overview of the history of the term 'Celt' in her article, 'Rethinking Celtic Cornwall'; for her quote, see p. 90.

22. Hale, 'Rethinking Celtic Cornwall', p. 90; Hale acknowledges the Biblical allusion in the phrase: John 6:12.

23. Grimm, *Teutonic Mythology*; for a discussion of the place of this phrase and the assertion it makes in the development of folklore studies see Jack Zipes, editor, *The Oxford Companion to Fairy Tales* (Oxford: University Press, 2015, second edition), p. 538.

24. Smith, Elder and Co., editors, *Dictionary of National Biography* (New York: Macmillan, 1908, second edition); Briggs, *An Encyclopedia of Fairies*, pp. 226–27; and obituary, *The Times*, 20 October 1887, p. 5; Issue 32208; col. F: https://en.wikisource.org/wiki/The_Times/1887/Obituary/Robert_Hunt (accessed 1 May 2010); see also Amy Hale, 'Cornish', from *Celtic Culture: A Historical Encyclopedia*, Volumes 1–5 by John T. Koch, editor (Santa Barbara, California: ABC-CLIO, 2006), p. 761; and Alan Pearson, *Robert Hunt, F.R.S. (1807–1887)* (Federation of Old Cornwall Societies, 1976).

25. Dorson, *The British Folklorists*, p. 323.

26. Ibid., p. 319 and p. 323.

27. Briggs, *An Encyclopedia of Fairies*, p. 34; besides his first volume, the 'first series', published in 1870, previously cited, see also William Bottrell's *Traditions and Hearthside Stories of West Cornwall* (Penzance: Beare and Son, 1873, second series); the final volume (Penzance: F. Rodda, 1880) appeared with the title *Stories and Folk-Lore of West Cornwall*. Simon Young, 'Five Notes on Nineteenth-Century Cornish Changelings', *Journal of the Royal Institution of Cornwall* (2013), pp. 73–77, provides an excellent analysis of Hunt and Bottrell, including their relationship as collectors and authors.

28. Margaret Ann Courtney and T.Q. Couch, *Glossary of Words in Use in Cornwall* (London: Trübner and Co., 1880). Couch contributed information on the eastern part of Cornwall. See also Courtney's *Cornish Feasts and Folk-lore* (Penzance: Beare and Son, 1890).

29. James Orchard Halliwell-Phillipps, *Rambles in Western Cornwall by the Footsteps of the Giants, with Notes on the Celtic Remains of the Land's End District and the Islands of Scilly* (London: J.R. Smith, 1861).

30. William Purcell, *Onward Christian Soldier: A Life of Sabine Baring-Gould, Parson, Squire, Novelist, Antiquarian, 1834–1924* (London: Longmans Green, 1957).

31. William Henry Kearley Wright, *West-Country Poets: Their Lives and Works* (London: Elliot Stock, 1896), pp. 303–4.

32. The volume in question was reissued: William Copeland Borlase, *The Age of the Saints: A Monograph of Early Christianity in Cornwall with the Legends of the Cornish Saints and an Introduction Illustrative of the Ethnology of the District* (Somerset, UK: Llanerch, 1995 [1893]), pp. xii–xiii, pp. 16–25.

33. Charlotte S. Burne, 'Short Notice: Legends and Tales of North Cornwall', *Folklore*, 19:4 (1908), p. 508.

34. Enys Tregarthen, *The Piskey-Purse: Legends and Tales of North Cornwall* (London: Gardner, Darton and Co., 1905); *North Cornwall Fairies and Legends* (London: Gardner, Darton and Co., 1906); and see the newer publication under her authorship, collected by Elizabeth Yates, *Pixie Folklore and Legends* (New York: Avenel, 1996; originally published as *Piskey Folk: A Book of Cornish Legends*), pp. 1–3. Simon Young '"Her Room Was Her World": Nellie Sloggett and North Cornish Folklore', *Journal of Ethnology and Folkloristics* (2017; http://www.jef.ee). Michael Dylan Foster and Jeffrey A. Tolbert offer an innovative way to consider the work of people such as Enys Tregarthen: see their *The Folkloresque: Reframing Folklore in a Popular Culture World* (Boulder: University of Colorado Press, 2016).

35. Robert Morton Nance, 'Cornish Beginnings', *Old Cornwall* (5:9) 1958. See also the obituary for Nance in *The Times*, 28 May 1959; Peter W. Thomas and Derek R. Williams, *Setting Cornwall on its Feet—Robert Morton Nance 1873–1959* (London: Francis Boutle, 2007); Derek R. Williams, *Henry and Katharine Jenner: A Celebration of Cornwall's Culture, Language and Identity* (London: Francis Boutle, 2004); and Tony Deane and Tony Shaw, *The Folklore of Cornwall* (Totoway, New Jersey: Rowman and Littlefield, 1975), p. 11, pp. 13–15.

36. Justin Brooke, '(Alfred) Kenneth Hamilton Jenkin (1900–1980)' from the *Oxford Dictionary of National Biography* (Oxford: Oxford University Press, 2004). See Jenkin's *The Cornish Miner: An Account of his Life above and underground from Early Times* (London: Allen and Urwin, 1962 [1927]); *Cornwall and the Cornish: Story, Religion, and Folk-Lore of 'The Western Land'* (London: J.M. Dent and Sons, 1933); and *Cornish Homes and Customs* (London: J.M. Dent and Sons, 1934).

37. Walter Yeeling Evans-Wentz, *The Fairy Faith in Celtic Countries* (New York: Citadel, 1990 [1911]), p. 170.

38. Carl Phillips, 'A "mystic message to the world": Henry Jenner, W.Y. Evans-Wentz and the fairy-faith in "Celtic" Cornwall', *Cornish Studies: Second Series*, 19, Philip Payton, editor (Exeter: University of Exeter Press, 2012), pp. 123–39.

39. William H. Paynter, *The Cornish Witch-finder—William Henry Paynter and the Witchery, Ghosts, Charms and Folklore of Cornwall*, selected and introduced by Jason Semmens (St Agnes, UK: Federation of Old Cornwall Societies, 2008); Jason Semmens, '"Whyler Pystry": A Breviate of the Life and Folklore-Collecting Practices of William Henry Paynter (1901–1976) of Callington, Cornwall', *Folklore*, 116:1 (2005), pp. 75–94; William H. Paynter, *Cornish Witchcraft: The Confessions of a Westcountry Witch-finder*, with a forward by Jason Semmens (Liskeard: Privately Printed, 2016).

40. Jacqueline Simpson, *British Dragons* (London: Batsford, 1980), pp. 103–5, suggests that the Padstow 'Obby 'Oss may have originally been a 'Hobby Dragon'.

41. Hunt, *Popular Romances of the West of England*, p. 21.

42. Ibid., p. 30.

43. Ibid., p. 23.

44. Bottrell, *Traditions and Hearthside Stories of West Cornwall* (1870), p. vii.

45. Hunt, *Popular Romances of the West of England*, pp. 23–25, and see his discussions throughout.

46. Courtney, *Cornish Feasts and Folk-Lore*, p. 56.

47. Hale, 'Rethinking Celtic Cornwall', p. 87.

48. Two dictionaries in the Oxford series devoted to mythology and folklore, volumes dealing with Celtic mythology on the one hand and English folklore on the other, include numerous references to Cornwall, a place shared by both topics in the minds of the editors. See Jacqueline Simpson and Steve Roud, *A Dictionary of English Folklore* (Oxford: Oxford University Press, 2000) and James MacKillop, *A Dictionary of Celtic Mythology* (Oxford: Oxford University Press, 1998).

49. Amy Hale, 'Genesis of the Celto-Cornish Revival? L.C. Duncombe-Jewell and the Cowethas Kelto-Kernuak', Philip Payton, editor, *Cornish Studies: Second Series*, 5 (Exeter: University of Exeter Press, 1997), pp. 100–11.

50. Dorson, *The British Folklorists*, pp. 343–439. Karen B. Golightly, 'Who put the Folk in Folklore?: Nineteenth-Century Collecting of Irish Folklore from T. Crofton Croker to Lady Augusta Gregory' (Carbondale: Southern Illinois University, 2007). Bernhard Maier, *Dictionary of Celtic Religion and Culture*, translated by Cyril Edwards (Woodbridge, UK: Boydell Press, 1997).

Chapter 2: The Droll Tellers

1. P.A.S. Pool, *The Life and Progress of Henry Quick of Zennor* (St Ives: W.J. Rowe, 1963), p. 31; Pool borrowed the text from Bottrell, *Traditions and Hearthside Tales of West Cornwall* (1870), p. 69.

2. Von Sydow was an early proponent of the idea of active and passive bearers of oral tradition. See his 'On the Spread of Tradition', from his *Selected Papers on Folklore*, pp. 11–43. And see Kenneth S. Goldstein, 'On the Application of the Concepts of Active and Inactive Traditions to the Study of Repertory', *The Journal of American Folklore*, 84:331 (Jan–Mar 1971), pp. 62–67.

3. James H. Delargy (Séamus Ó Duilearga), 'The Gaelic Story-Teller with some notes on Gaelic Folk-Tales' (The Sir John Rhŷs Lecture, presented 28 November 1945; published 1946); and see his 'The Gaelic Story-Teller—No Living Counterpart in Western Christendom', *Ireland of the Welcomes*, 1:1 (1952), pp. 2–4. Dundes reproduced his original article in *International Folkloristics*, pp. 153–76; references to Delargy's article employ page numbers from this edition. Dundes, p. 157, further recommends additional sources to be considered in the context of storytellers: *Peig: The Autobiography of Peig Sayers of the Great Blasket Island*, translated by Bryan MacMahon (Syracuse, New York: Syracuse University Press, 1974; originally published in Gaelic in 1938) and her sequel, *An Old Woman's Reflections*, translated by Séamus Ennis (Oxford: Oxford University Press, 1962); and Henry Glassie, *Passing the Time in Ballymenone: Culture and History of an Ulster Community* (Philadelphia: University of Pennsylvania Press, 1982). Gun Herranen provides an example of a Finnish-Swedish storyteller, Berndt Strömberg (1822–1910), discussing the creativity of the tradition bearer. Herranen's article, 'The Storyteller's Repertoire', appears in Reimund Kvideland and Henning K. Sehmsdorf, editors, *Nordic Folklore: Recent Studies* (Bloomington: University of Indiana Press, 1989), pp. 63–69.

4. George Denis Zimmermann, *The Irish Storyteller* (Dublin: Four Courts Press, 2001).

5. Ibid., p. 316.

6. James A.H. Murray, editor, *A New English Dictionary on Historical Principals, D and E, Volume III* (Oxford: Clarendon Press, 1897; referred to as the *Oxford English Dictionary* after 1933), pp. 675–76, referring to Hunt's 1865 book; see also Joseph Wright, *The English Dialect Dictionary: Volume II. D–G* (London: Henry Frowde, Amen Corner, 1900), p. 180.

7. Carew, *Survey of Cornwall*, pp. 308–9.

8. An Irish storyteller could also be known as *sgéalaí* or *sgéaltóir* depending on the type of stories told. See Zimmerman, *The Irish Storyteller*, pp. 430–31. For the *cyfarwyddiaid*, see Sioned Davies, 'Storytelling in Medieval Wales', *Oral Tradition*, 7/2 (1992), pp. 231–57. Zimmerman differentiates between sedentary local storytellers and travelling storytellers who depended on hosts for room and board, pp. 434–36.

9. Briggs, *An Encyclopedia of Fairies*, p. 426. With more information, it would be possible to address the subject of gender and Cornish storytelling. In Ireland, ample evidence exists to demonstrate that many women were active bearers of tradition; documented travelling professionals were generally men, but that observation may speak more to the prejudice of the early male folklore collectors than to reality.

10. Hunt, *Popular Romances of the West of England*, p. 28.

11. Delargy, 'The Gaelic Story-Teller', p. 159.

12. Ibid., p. 158.

13. Ibid., pp. 160–61.

14. Ibid., p. 161.

15. Ibid., p. 166.

16. Ibid., p. 176.

17. Jackson, *The Oldest Irish Tradition*.

18. Zimmermann, *The Irish Storyteller*, pp. 440–44. Dundes, in an essay introducing the work of Arnold van Gennep (1873–1957), points out that 'van Gennep ... understood that folklore was "living" rather than wrongly considered solely to be "dead" survivals from the past': Arnold van Gennep, *The Rites of Passage*, p. 100, from Dundes, *International Folkloristics*, pp. 99–108.

19. Zimmermann, *The Irish Storyteller*, p. 443.

20. As cited by Hunt, *Popular Romances of the West of England*, p. 26, from Carew, *Survey of Cornwall*, pp. 308–9.

21. Hunt, *Popular Romances of the West of England*, p. 28. Bottrell's two droll tellers may or may not have been distinct from the two Hunt indicates he had known. Both mention Uncle Anthony James. Hunt's two droll tellers in 1829 are seemingly distinct from Uncle Anthony James and Billy Frost, mentioned by Bottrell.

22. Bottrell, *Traditions and Hearthside Stories of West Cornwall* (1870), p. vi.

23. Hunt, *Popular Romances of the West of England*, p. 26. William Bottrell lent Hunt some of his material before publishing on his own; see Young, 'Five Notes on Nineteenth-Century Cornish Changelings', p. 73.

24. Hunt, *Popular Romances of the West of England*, p. 27.

25. Bottrell, *Traditions and Hearthside Stories of West Cornwall* (1870), p. 63.

26. Ibid., p. vi.

27. This is as quoted by Hunt, apparently drawing on Bottrell for insight; see Hunt, *Popular Romances of the West of England*, p. 26.

28. Ibid., pp. 91–95. Simon Young refers to this poem as 'arguably the only genuine droll piece to survive', by which he means in rhyme and intact. See his article, 'Five Notes on Nineteenth-Century Cornish Changelings', p. 54.

29. Courtney, *Cornish Feasts and Folk-lore*, pp. 126–27. McMahon in 'Folklore, Loss, and Social Change in Nineteenth Century Cornwall' points out that 'whether the droll-tellers and the itinerant balladeers were the same people is hard to say', p. 35. McMahon adds in note 19 that 'Alan Kent thinks not but their roles may have overlapped to some extent.': see Alan M. Kent, *The Literature of Cornwall: Continuity, Identity, Difference, 1000–2000* (Bristol: Redcliffe Press, 2000).

30. Hunt, *Popular Romances of the West of England*, p. 27; 'Barbara Allen', which has deep historical roots, appears in the Child collection as number 84; Francis James Child, *The English and Scottish Popular Ballads* (Boston: Houghton, Mifflin, 1886–1898).

31. Hunt, *Popular Romances of the West of England*, p. 26.

32. Future enquiry might consider how similar the tradition of rhyme and song of the Cornish droll tellers was to the long-standing institution of the English ballad writers, but that is beyond the scope of this study.

33. Bottrell, *Traditions and Hearthside Stories of West Cornwall* (1870), p. vi.

34. Young, 'Five Notes on Nineteenth-Century Cornish Changelings', p. 74.

35. John Rule, *Essays in Eighteenth and Nineteenth Century Social History* (Clio Publishing: Southampton, 2006), p. 269.

36. Philip Payton, 'Bridget Cleary and Cornish Studies: Folklore, Story-telling and Modernity', *Cornish Studies: Second Series*, 13, Philip Payton, editor (Exeter: University of Exeter Press, 2005), pp. 194–215; Angela Bourke, *The Burning of Bridget Cleary: A True Story* (New York: Viking, 2000).

37. Vladímir Propp, *Morphology of the Folktale*, translated by Laurence Scott and revised and edited by Louis A. Wagner (Austin: University of Texas Press, 1968 [1928]). Propp's work appeared in English in 1958. Propp's position influenced Dundes in his dissertation: *The Morphology of North American Indian Folktales* (Helsinki: FF Communications, 195, 1964). Axel Olrik's essay appeared as 'Epische Gesetze der Volksdichtung', *Zeitschrift für Deutsches Altertum*, 51 (1909), pp. 1–12: reprinted in translation, Dundes, editor, *The Study of Folklore* (Berkeley: University of California Press, 1965), pp. 129–41. Any radical stance asserting that nineteenth-century folk narrative is of recent origin is softened here by finding a middle ground between tradition and change.

38. For the delayed analysis of legends, see Bo Almqvist, 'Irish Migratory Legends on the Supernatural: Sources, Studies, and Problems', *Béaloideas*, 59 (1991), pp. 1–43. Folktales were relatively rare in English collections as well: see Dorson, *The British Folklorists*, p. 160.

39. Reimund Kvideland and Henning K. Sehmsdorf, editors, *Scandinavian Folk Belief and Legend* (Minneapolis: University of Minnesota Press, 1988), pp. 12–13.

40. Sveinsson, *The Folk-Stories of Iceland*, p. 69. Sveinsson goes on to indicate that 'there are references to distinguished *rímur*-chanters in Iceland, and some vagrants were good story-tellers, but their livelihood did not depend on it and I know of no instance of anyone who ever made story-telling his profession'. By contrast, Cornwall's professional droll tellers are even more remarkable.

41. The idea that the preservation of tradition is often more a process of invention than conservation is discussed by Merv Davey, 'As is the Manner and the Custom: Identity and Folk Tradition in Cornwall' (Exeter: University of Exeter, Doctoral Thesis, September 2011), pp. 15–50.

Chapter 3: Folkways and Stories

1. This and the following paragraphs refer to A.L. Rowse, *A Cornish Childhood*, which originally appeared in 1942; page numbers are from the Cardinal edition

(London, 1975): p. 8, 'A Neck'; p. 8, Christmas mumming of St George and the dragon; p. 8, shivaree; p. 10, St Austell Feast Week; p. 11, Summercourt Fair; p. 38, clock stop as omen of death; p. 44, magpie numbers as predictor of the day; p. 47, 'laugh like a pisky'; p. 49, seeing ghosts; p. 50, Christmas carols; p. 51, game of twelve; p. 68, songs from the Crimean War and the Czar and his long league boots; p. 78, St Michael's Mount; p. 78 submerged forests and ringing bells of submerged churches; p. 98, a witch; p. 102, white hawthorn flowers regarded as bad luck; p. 125, traditional children's games of rounders and skippety-bed; p. 132, sympathetic magic; p. 180, kissing gates; p. 206, Flora dance at end of WWI; p. 229, traditional songs; p. 239, elf and fairy references; p. 258, money spider; p. 264, returning for a forgotten item as unlucky and a threepenny bit as good luck. John Rule, *Essays in Eighteenth and Nineteenth Century Social History*, pp. 268–89, discusses the St Austell Feast week, together with similar festivals.

2. The distinction between legend and folktale can be much vaguer than described here. Almqvist suggests that it might be better to define a legend as 'a story that often is believed': Bo Almqvist, 'Irish Migratory Legends on the Supernatural', pp. 41–42.

3. Aarne and Thompson, *The Types of the Folktale*; Uther, *The Types of International Folktales*. The work of Vladímir Propp is an important critique of the Finnish method; see his *Morphology of the Folktale*. Propp is discussed in Chapter 2 and in the Conclusion in the context of the role of the droll teller.

4. The number of Irish folktale types is slightly less than three hundred when examples of direct transcriptions from foreign published sources are discounted as demonstrated by Ronald M. James, 'A Year in Ireland: Reflections on a Methodological Crisis', *Sinsear: The Folklore Journal*, 4 (1982–1983), pp. 4–5, pp. 83–90; see Seán Ó Súilleabháin and Reidar Th. Christiansen, *The Types of the Irish Folktale* (Helsinki: FF Communications 188, 1967). Zimmermann, *The Irish Storyteller*, p. 449, indicates that Ireland has 'some seven hundred' of what he calls 'international plot types', citing Ó Súilleabháin and Christiansen. Zimmermann is probably referring to subtypes, but he may also be including migratory legends.

5. Another cycle of stories is classified as ATU 328, 'The Boy Steals the Giant's Treasure', which is better known than 'Strong Hans' thanks to a popular version of the folktale, 'Jack and the Beanstalk'. Halliwell-Phillipps, *Rambles in Western Cornwall*, pp. 7–11, refers to encountering this cycle of stories in west Cornwall. With its 'Cornish' hero, the story of 'Jack and the Beanstalk' appeared in Edwin Sidney Hartland, *English Fairy and other Folk Tales* (London: C.E. Brock, 1890), pp. 28–34. The scant evidence of the questionable Halliwell-Phillipps aside, this is apparently not a Cornish folktale; English storytellers probably placed it in the peninsula because they believed it was home to giants; see Chapter 9.

6. Bottrell is quoted in Hunt, *Popular Romances of the West of England*, p. 27. For other examples of ATU 365, see Hunt's 'The Spectre Bridegroom', p. 233; 'The Lovers of Porthangwartha', p. 247; and 'The Execution and Wedding', p. 256.

7. Christiansen, *The Migratory Legend*. Migratory legends are also called 'testimonial legends'. Von Sydow used the term 'fabulate' for a variety of traditional narratives including what is referred to here as migratory legends, but the term 'fabulate' is less useful for this discussion.

8. For a discussion of Cornish variants, see Chapter 5. See also Christiansen, *The Migratory Legends*.

9. Hunt, *Popular Romances of the West of England*, pp. 152–55, and Bottrell, *Traditions and Hearthside Stories of West Cornwall* (1870), pp. 64–70; See also Briggs, *An Encyclopedia of Fairies*, pp. 272–75.

10. Hunt, *Popular Romances of the West of England*, p. 366; see also Dáithí Ó hÓgáin, 'Migratory Legends in Medieval Irish Literature', *Béaloideas*, 60/61 (1992/1993), pp. 57–74; and Barry O'Reilly, 'River Claiming its Due and the Sod of Death Predestined (ML 4050 and MLSIT 4051): Two Legends of Fate in Irish Tradition', *Béaloideas*, 59 (1991), pp. 83–90.

11. The situation in Scandinavia is complex because of different dialects and languages as well as extensive geography. For troll beliefs see Elisabeth Hartmann, *Die Trollvorstellungen in den Sagen und Märchen der Skandinavischen Völker* (Eberhard Karls Universität Tübingen, 1936). Much has been written on Celtic supernatural beings; see, for example, Evans-Wentz, *The Fairy Faith in Celtic Countries*. More recently, see Peter Narváez, editor, *The Good People: New Fairylore Essays* (Lexington: University of Kentucky, 1997); Lizanne Henderson and Edward J. Cowan, *Scottish Fairy Belief: A History* (East Lothian, Scotland: Tuckwell Press, 2001); Patricia Lysaght, *The Banshee: The Irish Death Messenger* (Boulder, Colorado: Roberts Rinehart, 1986), and Simon Young and Ceri Houlbrook, editors, *Magical Folk: British and Irish Fairies at Home and Abroad* (London: Gibson Square, 2017). There are many other terms used in northern Europe. Polynesia also includes the rare concept of social supernatural beings.

12. This discussion does not mention ballads, riddles and other forms of oral tradition, all of which warrant study.

13. Dundes, *International Folkloristics*, p. 156.

14. In this context, consider Davey, 'As is the Manner and the Custom' and Simon Reed, *The Cornish Traditional Year* (London: Troy Books, 2011).

15. Thomas, *Studies in the Folk-Lore of Cornwall: II. The Sacrifice*.

16. See Hunt, *Popular Romances of the West of England*, pp. 385–86; Courtney, *Cornish Feasts and Folk-lore*, pp. 52–53; Jenkin, *Cornish Homes and Customs*, pp. 153–57; Rowse. *A Cornish Childhood*, p. 8. See also Deane and Shaw, *Folklore of Cornwall*, pp. 167–68; Payton, *Cornwall: A History*, p. 20; and Iorwerth C. Peate, 'Corn Ornaments', *Folklore*, 82:3 (Autumn 1971), p. 177.

17. James Frazer, *Spirits of the Corn and of the Wild*, Volume 1 (*The Golden Bough*, Volume 7; London: Macmillan, 1912, third edition), pp. 264–69. Frazer also cites Devonian and Welsh examples in addition to his material from Cornwall.

18. Simpson and Roud, *A Dictionary of English Folklore*, p. 168.

19. See, for example, Jacqueline Simpson, *Scandinavian Folktales* (London: Penguin Books, 1988), pp. 174–75; Reidar Th. Christiansen, *Folktales of Norway*, translated by Pat Shaw Iversen (Chicago: University of Chicago Press, 1964), pp. 139–40. See also Simpson, 'Fairy Queens and Pharisees' from Young and Houlbrook, editor, *Magical Folk*, pp. 28–29.

20. An online recollection by John Bennallick of St Wenn, Cornwall, includes an eloquent description of the last sheaf as containing the power of the field, so the meaning of the tradition was apparently not completely lost: http://www. storylines.org.uk/2013/05/21/the-cornish-tradition-of-crying-the-neck/ (accessed 29 July 2016).

21. Wilhelm Mannhardt was an early proponent of the idea that these harvest festivals harken back to homages to fertility deities. For an evaluation of Mannhardt, see Dundes, *International Folkloristics*, pp. 15–19 and pp. 21–22. For an early assessment of Mannhardt, see von Sydow's 1934 article in *Folklore*, 'The Mannhardtian Theories about the Last Sheaf and the Fertility Demons from a Modern Critical Point of View', reprinted in *Selected Papers on Folklore*, pp. 89–105; for the Scandinavian tradition about the potency of the final grains of harvest, see von Sydow's brief article from the same collection: 'The Ideas of the "First" and the "Last" in the Folk Traditions, Especially in Harvest Rites', pp. 163–66.

22. Dundes, *The International Folkloristics*, p. 25.

Chapter 4: Piskies, Spriggans and Buccas

1. Bottrell, *Traditions and Hearthside Stories of West Cornwall* (1873), pp. 95–102. Jeremy Harte, *Explore Fairy Traditions* (Loughborough, United Kingdom: Heart of Albion, 2004), pp. 43–44, asserts that this story is typical of what can be found in Ireland, but the motifs he cites are no more Irish than Norwegian or Swedish: they are simply part of the broad regional tradition, and there is no reason to see the Cornish story as being somehow foreign in its origin. For a discussion of this, see Young, 'Five Notes on Nineteenth-Century Cornish Changelings'. Perhaps Harte was inspired by Katharine Briggs, 'The Fairies and the Realms of the Dead', *Folklore*, 81:2 (Summer 1970), pp. 81–96, in which she considers the way this Cornish legend and various Irish counterparts deal with the subject of fairies and the dead. Briggs is not suggesting a direct connection between the legends; she is merely considering how they treat the subject.

2. Von Sydow, *Selected Papers on Folklore*, pp. 60–85. See also Bringéus, *Carl Wilhelm von Sydow*.

3. Bottrell, *Traditions and Hearthside Stories of West Cornwall* (1870), p. 169.

4. Briggs, *An Encyclopedia of Fairies*, pp. 141–43; and see Briggs, *Folktales of Britain: Legends*, pp. 348–50. She describes Bottrell's story with motifs C.211.1, Tabu: eating in Fairyland; F.370, Visit to Fairyland; F.372, Fairies take human nurse to

attend fairy child; F.375, Mortals as captives in Fairyland; F.377, Supernatural lapse of time in Fairyland; F.251.2, Fairies as souls of departed; F.234.1.15, Fairy in form of a bird; F.385.1, Fairy spell averted by turning coat.

5.   Hunt, *Popular Romances of the West of England*, p. 80; Evans-Wentz, *The Fairy Faith in Celtic Countries*, pp. 164–65. Consider the article by Simon Young, 'Against Taxonomy: The Fairy Families of Cornwall', Philip Payton, editor, *Cornish Studies: Second Series*, 21 (Exeter: University of Exeter Press, 2014), pp. 223–37; Young argues that Hunt, influenced by the sciences, employed a rigid taxonomy of the fairy folk of Cornwall but that Bottrell's idea of 'types' is more fluid. He also argues that Bottrell's approach is more like that which would be found among people. This conclusion is echoed by other folklorists: see Hartmann, *Die Trollvorstellungen in den Sagen und Märchen der Skandinavischen Völker*, for example. Echoing Young's argument about nineteenth-century preoccupation with taxonomy, see Ármann Jakobsson, 'Beware of the Elf! A Note on the Evolving Meaning of *Álfar*', *Folklore* 126:2 (July 2015), pp. 215–23. Critiques of taxonomies of supernatural beings should not be taken to suggest that indexes of story types are not a valid means to organize and study folklore.

6.   Mermaids and the merfolk (see Chapter 7) have many of the same characteristics as fairies and some stories overlap, but the distinct environment of the sea makes it useful to discuss them separately. The same is true of knockers in the mines (see Chapters 10 and 11).

7.   Reidar Th. Christiansen, 'Some Notes on the Fairies and the Fairy Faith', *Béaloideas*, 39/41 (1971–1973), pp. 95–111.

8.   Murray, *A New English Dictionary on Historical Principals, O and P, Volume VII* (1909), p. 924. Nicolas Udall, translator. *The Apophthegmes of Erasmus* (London: Kingston, 1564; reprinted, Boston, Lincolnshire: Robert Roberts, 1877). Mark Norman and Jo Hickey-Hall suggest that 'piskie' is a dialect mutation of pixie in a corner of Britain where 'it was common for pairs of letters to be transposed. For example, in local dialect you would "aks" a question rather than "ask"; hence piskey instead of pixie. Piskie is still very common in Devon.' The suggestion that the term may be etymologically related to the name 'Picts' stretches credibility. See their article 'Pixies and Pixy Rocks' from Young and Houlbrook, editors, *Magical Folk*, p. 240, note 1.

9.   Evans-Wentz, *The Fairy Faith in Celtic Countries*, p. 171 and p. 182. The indication that this came from a woman dead for half a century dates the information to the mid-nineteenth century. The inclination to abduct babies was confirmed by people in the neighbourhood of Newlyn and St Just, pp. 176–77; from someone from St Just, p. 181; and from Sennen Cove, p. 182.

10. Ibid., pp. 174–75, and for this paragraph in general, pp. 172–75; the evidence from Newlyn is from page 179. For evidence of piskies dancing in circles, see pp. 181–82.

11. Ibid., p. 183.

12. Ibid., p. 175, and see p. 182.

13. Ibid., pp. 177–79. The idea that piskies were the spirits of the dead 'come back in the form of little people' came from someone born in 1825 on St Michael's Mount, p. 179; and on 'dead-born children', p. 183. On the interplay between the ideas of the dead and fairies, see Briggs, 'The Fairies and the Realms of the Dead'; and see John P. Brennan and Jane Garry, 'Otherworld Journeys: Upper and Lower Worlds' from Jane Garry and Hasan El-Shamy, editors, *Archetypes and Motifs in Folklore and Literature: A Handbook* (London: M.E. Sharpe, 2005), pp. 196–97. Because pre-modern Europeans counted the evening as the beginning of All Saints Day, the first day of November began at what is now regarded as sunset on 31 October.

14. Two benchmark studies dealing with northern European fairies with an emphasis on Britain and Ireland are both by Katharine Briggs: *The Fairies in Tradition and Literature* (London: Routledge and Kegan Paul, 1967) and *The Vanishing People: Fairy Lore and Legends* (New York: Pantheon, 1978); see also Carole G. Silver, *Strange and Secret Peoples: Fairies and Victorian Consciousness* (Oxford: Oxford University Press, 1999).

15. Hartmann, *Die Trollvorstellungen in den Sagen und Märchen der Skandinavischen Völker*; the term 'troll' is problematic because various places apply it to indicate different types of supernatural beings, but in some locations, particularly parts of Sweden and Denmark, variations of the term indicate a social supernatural being much like the fairies of Britain and Ireland. On the issue of terms for the super-natural being used differently in various locations, see Sveinsson, *The Folk-Stories of Iceland*, pp. 159–61. For Bo Almqvist, see his excellent collection of studies, edited by Éilís Ní Dhuibhne and Séamas Ó Catháin, *Viking Ale: Studies on Folklore Contacts between the Northern and the Western Worlds* (Aberystwyth: Boethius, 1991). On von Sydow, see Bringéus, *Carl Wilhelm von Sydow*. It is also worth noting that in the 1920s and 1930s Liljeblad helped organize the folklore archives in Uppsala, Sweden, and in Dublin, Ireland.

16. This legend appears to be behind a Cornish story related to mermaids where the abode of the supernatural beings is beneath the waves; see Chapter 8.

17. Coincidentally, Lotte Motz addresses the issue of relative size regarding giants, which could appear large but also small: 'Giants in Folklore and Mythology: A New Approach', *Folklore*, 93:1 (1982), pp. 70–84, especially pp. 73–74.

18. Simon Young gives eloquent voice to the radically different ways pre-industrial people viewed, and modern enthusiasts view, fairies; see his 'Fairy Holes and Fairy Butter', Young and Houlbrook, editors, *Magical Folk*, p. 80.

19. See motifs F.365.1; F.243; troll's food F.455.4.2.

20. Bottrell, *Stories and Folk-Lore of West Cornwall*, p. 194.

21. John H. Fisher, editor, *The Complete Poetry and Prose of Geoffrey Chaucer* (New York: Holt, Rinehart and Winston, 1977), p. 120.

22. Linda-May Ballard, 'Fairies and the Supernatural on Reachrai', in Narváez, *The Good People*, p. 91; note 9; and see Young, 'Five Notes on Nineteenth-Century Cornish Changelings', p. 67.

23. Marjorie T. Johnson, *Seeing Fairies: From the Lost Archives of the Fairy Investigation Society, Authentic Reports of Fairies in Modern Times* (San Antonio, Texas: Anomalist Books, 2014).

24. *The Packet*, 22 August 2017.

Chapter 5: Piskies and Migratory Legends

1. Bottrell, *Traditions and Hearthside Stories of West Cornwall* (1873), pp. 73–76.

2. Hunt, *Popular Romances of the West of England*, pp. 107–9.

3. Christiansen, *The Migratory Legend*, p. 178.

4. See Ann Helene Bolstad Skjelbred, '"These Stories will not lead you to Heaven": An Encounter with Two Sami Narrators', *Folklore*, 112:1 (2001), p. 61. This source includes an account about a man obtaining a fairy cow by throwing his knife over it, but the supernatural being subsequently reclaimed the cow, maintaining that the man had ruined the beast by milking it into an iron bucket rather than one of wood. And see Jessica Hemmings, '"Bos Primigenius" in Britain: Or, Why do Fairy Cows Have Red Ears?', *Folklore*, 113:1 (2002), pp. 71–82. For sea cows, see Jacqueline Simpson, *Icelandic Folktales and Legends* (Berkeley: University of California Press, 1972), pp. 94–96.

5. Simpson, *Icelandic Folktales and Legends*, pp. 23–25.

6. Reimund Kvideland and Henning K. Sehmsdorf, editors, 'Binding the Cattle of the Mound Folk', from *Scandinavian Folk Belief and Legend*, pp. 232–33.

7. Robin Gwyndaf, 'Fairylore: Memorates and Legends from Welsh Oral Tradition', from Narváez, *The Good People*, pp. 189–90.

8. Evans-Wentz, *The Fairy Faith in Celtic Countries*, p. 143, p. 147, and pp. 203–4, mentions fairy cattle in Welsh tradition and in Brittany. These stories feature the idea of fairies keeping cattle, but they do not include the initial episode dealing with acquisition that one normally finds in Scandinavian tradition. See also the legend of Llyn Barfog from Wirt Sikes, *British Goblins, Welsh Folk-lore, Fairy Mythology, Legends and Traditions* (London: S. Low, Marston, Searle and Rivington, 1880), pp. 37–38.

9. Bo Almqvist, 'Crossing the Border: A Sampler of Irish Migratory Legends about the Supernatural', *Béaloideas*, 59 (1991), pp. 209–17, pp. 219–78, and see especially p. 272. Almqvist cites Séamas Ó Catháin, 'A Tale of Two Sittings—Context and variation in a fairy legend from Tyrone', *Béaloideas*, 48–49 (1980–1981), pp. 135–47.

10. Brian Earls, 'Supernatural Legends in Nineteenth-Century Irish Writing', *Béaloideas*, 60–61 (1992–1993), pp. 93–144, especially p. 134.

11. Briggs, who often draws on Hunt and Bottrell for her British compendium, does not list a variant of ML 6055. Briggs, *Folk Tales of Britain*.

12. Christiansen, *The Migratory Legend*. See also, Briggs, *The Fairies in Tradition and Literature*, pp. 33–47 and Briggs, *The Vanishing People*, pp. 53–65.

13. Hunt, *Popular Romances of the West of England*, pp. 129–30. Hunt quotes from a tale told by Thomas Quiller Couch in *Notes and Queries*. Briggs, *Folk Tales of Britain: Legends*, pp. 482–83, describes this with the following motifs: F.346(c), Fairy helps mortal with threshing; F.381.3(a), Tabu: mortal for whom fairy works must not give fairy gifts, especially clothing. The story of 'The New Suit' has enjoyed a lengthy history thanks in part to its publication in the collection of the Brothers Grimm: see story number 391.

14. Evans-Wentz, *The Fairy Faith in Celtic Countries*, p. 172.

15. Ibid., p. 184. Again, the spelling of 'piskie' appears differently in various sources.

16. Couch and Couch, *The History of Polperro*, pp. 136–37; as cited by M.A. Courtney, 'Cornish Folk-lore', *The Folk-Lore Journal* (1887), p. 5, pp. 180–81. Couch recounts the story that also appears in Hunt, *Popular Romances of the West of England*, as 'The Piskie Thresher'.

17. Couch and Couch, *History of Polperro*, p. 137.

18. Hunt, *Popular Romances of the West of England*, p. 82. Briggs, *An Encyclopedia of Fairies*, p. 45, suggests the possibility 'that "Browney" is the name of the bees themselves.' While this might have been the case, that was clearly not Hunt's understanding of the tradition.

19. Simon Young, 'The Phantom Cornish Browney', *Devon and Cornwall Notes and Queries* 41:10 (Autumn 2016), pp. 323–27; and see Hitchins and Drew, *The History of Cornwall*, p. 142. Bottrell, *Stories and Folk-Lore of West Cornwall*, p. 92, makes a reference to 'rattling pewter plates or brass pans to frighten swarming bees home, or to make them settle', but this is not told in the context of a brownie-like entity.

20. Tregarthen, *Pixie Folklore and Legends*, pp. 89–95.

21. Ibid., p. 194; Evans-Wentz, *The Fairy Faith in Celtic Countries*, pp. 164–65.

22. Readers may recognize this legend as the source of J.K. Rowling's elfin character named Dobby, the sad creature who is enslaved until someone gives him a new set of clothes. Rowling drew directly on folklore: Briggs, who may have been Rowling's source, describes 'Dobby' as 'a friendly name for a hobgoblin in Yorkshire and Lancashire. He is very like a brownie.' Jacqueline Simpson refers to this aspect of Rowling's writings in her essay, 'On the Ambiguity of Elves', *Folklore*, 122 (2011), p. 77. Briggs, *An Encyclopedia of Fairies*, p. 103.

23. Almqvist, 'Irish Migratory Legends on the Supernatural', p. 35.

24. Although he does not employ the cup motif and the adversaries are witches, Robert Burns apparently looked to this legend when he crafted his poem, 'Tam o' Shanter'.

25. Bottrell, *Stories and Folk-Lore of West Cornwall*, pp. 92–94.

26. Hunt, *Popular Romances of the West of England*, p. 90. Trencrom Hill is on the north-west coast of Cornwall.

27. Ibid., p. 98. Briggs, *Folk Tales of Britain: Narratives*, p. 757, identifies this as Tale Type AT 503 III; and she notes the following motifs: F.340, Gifts from fairies; F.211.9,

Fairyland under hollow knoll; F.239.4.3, Fairy is tiny; F.262.3.6, Fairy music causes joy; F.456.1, Spriggans; F.350, Theft from fairies; F.361.2.3, Fairies bind man fast to ground after he has attempted to capture fairy prince and princess. Aarne and Thompson, *The Types of the Folktale*, describe the third part of 503 (i.e. 503 III) as involving the punishment of an avaricious and bungling person. See also Jennifer Westwood and Jacqueline Simpson, *The Lore of the Land: A Guide to England's Legends, from Spring-Heeled Jack to the Witches of Warboys* (London: Penguin Books, 2005), pp. 97–100.

28. Blight, *A Week at the Land's End*, pp. 194–95.

29. Ibid., pp. 195–97.

30. Hunt, *Popular Romances of the West of England*, p. 103.

31. Hunt's emphasis. See Ibid., pp. 102–3. Briggs, *Folk Tales of Britain: Legends*, p. 357, notes motifs F.268.1, Burial service for Fairy Queen is held at night in Christian church; F.361.3, Fairies take revenge on mortal who spies on them. Compare Simpson, 'Fairy Queens and Pharisees' from Young and Houlbrook, editors, *Magical Folk*, p. 26.

32. Hunt, *Popular Romances of the West of England*, pp. 113–14; Briggs, *Folk Tales of Britain: Legends*, p. 479, adds motifs: F.385.1, Fairy spell averted by turning coat; F.351.2, Theft of money from fairies by frightening them away from it; F.361.2, Fairy takes revenge for theft.

33. Couch and Couch, *History of Polperro*, pp. 137–38.

34. Sabine Baring-Gould, *A Book of the West: Being an Introduction to Devon and Cornwall*, II (London: Methuen and Company, 1899), pp. 107–8; see also Westwood and Simpson, *The Lore of the Land*, p. 108. The discovery of a golden cup at Rillaton caused a stir in view of this story; see Philip Payton, *Cornwall* (Fowey: Alexander Associates, 1996), pp. 40–41; and Payton, *Cornwall: A History*, p. 34.

35. Kimberly Ball, 'Legend as Metatradition', *Fabula*, 53:102 (December 2012), p. 2. See also Séamas Ó Catháin, 'The Robbers and the Captive Girl: Ancient Antecedents and Other Elements of a Rare Irish Legend Type', *Béaloideas*, 62/63 (1994/1995), pp. 109–46.

36. Ball, 'Legend as Metatradition', pp. 2–3, quoting and translating from Inger Lövkrona, *Det bortrövade dryckeskarlet: En sägenstudie* (Lund: Skrifter från Folklivsarkivet I Lund 24, 1982), p. 44.

37. This is described by Donald Haase, editor, *The Greenwood Encyclopedia of Folktales and Fairy Tales, Volume One* (London: Greenwood Press, 2008), p. 296; see also Young, 'Fairy Holes and Fairy Butter' from Young and Houlbrook, editors, *Magical Folk*, p. 87.

38. Hunt, *Popular Romances of the West of England*, pp. 88–90. Briggs, *Folk Tales of Britain: Legends*, p. 484, sees this as ML 5006*. Motifs: F.282.2(b), Fairies say 'Ho! And away for Par Beach!'. They fly away (Baughman); F.282.4*(b), Mortal travels with fairies. He drinks too much in wine-cellar where they revel. He is being hanged by owner when a fairy appears and tells him to use the formula he had

used the night before. He escapes (Baughman). Briggs notes that 'similar tales are told of witches'. It is reminiscent of Migratory Legend 6050, 'The Fairy Hat' in such a way that ML 5006* may be regarded as a subvariant of ML 6050. The asterisk associated with migratory legend type ML 5006* indicates an addition to the initial type index of Christiansen.

39. Couch and Couch, *History of Polperro*, pp. 135–36, as cited by M.A. Courtney, *The Folk-Lore Journal*, 5 (1887), pp. 180–81. Also discussed by Edwin Sidney Hartland, *The Science of Fairy Tales: An Enquiry into Fairy Mythology* (New York: Scribner and Welford, 1891), pp. 147–48.

40. Briggs, *The Vanishing People*, pp. 47–49, pp. 128–29.

41. Tregarthen, *Pixie Folklore and Legends*, pp. 11–12.

42. Ibid., p. 12.

43. Uther, *The Types of International Folktales, Part I*, pp. 415–16; tale number 180 in the Grimm collection.

Chapter 6: Seeking the Companionship of People

1. Moses Pitt, *An Account of one Ann Jefferies* (London: Richard Cumberland, 1696), pp. 7–9; the text was republished by Hunt, *Popular Romances of the West of England*, pp. 470–71, which provides most of the quotes here, featuring regularized spelling; see also Briggs, *An Encyclopedia of Fairies*, pp. 239–42; Peter Marshall, 'Ann Jefferies and the Fairies: Folk Belief and the War on Scepticism in Later Stuart England', from Angela McShane and Garthine Walker, editors, *The Extraordinary and the Everyday in Early Modern England* (Houndsmills, Basingstoke, Hampshire, UK: Palgrave MacMillan, 2010), pp. 127–41; James Elimalet Smith, *Legends and Miracles and other Curious and Marvellous Stories of Human Nature* (London: B.D. Cousins, 1837), pp. 49–54. 'Ann' appears in later publications as 'Anne'.

2. Pitt, *An Account of one Ann Jefferies*, pp. 10–11.

3. Ibid., p. 16.

4. Ibid., p. 16, pp. 19–20; quotes here are from Hunt, *Popular Romances of the West of England*, pp. 470–71.

5. For supernatural beings abducting people in northern Europe, see Hartmann, *Die Trollvorstellungen in den Sagen und Märchen der Skandinavischen Völker*; Briggs, *The Vanishing People* and *The Fairies of Tradition and Literature*; and Carole G. Silver, 'Abductions', Garry and El-Shamy, *Archetypes and Motifs in Folklore and Literature*, pp. 381–88; Norman and Hickey-Hall, 'Pixies and Pixy Rocks' from Young and Houlbrook, editors, *Magical Folk*, pp. 44–45. Simon Young provides an excellent overview of the folklore of being 'pixy-led'; see his 'Pixy-Led in Devon and the South-West', *The Devonshire Association Transactions*, 148 (June 2016), pp. 311–36.

6. Hunt, *Popular Romances of the West of England*, pp. 83–85. This story is echoed by Hunt's 'The Fairy Widower', pp. 114–18, which involves many of the same motifs

except that the woman in question lives at the home of her employer and his son. Briggs, *Folktales of Britain: Legends*, p. 375, incorrectly sees this as ML 4075, 'Visit to the Blessed Islands'. She further notes: 'This is a rather more romantic version of the "Cherry of Zennor" story.'

7. Christiansen, *The Migratory Legends*, pp. 91–99. For a general discussion of the legend, see Briggs, *The Fairies in Tradition and Literature*, pp. 142–45; and Briggs, *The Vanishing People*, pp. 93–100.

8. 'The Fairy Ointment', Hunt, *Popular Romances of the West of England*, pp. 109–11; 'Cherry of Zennor', Ibid., 120–26; and 'How Joan lost the sight in her eye', Ibid., pp. 111–13. For a list of Cornish examples, see the appendix.

9. Evans-Wentz, *The Fairy Faith in Celtic Countries*, pp. 175–76.

10. Ibid., p. 182.

11. Couch and Couch, *History of Polperro*, pp. 138–39. Tony Deane and Tony Shaw reproduced this story without attribution in their *Folklore of Cornwall* (Stroud, Gloucestershire: Tempus, 2003), p. 63.

12. Tregarthen, *Pixie Folklore and Legends*, pp. 77–88.

13. Bray, 'The Fairy Midwife' from *Traditions, Legends, Superstitions*, pp. 183–88; Joseph Jacobs adapts this story for his *English Fairy Tales*.

14. Mabel Quiller-Couch, *Cornwall's Wonderland* (London and Toronto: J.M. Dent and Sons, n.d., *c*.1914), pp. 68–92.

15. See the motifs: F.376, Mortal as servant in Fairyland; F.372, Fairies take human nurse to wait on fairy child.

16. Uther, *The Types of International Folktales*, I, pp. 280–81.

17. Críostóir Mac Cárthaigh, 'Midwife to the Fairies (ML 5070): The Irish Variants in their Scottish and Scandinavian Perspective', *Béaloideas*, 59 (1991), pp. 133–43. The article draws on an unpublished dissertation. Mac Cárthaigh's work is discussed by Alan Bruford, 'Trolls, Hillfolk, Finns, and Picts' in Narváez, *The Good People*, p. 126.

18. Cornwall is inserted here; Mac Cárthaigh apparently groups the Cornish material with England.

19. The assertion that ATU 476** does not occur in Britain south of Scotland is based on the review of Hans-Jörg Uther's index by Jonathan Roper who suggests that Uther used a problematic source for a supposed English variant of ATU 476**. See his 'Review Essay', *Folk Life*, 45 (2007), pp. 124–27. For an example of the toad motif, see 'Midwife to the *Huldre*-folk at Ekeberg', Christiansen, *Folktales of Norway*, pp. 105–8. Under the supervision of von Sydow, Hartmann in her 1936 treatment of troll-related folklore speculated that the story of the midwife was of Celtic origin and that it diffused to Scandinavia. See her *Die Trollvorstellungen in den Sagen und Märchen der Skandinavischen Völker*.

20. Gervase of Tilbury, discussed by E. Sidney Hartland, 'Peeping Tom and Lady Godiva', *Folklore*, 1:2 (1890), pp. 207–26; see pp. 208–9, which includes a treatment of 'The Midwife to the Fairies'. Thomas Keightley addresses this early

source, providing the text in his *The Fairy Mythology* (London: Bradbury and Evans, 1860), pp. 465–66.

21. Henderson and Cowan classify this account as Migratory Legend 5070; see their *Scottish Fairy Belief*, p. 102; and see R.J. Stewart, *Robert Kirk: Walker between Worlds, a New Edition of The Secret Commonwealth of Elves, Fauns and Fairies* (Dorset: Element, 1990), p. 37.

22. Child Ballad number 40, Child, *The English and Scottish Popular Ballads*; also known as 'The Queen of Elfland's Nourice': Bertrand Harris Bronson, editor, *The Singing Tradition of Child's Popular Ballads (Abridgement)* (Princeton: Princeton University Press, 1976), p. 103.

23. Grimm and Grimm, *The Complete Grimm's Fairy Tales*, Number 39II. Andrew Lang published a version in his *Lilac Fairy Book* (London: Folio, 2012 [1910]), pp. 39–42. 'The Fairy Nurse' was borrowed from *Legendary Fictions of the Irish Celts* by Patrick Kennedy, which first appeared in 1866.

24. Mac Cárthaigh, 'Midwife to the Fairies (ML 5070)', p. 140, p. 142. And see Hunt, *Popular Romances of the West of England*, pp. 120–26.

25. Mac Cárthaigh provides an Irish example of this legend with the pregnant frog motif, and the water that allowed the seeing of the supernatural: IFC Ms. 850: pp. 167–73. Recorded 1 August 1942 by Liam Mac Coisdeala, Kilkerrin, Co. Galway.

26. This is not a comprehensive examination of all British expressions of ML 5070 south of Scotland, but even a cursory look yields insight. Briggs discusses related topics in *An Encyclopedia of Fairies*. Briggs, *Folk Tales of Britain: Legends*: 'The Fairy Midwife: I' (Somerset), pp. 360–61; 'The Fairy Midwife II' (northern England), pp. 361–62; 'Fairy Ointment' (northern England), p. 364; 'The Little Man's Gift' (Lancashire), pp. 442–43; 'Marie Kirstan the Midwife' (Shetland), pp. 450–51; 'The Midwife' (Scotland), p. 468; 'The Woman who Suckled a Fairy' (Galloway), pp. 567–68.

27. Sir John Rhŷs, *Celtic Folklore: Welsh and Manx*, 1 (Oxford: Clarendon Press, 1901), pp. 98–99; Evans-Wentz, *The Fairy Faith in Celtic Countries*, p. 136; D. Parry-Jones, *Welsh Legends and Fairy Lore* (New York: Barnes and Noble, 1992 [1953]), pp. 53–57.

28. Paul Sébillot, *Traditions et Superstitions de La Haute Bretagne, Volume I* (Paris: Maison Neuve, 1882), p. 109. This is cited by G.J.C. Bois, *Jersey Folklore and Superstitions, Volume Two* (Central Milton Keynes: Author House, 2010), p. 137. Bois discusses similar stories from Jersey, pp. 134ff. Evans-Wentz also discusses Sébillot's example in his *The Fairy Faith in Celtic Countries*, pp. 204–5.

29. Lewis Spence, *Legends and Romances of Brittany* (Mineola, New York: Dover, 1997), pp. 75–80, p. 82.

30. The absence of the midwife motif in Cornwall, except for the problematic summary offered by Deane and Shaw and the equally problematic stories by Couch and Couch and Tregarthen, suggest that this version of ML 5070 may not have crossed the Tamar into Cornwall, or if it did, it did not thrive there.

31. Several websites, none of which have academic credibility and therefore need not be mentioned specifically, allude to the similarity between the novel and the legend. See, however, Jacqueline Simpson, 'The Functions of Folklore in "Jane Eyre" and "Wuthering Heights"', *Folklore*, 85:1 (January 1974), pp. 47–61. Motif C.611, the forbidden chamber, is found in a variety of folktales, and especially in ATU 311 and a related type, ATU 312, Bluebeard.

32. In the Grimm's collection, see tale 39III. For a general discussion of changelings, see Briggs, *The Fairies in Tradition and Literature*, pp. 136–42; and Briggs, *The Vanishing People*, pp. 100–3.

33. See, for example, S. Eberly, 'Fairies and the Folklore of Disability: Changelings, Hybrids, and the Solitary Fairy', in Narváez, *The Good People*. Hartmann, *Die Trollvorstellungen in den Sagen und Märchen der Skandinavischen Völker*, also explores this idea.

34. See, for example, Hartland, *The Science of Fairy Tales*, pp. 93–134, and more recently, Séamas Mac Philib, 'The Changeling (ML 5058): Irish Versions of a Migratory Legend in their International Context', *Béaloideas*, 59 (1991), pp. 121–31.

35. Bottrell, *Traditions and Hearthside Stories of West Cornwall* (1870), p. 42.

36. Couch and Couch, *History of Polperro*, p. 133.

37. Evans-Wentz, *The Fairy Faith in Celtic Countries*, p. 171.

38. Hunt, *Popular Romances of the West of England*, pp. 86–87; see Young, 'Five Notes on Nineteenth-Century Cornish Changelings', pp. 57–61.

39. Young, 'Five Notes on Nineteenth-Century Cornish Changelings', pp. 51–79. See also his 'Some Notes on Irish Fairy Changelings in Nineteenth-Century Newspapers', *Béascna*, 8 (2013), pp. 34–47.

40. Briggs, *Folk Tales of Britain*, includes several variants from elsewhere in Britain.

41. Hunt, *Popular Romances of the West of England*, pp. 91–95. It is summarized in prose by Margaret Ann Courtney in her *Cornish Feasts and Folk-Lore*, pp. 126–28.

42. Hunt, *Popular Romances of the West of England*, pp. 95–96. Couch and Couch, *History of Polperro*, pp. 134–35, includes a similar story with slightly different spellings and words.

43. The legend also appears in the folktale type index as ATU 113A, 'Pan is Dead'. The story has an ancient pedigree, appearing in Plutarch's *De defectu oraculorum*. See also William F. Hansen, *Ariadne's Thread: A Guide to International Tales Found in Classical Literature* (Ithaca, New York: Cornell University Press, 2002), pp. 131–36. For a useful recent analysis of the type, see John Lindow, 'Cats and Dogs, Trolls and Devils: At Home in Some Migratory Legend Types', *Western Folklore*, 69:2 (Spring 2010), pp. 163–79. Christiansen, *The Migratory Legend*, p. 142.

44. Hunt, *Popular Romances of the West of England*, pp. 450–51; Briggs, *Folktales of Britain: Legends*, pp. 504–5.

45. Tregarthen, *Pixie Folklore and Legends*, pp. 37–57, and see her *The Piskey-Purse*, pp. 59–110.

Chapter 7: Mermaids

1. As indicated previously, the term 'uncle' does not imply kinship; traditional Cornish society used the term as a sign of respect. Quotes are from Bottrell, *Traditions and Hearthside Stories* (1870), pp. 63–70. See also Westwood and Simpson, *The Lore of the Land*, p. 96.

2. Hunt, *Popular Romances of the West of England*, pp. 152–55.

3. Jenkin, *Cornwall and the Cornish*, p. 269.

4. Christiansen, *The Migratory Legends*. An early example of this appears in the thirteenth-century work of Gervase of Tilbury, *Otia Imperialia*; see Keightley, *The Fairy Mythology*, p. 466, who provides the text.

5. Hunt, *Popular Romances of the West of England*, 'The Voice from the Sea', p. 366; see also Hunt's 'The Pirate-Wrecker and the Death Ship', pp. 359–62; in addition, the story occurs in Sabine Baring-Gould, *Book of Folk-Lore* (London: Collins, 1913), pp. 114–15. Briggs, *Folk Tales of Britain: Legends*, offers no catalogue number for 'The Story of the Mermaid and the Man of Cury' in her collection of narratives. In *An Encyclopedia of Fairies*, p. 275, Briggs classifies it as ML 4080, 'The Mermaid Wife', which is discussed in this chapter in the context of another legend. ML 4080 is far removed from this story and the classification is clearly in error, which is perhaps why she did not repeat the assertion in her collection of British oral tradition.

6. Migratory Legend 4050, 'The hour is come but the man is not', would represent a sixth type when it is associated with the character of the mermaid. This link may not have been typical in Cornish tradition, so it is not included in this list.

7. Hunt, *Popular Romances of the West of England*, pp. 151–52, describes traditions associated with 'The Mermaid's Rock' involving the supernatural being singing as a prediction of storms and her drowning any young men who swam to her rock. Courtney, *Cornish Feasts and Folk-Lore*, p. 134, also maintains that the mermaid's mirror and comb were treasured keepsakes, both of which could grant the bearer the power to charm away diseases. Stephanie Kickingereder, *The Motif of the Mermaid in English, Irish, and Scottish Fairy- and Folk Tales* (Diplomarbeit, Universität Wien; Philologisch-Kulturwissenschaftliche Fakultät; BetreuerIn: Franz-Karl Wöhrer, 2008), provides an overview of mermaid folklore with some discussion of Cornish material. Kickingereder employs literary analysis as the core of her work, and lacking comparative folklore method, her conclusions have less application here. See also Gregory Darwin, 'On Mermaids, Meroveus, and Mélusine: Reading the Irish Seal Woman and Mélusine as Origin Legend', *Folklore*, 115:2 (2015), pp. 123–41.

8. Llewellynn Jewitt, 'The Mermaid of Legend and of Art', *The Art Journal* (1875–1887), New Series, 6 (1880), pp. 117–20, 170–72 and 230–33; Arthur Waugh, 'The Folklore of the Merfolk', *Folklore*, 71:2 (June 1960), pp. 73–84; Westwood and Simpson, *The Lore of the Land*, pp. 120–21.

9. Bo Almqvist, 'Of Mermaids and Marriages: Seamus Heaney's "Maighdean Mara" and Nula Ní Dhomhnaill's "an Mhaighdean Mhara" in the Light of Folk Tradition', *Béaloideas*, 58 (1990), p. 1. See also Dáithí Ó hÓgáin, *The Lore of Ireland: An Encyclopaedia of Myth, Legend and Romance* (Cork: Boydell, 2006), pp. 342–45.

10. Almqvist, 'Of Mermaids and Marriages', pp. 2–4. In addition, Barbara Fass Leavy, *In Search of the Swan Maiden: A Narrative on Folklore and Gender* (New York: New York University Press, 1995) notes the similarity of the 'Scottish' seal maiden story to that of the swan and her feather cloak, pp. 33–37, pp. 46–47. Carl Wilhelm von Sydow, 'Folktale Studies and Philology: Some Points of View' (in Dundes, *The Study of Folklore*, pp. 223–24) argues that Tale Type ATU 400, 'The Swan Maidens', is ancient; he criticizes the 1919 conclusion of Helge Holmström, his first doctoral student, who in *Studies on the Swan Maiden Motif* suggests that the folktale originated in India. See also Arthur Thomas Hatto, 'The Swan Maiden: A Folktale of North European Origin?', *Bulletin of the School of Oriental and African Studies*, 24:2 (1961), pp. 326–52. Hatto found the distribution of the motif as possibly linked to the Arctic and sub-Arctic and tied to 'the distribution and migratory breeding patterns of swans, geese, and cranes'. How the folktale is linked to, affected by, or influenced the legend ML 4080, 'The Mermaid Wife' is beyond the scope of this chapter, but the similarity is clear.

11. Almqvist, 'Of Mermaids and Marriages', p. 8, agrees with previous scholars that the legend of the marriage to the mermaid, ML 4080, probably diffused during the Viking Age from either Ireland or Scotland 'directly or via Orkney and Shetland mainly to Iceland and the Faroe Islands, where influences from Irish and Scottish-Gaelic traditions are on the whole stronger than in the other Nordic Countries'. He points out that previous scholars including Liestøl and Matras (see his note 16) refer to the source as 'Celtic', but as Almqvist indicates, 'it would have been more correct if they had referred to the legend as Irish and Scottish Gaelic rather than "Celtic", since it is not found in Wales and Brittany'. Of course, Brittany has its own water beings and Wales has lake creatures, both of whom appear in stories, interacting with people. That said, Almqvist does not recognize ML 4080 as occurring in material from Brittonic-speaking areas.

12. Bottrell, *Traditions and Hearthside Stories* (1873), pp. 288–89. The story is discussed by Philip Hayward, 'Senara, Zennor, and the Mermaid Chair: Transplanting Cornish Folklore to a Fictional American Island', and by Caradoc Peters, 'The Mermaid of Zennor—A Mirror on Three Worlds', both in *Cornish Studies: Third Series*, 1, Garry H. Tregidga, editor (Exeter: University of Exeter Press, 2015).

13. For a full discussion of the motif of the magic cap, see Almqvist, 'Of Mermaids and Marriages'. See also Waugh 'The Folklore of the Merfolk', p. 77. Einar Ólafur Sveinsson identifies this legend in a seventeenth-century Icelandic text. See his *The Folk-Stories of Iceland*, pp. 102–4.

14. Boria Sax, *The Serpent and the Swan: The Animal Bride in Folklore and Literature* (Blacksburg, Virginia, 1998) cites Friedrich de la Motte Fouqué who wrote the

short story 'Undine' inspired by Paracelsus, *Liber der nymphen*. See also the opera by Marjory Kennedy-Fraser and Sir Granville Bantock, 'The Seal-Woman' (1906). As mentioned above, see Tale Type ATU 400 in Antti Aarne and Stith Thompson, *The Types of the Folktale* and in Hans-Jörg Uther, *The Types of International Folktales*, 1, pp. 194–98, pp. 231–33, pp. 273–74. Almqvist, 'Of Mermaids and Marriages', p. 8, discusses the material; on 'Völundarkiða', which may be as early as the ninth century, see Almqvist, p. 2, fn. 5.

15. Christiansen, *The Migratory Legends*, p. 99. Christiansen discusses this legend type in his 'Some Notes on the Fairies and the Fairy Faith', pp. 107–10.

16. See, for example, Jewitt, 'The Mermaid of Legend and of Art'; and see Doris Jones-Baker, 'The Graffiti of Folk Motifs in Cotswold Churches', *Folklore*, 92:2 (1981), pp. 160–67.

17. Peters, 'The Mermaid of Zennor'.

18. Hunt, *Popular Romances of the West of England*, p. 152. For Padstow, see p. 151.

19. Courtney, *Cornish Feasts and Folk-Lore*, p. 134.

20. Hunt, *Popular Romances of the West of England*, pp. 367–68; Bottrell, *Traditions and Hearthside Stories* (1873), p. 247. In this case, the mermaid is referred to as a 'hooper', a term sometimes applied to mermaids in Cornwall.

21. Hunt, *Popular Romances of the West of England*, pp. 155–70.

22. Reverend Sabine Baring-Gould, *The Vicar of Morwenstow: A Life of Robert Stephen Hawker, M.A.* (New York: Thomas Whittaker, 1888), pp. 26–27; the alternative ending appears in Piers Brendon, *Hawker of Morwenstow: Portrait of a Victorian Eccentric* (London: Pimlico, 2002), p. 42, as quoted by http://www.strangehistory.net/2011/08/27/cornish-mermaid-half-priest-half-fish/ (accessed 28 September 2017).

23. The Cornish mermaid legends do not have counterparts in Katharine Briggs's extensive collection of British folktales and legends. Briggs and Baughman include some Cornish material in their catalogues of British folklore, but they did not identify legend type numbers for these stories, describing them instead with motif numbers without clear counterparts elsewhere. This reinforces the conclusion that these types are unique to Cornwall.

Chapter 8: The Spectre Bridegroom

1. Calvin Thomas, *An Anthology of German Literature* (Boston: D.C. Heath, 1906), pp. 387–91.

2. 'The Suffolk Miracle' appeared in many forms, the earliest of which may date to 1689: Child, *The English and Scottish Popular Ballads*, Part 9, p. 67 cites a broadsheet printed for W. Thackeray and T. Passenger, providing the year 1689 followed by 'The date added by Wood'.

3. 'Sweet William's Ghost' is Scottish. Thomas Percy, *Reliques of Ancient English Poetry: Volume III* (London: J. Dodsley, 1775), pp. 120–24. Child, Part 9, includes

several versions of each ballad. In 'Fair Margaret and Sweet William', the roles are reversed, removing the story a step further from the tradition discussed here.

4. Briggs, *Folk Tales of Britain: Legends*, p. 34, lists five variants of Tale Type ATU 365; 'The Suffolk Miracle' and 'The Fair Maid of Clifton' are both ballads, but the latter was collected from an oral source. The other three are legends from oral tradition, all from Cornwall.

5. Bottrell, *Traditions of the Hearthside* (1870), pp. 468–527. The analysis presented here does not purport to be international in a comprehensive way; the observation regarding length is supported by a discussion of variants in Ireland: Ríonach Uí Ógaín and Anne O'Connor, '"Spor ar An gCois Is gan An Chos Ann": A Study of "The Dead Lover's Return" in Irish Tradition', *Béaloideas*, 51 (1983), pp. 126–44.

6. Bottrell, *Traditions of the Hearthside* (1870), pp. 478–79.

7. Ibid., pp. 508.

8. Aarne and Thompson, *The Types of the Folktale*, pp. 127; Uther, *The Types of International Folktales*, pp. 229–30. Briggs, *Folk Tales of Britain: Legends*, p. 34. Sven S. Liljeblad, in his *Introduction to Folklore* (self-published, 1966), p. 113, for example, refers to 'The Dead Bridegroom Carries off His Bride' as both a folktale and as a testimonial legend.

9. For a Japanese variant, see Hiroko Ikeda, *A Type and Motif Index of Japanese Folk-Literature* (Helsinki: FF Communications No. 209, 1971), pp. 95–96, but it is unclear if this isolated example is related to the European tradition. For the Irish material, see Uí Ógaín and O'Connor, 'Spor ar An gCois Is gan An Chos Ann'. For Iceland, see Jón Arnason, *Icelandic Legends*, translated by George E.J. Powell and Eiríkur Magnússon (London: R. Bentley, 1864), pp. 173–77. For Sweden, see Reimund Kvideland and Henning K. Sehmsdorf, editors, *All the World's Reward: Folktales Told by Five Scandinavian Storytellers* (Seattle: University of Washington Press, 1999), pp. 219–20. A Hungarian variant appears in János Kriza, János Erdélyi, Gyula Pap, et al., *The Folk-Tales of the Magyars*, translated by W. Henry Jones and Lewis L. Knopf (London: The Folk-Lore Society, 1889), pp. 278–82.

10. Thomas, *An Anthology of German Literature*, pp. 387–91.

11. In the modern urban legend, 'The Vanishing Hitchhiker', the apparition borrows a garment, which she typically leaves on her tombstone as proof that the story is true. Jan Harold Brunvand, *Too Good to be True: The Colossal Book of Urban Legends* (New York: W. W. Norton and Company, 1999), pp. 231–34.

12. Hunt, *Popular Romances of the West of England*, pp. 233–39. Hunt's 'The Spectre Bridegroom' appeared in 1865 before Bottrell's 1870 publication. Hunt, however, used Bottrell's notes on occasion, and it appears from the nature of the details in the two versions that the tale passed from Bottrell to Hunt and not in the opposite direction. Perhaps because it is abridged, Hunt's version appears in other collections and online, even though the extensive details suggest Bottrell probably captures what was closer to the oral presentation.

13. Bottrell, *Traditions of the Hearthside* (1873), pp. 149–53.

14. Ibid., p. 153.

15. Hunt, *Popular Romances of the West of England*, p. 247.

16. Ibid., pp. 26–27. Hunt refers to someone as the source for this information, but given the context, it is certainly Bottrell.

17. Briggs, *Folk Tales of Britain: Legends*, pp. 802–3, suggests that the Cornish legend, 'The Execution and Wedding', which she calls 'Yorkshire Jack', is another variant of Tale Type ATU 365. This story from Hunt may be related to this complex, but even if that is the case, it deviates considerably, featuring the woman's death at the gallows. She then returns with the devil to find Jack aboard a ship and sweeps him away with a large wave to an eternity married to her in the company of Satan. Hunt, *Popular Romances of the West of England*, pp. 256–58. Deane and Shaw, *Folklore of Cornwall* (1975), pp. 81–82 and pp. 108–9 discuss variants, summarizing stories from Hunt and Bottrell. They consequently add nothing to this discussion.

18. Uí Ógaín and O'Connor, 'Spor ar An gCois Is gan An Chos Ann', p. 132.

19. Ibid., p. 133.

20. Arnason, *Icelandic Legends*, pp. 173–77.

21. Child, *The English and Scottish Popular Ballads*, Part 9, pp. 63–64. And see Sébillot's story 'Les Deux Fiancés', in *Traditions et Superstitions de La Haute Bretagne*, pp. 197–99.

22. There are numerous histories of ghosts in various societies and across the expanse of history and literature. See, for example, Owen Davies, *The Haunted: A Social History of Ghosts* (New York: Palgrave Macmillan, 2007) and R.C. Finucane, *Ghosts: Appearance of the Dead and Cultural Transformation* (Amherst, New York: Prometheus, 1996). See also an overview essay from a folklore point of view: Jane Garry and Janet L. Langlois, 'Ghosts and Other Revenants' from Garry and El-Shamy, *Archetypes and Motifs in Folklore and Literature*, pp. 181–87.

23. Juha Pentikäinen, 'The Dead without Status', from Kvideland and Sehmsdorf, *Nordic Folklore*, pp. 128–34, originally appearing in *Temenos*, 1969; Uí Ógaín and O'Connor cite Pentikäinen in their article. See also Jacqueline Simpson, 'Repentant Soul or Walking Corpse? Debatable Apparitions in Medieval England', *Folklore*, 114:3 (2003), pp. 389–402; and G. David Keyworth, 'Was the Vampire of the Eighteenth Century a Unique Type of Undead-corpse?', *Folklore*, 117:3 (2006), pp. 241–60.

24. Lee M. Hollander, translated with introduction and explanatory notes, *The Poetic Edda* (Austin: University of Texas Press, 1962), pp. 190–202. Hollander remarks on the importance of the 'Second Lay of Helgi the Hunding-Slayer/Helgakviða Hundingsbana II' in relation to the story of 'The Dead Bridegroom Carries off His Bride'.

25. Liljeblad, *Introduction to Folklore*, p. 113, notes the significance of this medieval lay in the context of the legend of 'The Dead Bridegroom Carries off His Bride'. In communication with the author, c. 1977, Liljeblad described how the pre-Christian

motif was apparently different from its later Christian counterpart in that the woman willingly spent the night with the corpse, an act of devotion that would have violated Christian sensibilities. Eric Shane Bryan takes up the issue of how this story transformed from its earlier roots to its later manifestations in Iceland; Bryan quotes my earlier article that I used in the writing of this chapter. See his 'The Moon Glides, Death Rides: Pejoration and Aborted Otherworldly Journeys in "The Dead Bridegroom Carries off his Bride" (ATU 365)', *Intégrité: A Faith and Learning Journal*, 16:1 (Spring 2017), pp. 13–30.

26. Aarne published his German-language tale type index in 1910; Thompson translated and enlarged Aarne's work, publishing his first edition in 1929.

27. Von Sydow, 'Geography and Folk-Tale Oicotypes'.

28. Thompson, *The Folktale*, p. 41. Child, *The English and Scottish Popular Ballads*, p. 60, also maintains that there was a Slavic origin for the tale, and this may have influenced Thompson.

Chapter 9: Giants

1.   Bottrell, *Traditions and Hearthside Stories of West Cornwall* (1870), p. 9.

2.   Barbara C. Spooner, 'The Giants of Cornwall', *Folklore*, 76:1 (Spring 1965), pp. 16–32. This overview presents a catalogue of existing material without analysis. See also her 'Jack and Tom in "Drolls" and Chapbooks', *Folklore*, 87:1 (Spring 1976), pp. 105–12.

3.   Geoffrey of Monmouth, *The History of the Kings of Britain*, p. 22. John Clark, 'Gogmagog Again', *3rd Stone*, 44 (Autumn 2002), pp. 38–43, takes up the question of the origin of the name 'Gogmagog'.

4.   Monmouth, *The History of the Kings of Britain*, pp. 151–52, has an additional tale of King Arthur killing a giant at St Michael's Mount. Hunt, *Popular Romances of the West of England*, p. 44, retells the story of Corineus and Gogmagog, implying that it was Cornish. Hunt's version was in turn reproduced by Briggs, *Folktales of Britain: Legends*, p. 808, again suggesting a Cornish origin for the story.

5.   John Weever (1576–1632), *Ancient Funeral Monuments, of Great Britain, Ireland, and the Islands Adjacent*, p. 183 (from a 1767 edition) provided (and presumably translated) the text of the fourteenth-century Latin poem by John Havillan. On Havillan, see R.N. Worth, *West Country Garland: Selected from the writings of the poets of Devon and Cornwall* (London: Houlston, 1875), p. vii.

6.   Carew, *Survey of Cornwall*.

7.   John Milton, *The History of Britain* (London: Chiswell, 1695 [1670]; https://books. google.com/books?id=EA4-AQAAMAAJ&pg=PA3&source=gbs_selected_pages &cad=3#v=onepage&q&f=false; accessed 16 July 2017), pp. 18–20.

8.   Caitlin R. Green, 'Tom Thumb and Jack the Giant-Killer: Two Arthurian Fairy Tales?', *Folklore*, 118:2 (2007), pp. 123–40. And see Green's 'Jack and Arthur: An

Introduction to Jack the Giant-Killer', *The Arthuriad*: 1 (http://www.arthuriana. co.uk/arthuriad/Arthuriad_VolOne.pdf; accessed 9 April 2017), pp. 1–4 and p. 8. According to Green, the story of Jack was a relatively recent invention, dating to the eighteenth century.

9. 'The Giant's Causeway', *The Dublin Penny Journal*, 1.5 (1832), p. 33. For Devil's Dyke and Wade's Causeway, see Simpson and Roud, *Oxford Dictionary of English Folklore*, p. 95 and p. 144, respectively.

10. Courtney, *Cornish Feasts and Folk-Lore*, pp. 56–57; Hitchins and Drew, *The History of Cornwall*, p. 392, p. 402; Westwood and Simpson, *The Lore of the Land*, p. 92, p. 95, p. 96, p. 97, p. 108, pp. 628–29; Bottrell, *Traditions and Hearthside Stories of West Cornwall* (1870), pp. 49–50.

11. On Scandinavian giants and the problem of distinguishing them from trolls, see Hartmann's *Die Trollvorstellungen in den Sagen und Märchen der Skandinavischen Völker*. For a treatment of Anglo-Saxon giants and related entities, see Chris Bishop, 'Þyrs, ent, eoten, gigans—Anglo-Saxon Ontologies of "Giant"', *Modern Language Society*, 107:3 (2006), pp. 259–70.

12. J.R.R. Tolkien, *Farmer Giles of Ham*, edited by Christina Scull and Wayne G. Hammond (London: Harper Collins, 1999 [1949]), pp. 39–41.

13. Lotte Motz, 'The Rulers of The Mountain: A Study of the Giants of the Old Icelandic Texts', *Mankind Quarterly*, 20 (1979–1980), pp. 393–416, especially p. 413. Motz provides an inventory of attributes and descriptions in primary sources and later folklore.

14. Hunt credits his 'Corineus and Gogmagog' to Milton's seventeenth-century work, but as previously described, the story has roots in the work of Geoffrey of Monmouth and it appeared in other early sources. Hunt, *Popular Romances of the West of England*, pp. 44–46.

15. Bottrell, *Traditions and Hearthside Stories of West Cornwall* (1870), p. 19.

16. Halliwell-Phillipps, *Rambles in Western Cornwall by the footsteps of The Giants*.

17. Bottrell, *Traditions and Hearthside Stories of West Cornwall* (1870), pp. 10–46.

18. Ibid., pp. 49–50.

19. Hunt, *Popular Romances of the West of England*, p. 55.

20. See Briggs, *Folktales of Britain: Legends*, p. 816, for an example from Shropshire, involving throwing a key; Briggs also includes the motif, N.330, Accidental killing. An example from Somerset features a stone-throwing competition. Another from Yorkshire includes the motif of throwing a hammer back and forth, and the injuring of a giantess with a thrown rock; see Ibid., p. 825 and p. 827, respectively. The motif is also the explanation for the Whit Stones in Somerset: Leslie V. Grinsell, *Folklore of Prehistoric Sites in Britain* (Newton Abbot: David and Charles, 1976). Tolkien, *The Hobbit* (London: George Allen and Urwin, 1937); C.S. Lewis, *The Silver Chair* (London: Geoffrey Bles, 1953).

21. Snorri Sturluson, *The Prose Edda: Tales from Norse Mythology*, translated by Jean I. Young (Berkeley: University of California Press, 1954), pp. 103–5.

22. T.C. Paris, *A Hand-Book for Travellers in Devon and Cornwall* (London: John Murray, 1851), pp. 199–200.

23. Bottrell, *Traditions and Hearthside Stories of West Cornwall* (1870), p. 51.

24. Hunt, *Popular Romances of the West of England*, pp. 46–47. Several motifs apply here: F.531.6.6, Giants as builders of great structures; A.977.1.2(cb), Giant carrying apron load of stones drops them when apron string breaks (Baughman); and F.531.3.13, Giantess carries prodigious burden. See also Briggs, *Folktales of Britain: Legends*, p. 815.

25. Again, see motifs A.977.1.2(cb) and F.531.3.13; compare A.977.3.1, The Devil drops stones from apron, from England and Ireland, after Baughman. The motif of the broken apron string is best described in Thompson as A.963.1, Mountains from stones dropped from giant's clothes. He carries the stones in his clothes but loses them as he walks. Stith Thompson lists several examples including from Grimm, *Teutonic Mythology* (II, pp. 535–37); France (meaning Brittany) Sébillot IV, pp. 7–8; Sweden: Wessman 68 Nos., pp. 581–83; and Indonesian. The Indonesian example is unlikely to be historically related to the others.

26. Sidney Oldall Addy, editor, *A Glossary of Words Used in the Neighbourhood of Sheffield* (London: English Dialect Society, 1888), pp. lxvi–lxviii, p. 294. Patricia Monaghan, *The Encyclopedia of Celtic Mythology and Folklore* (New York: Facts on File, 2004), pp. 212–13; British Archaeological Association, *Collectanea Archaeologica Communications*, I (London: Longman, Green, Longman, and Roberts, 1862), p. 54; Sikes, *British Goblins*, p. 370; Bois, *Jersey Folklore and Superstitions, Volume Two*, p. 81; Eleanor Hull, 'Legends and Traditions of the Cailleach Bheara or Old Woman (Hap) of Beare,' *Folklore*, 48:3 (30 September, 1927), pp. 225–54, see especially pp. 245–48; Briggs, *The Fairies in Tradition and Literature*, pp. 79–80. For the association of Satan with this motif, consider the legend of 'The Devil's Footprints on Pendle and the Stones dropped by him on Apronful Hill' as discussed by David A. Borrowclough and John Hallam, 'The Devil's Footprints and Other Folklore: Local Legend and Archaeological Evidence in Lancashire', *Folklore*, 119:1 (April 2008), pp. 93–102. For a Yorkshire example, see Briggs, *Folktales of Britain: Legends*, p. 827.

27. T.G.E. Powell and G.E. Daniel, *Barclodiad y Gawres: The Excavation of a Megalithic Chamber Tomb in Anglesey, 1952–1953* (Liverpool: Liverpool University Press, 1956). For a treatment of giants in Wales, see John C. Grooms, *Giants in Welsh Folklore and Tradition* (Aberystwyth: University of Wales, dissertation, 1988).

28. Motz, 'Giants in Folklore and Mythology', p. 70; Carl Wilhelm von Sydow, 'Jätterna I mytologi och folktro', *Folkminnen och folktankar VI* (1919), pp. 52–96; Grimm, *Teutonic Mythology*, pp. 535–36, also provides Scandinavian examples of the motif. Motz argues against von Sydow's conjecture that giants were likely part of an early intellectual process that deduced that these sorts of supernatural beings must have existed.

29. The full text is from http://www.voicesfromthedawn.com/loughcrew/ (accessed 20 May 2017) with thanks to webmaster Howard Goldbaum for sorting out the issues surrounding the authorship of the primary source. Questions raised about Swift's authorship of the poem can be found in Eugene A. Conwell, 'On Ancient Sepulchral Cairns on the Loughcrew Hills,' *Proceedings of the Royal Irish Academy*, 9 (1864–1866), pp. 357–58.

30. Kathryn Rountree, *Crafting Contemporary Pagan Identities in a Catholic Society* (London: Routledge, Taylor and Francis Group, 2010), p. 29; Neil McDonald, *Malta and Gozo: A Megalithic Journey* (Neil McDonald: Megalithic Publishing, 2016), p. 329.

31. Bottrell, *Traditions and Hearthside Stories of West Cornwall* (1870), pp. 50–51; Hunt, *Popular Romances of the West of England*, pp. 73–75. Baughman classifies this under the grouping of murder by strategy (K.910, etc.) and as motif K.923, Murder by bleeding, taking more blood than victim realizes, and specifically as K.923(a), citing this Cornish story; see his *Type and Motif-Index of the Folktales of England and North America*, p. 354. See also Briggs, *Folktales of Britain: Legends*, p. 810. The motif G.520, Ogre deceived into self-injury is also appropriate to consider in this context.

32. Hunt, *Popular Romances of the West of England*, pp. 75–76. Hunt spells the location as 'Goran'.

33. Spooner, 'Cornwall and the Church that was shifted', pp. 270–75; Christiansen, *Migratory Legends*, pp. 201–9. This story is described by several motifs: D.2192.1, Church supernaturally moved at night (which according to Baughman appears in England and Scotland); D.2192, Work of day magically overthrown at night; F.531.6.6.1, Giants by night move building built my men in day. Sometimes the supernatural being is a ghost.

34. Ibid., pp. 209–14. Carl Wilhelm von Sydow discussed this legend at the beginning of his career: see his 'Studier i Finnsägnen och besläktade byggmästarsägner', 1. *Fataburen*, 2 (1907), pp. 65–78, pp. 199–218. His early work became a subject of dispute. For a summary of the academic discussion about the legend, see Martin Puhvel, 'The Legend of the Church-Building Troll in Northern Europe', *Folklore*, 72:4 (Winter 1961), pp. 567–83.

35. Bottrell, *Traditions and Hearthside Stories of West Cornwall* (1870), pp. 47–48; Thompson, *Motif Index*, identifies F.531.5.1, Giant friendly to man, as occurring in Powell's translation of Arnason's *Legends of Iceland*, I, p. 148. See also Sveinsson, *The Folk-Stories of Iceland*, pp. 164–66.

36. Christiansen, *Migratory Legends*.

37. See Green, 'Jack and Arthur', 1, who also points out that Hunt was unable to find the tradition when he was collecting in Cornwall: Hunt, *Popular Romances of the West of England*, pp. 303–4.

38. Motz, 'Giants in Folklore and Mythology', p. 71.

39. Brendan McMahon, 'Oedipus and identity in Victorian Cornwall: The Giant Stories', *Tradition Today*, 3 (December 2013), pp. 31–44, see especially p. 34. From: http://centre-for-english-traditional-heritage.org/TraditionToday3/TT3_McMahon_Giants.pdf (accessed November 22, 2015).

40. Manning, 'Jewish Ghosts, Knackers, Tommyknockers', pp. 229–32.

Chapter 10: Knockers in the Mines

1.   Hunt, *Popular Romances of the West of England*, pp. 90–91.

2.   Charlotte S. Burne, 'Staffordshire Folk and their Lore', *Folklore*, 7:4 (December 1896), p. 371. See also, Richard Suggett, 'The Fair Folk and Enchanters', an article dealing with Welsh folklore from Young and Houlbrook, editors, *Magical Folk*, p. 142.

3.   Lydia Fish, 'The European background of American miners' beliefs', in *Folklore Studies in Honour of Herbert Halpert*, Kenneth S. Goldstein and Neil V. Rosenberg, editors (St John's, Newfoundland: Memorial University of Newfoundland, 1980); Frazer, *Taboo and the Perils of the Soul*. Volume III of *The Golden Bough*, p. 407; Wolfgang Paul, *Mining Lore* (Portland, Oregon: Morris, 1970), pp. 469–85, pp. 818–20; Cedric E. Gregory, *Concise History of Mining* (New York: Pergamon, 1980), pp. 220–21; John Baragwanath, 'Pay Streak', *Cosmopolitan*, 60:5 (1936), p. 56; Hunt, *Popular Romances of the West of England*, p. 352; Wayland D. Hand, 'The Folklore, Customs, and Traditions of the Butte Miner', *California Folklore Quarterly*, 7 (1946), p. 3; and Jenkin, *The Cornish Miner*, p. 294. Bray's story, 'Pixy Gathon; or, The Tailor's Needle', features a mining supernatural being that is likely from neighbouring Devon; see her *A Peep at the Pixies*, pp. 17–37.

4.   Georgius Agricola, *De Animantibus Subterraneis Liber* (Basiliae: Apud Frobenium et Epicapium, 1549), pp. 77–79. See also Agricola's *De Re Metallica*, translated by Herbert Clark Hoover and Lou Henry Hoover (New York: Dover Publication, 1950), p. 217.

5.   E.T.A. Hoffmann, *Selected Writings of E.T.A. Hoffmann: The Tales*, Volume 1, edited and translated by Leonard J. Kent and Elizabeth C. Knight (Chicago: University of Chicago Press, 1969).

6.   Charles Kingsley, *Yeast: A Problem* (London: J.M. Dent and Sons, 1851), p. 255.

7.   Bottrell, *Traditions and Hearthside Stories of West Cornwall* (1873), pp. 186–93; the term 'fuggan' or 'figgy hobbin' is likely related to the Cornish word *hwiogan* (i.e. a pasty), a cognate of the Welsh, *chwiogen*, both meaning 'muffin' or 'simnel cake'; 'didjan' indicates a tiny piece: See Courtney, 'Cornish Folk-lore', p. 220.

8.   Hunt, *Popular Romances of the West of England*, p. 88; this legend is echoed in Elizabeth Mary Wright, *Rustic Speech and Folk-Lore* (New York: H. Milford, 1913), p. 199; Deane and Shaw, *The Folklore of Cornwall* (1975).

9.   Evans-Wentz, *The Fairy Faith in Celtic Countries*, p. 182. An informant from St Just attempted to make a distinction between knockers, who bestow bad luck, and other small underground people, who bring good luck.

10. Ibid., p. 177.

11. Ibid.

12. Wright, *Rustic Speech and Folk-Lore*; Jenkin, *The Cornish Miner*.

13. Deane and Shaw, *The Folklore of Cornwall* (1975).

14. For Bottrell, see his *Stories and Folk-Lore of West Cornwall*, pp. 193–94. See also Deane and Shaw, *Folklore of Cornwall* (2003), pp. 19–22; Wright, *Rustic Speech and Folk-Lore*, p. 200.

15. Hunt, *Popular Romances of the West of England*, p. 349; Jenkin, *The Cornish Miner*, pp. 294–97; Kingsley, *Yeast*.

16. Tregarthen, *Pixie Folklore and Legends*, pp. 171–85.

17. Manning, 'Jewish Ghosts, Knackers, Tommyknockers, and other Sprites of Capitalism in the Cornish Mines', p. 219.

18. Bottrell, *Stories and Folk-Lore of West Cornwall*, pp. 193–94, and for the second quote, see his *Traditions and Hearthside Stories of West Cornwall* (1873), p. 185. The grey zone separating the dead from fairies is well known: see Chapter 4, and see Briggs, 'The Fairies and the Realms of the Dead'.

19. John Rule, 'Some Social Aspects of the Cornish Industrial Revolution', from Roger Burt, editor, *Industry and Society in the South-West* (Exeter: University of Exeter Press, 1970), pp. 71–106; and see Rule's two publications, *The Experience of Labour in Eighteenth-Century English Industry* (New York: St. Martin's, 1981) and *The Labouring Classes in Early Industrial England: 1750–1850* (New York: Longman, 1986).

20. Keith Thomas, *Religion and the Decline of Magic* (London: Folio Society, 2012 [1971]; second edition in 1991, minor changes in the 2012 edition), p. 646.

21. George Orwell, *The Road to Wigan Pier* (New York: Harcourt, Brace, 1958 [1937]), p. 46.

22. Jenkin, *Cornwall and the Cornish*, pp. 216–17.

23. Payton, 'Bridget Cleary and Cornish Studies', pp. 194–215.

24. Alan M. Kent, '"Drill Cores": A Newly-found Manuscript of Cousin Jack Narratives from the Upper Peninsula of Michigan, USA', *Cornish Studies: Second Series*, 12, Philip Payton, editor (Exeter: University of Exeter Press, 2004), pp. 106–43.

Chapter 11: Tommyknockers, Immigration and the Modern World

1. Underground mining ceased in Grass Valley in the mid-1950s. F.W. McQuiston, Jr., *Gold: The Saga of the Empire Mine 1850–1956* (Grass Valley, California: Empire Mine Park Association, 1986).

2. F.D. Calhoon, *Coolies, Kanakas and Cousin Jacks: and Eleven Other Ethnic Groups who Populated the West during the Gold Rush Years* (Sacramento, California: Cal-Con

Publishers, 1986), pp. 320–21. Single jacks involved a solitary miner with a hammer and a drill, one to a hand; double jacking describes a miner swinging a larger, two-fisted sledgehammer while his partner held and rotated a drill bit.

3. Von Sydow, *Selected Papers on Folklore*, pp. 173–74.

4. John Rowe, 'Cornish Emigrants in America', *Folklife: Journal for the Society for Folklife Studies*, 3 (1965), p. 25.

5. Payton, *Cornwall: A History*, pp. 214–15, pp. 217–20.

6. John Rowe, *Hard Rock Men: Cornish Immigrants and the North American Mining Frontier* (New York: Barnes and Noble, 1974); Louis Albert Copeland, 'The Cornish in Southwest Wisconsin', *Wisconsin Historical Collections*, 14 (1898), pp. 301–4; and see Rowe, 'Cornish Emigrants in America', p. 25.

7. Philip Payton, *The Cornish Overseas* (Fowey, Cornwall: Alexander Associates, 1999); Rowe, *Hard Rock Men*; A.L. Rowse, *The Cousin Jacks: The Cornish in America* (New York: Charles Scribner's Sons, 1969); Arthur Cecil Todd, *The Cornish Miner in America* (Glendale, California: Arthur H. Clark, 1967); Calhoon, *Coolies, Kanakas and Cousin Jacks*; McQuiston, *Gold*.

8. Ronald M. James, *The Roar and the Silence: A History of Virginia City and the Comstock Lode* (Reno: University of Nevada Press, 1998); see also, Ronald M. James, 'Defining the Group: Nineteenth-Century Cornish on the Mining Frontier', *Cornish Studies: Second Series*, 2, Philip Payton, editor (Exeter: University of Exeter Press, 1994), pp. 32–47; and 'Home away from Home: Cornish Immigrants in Nineteenth-Century Nevada', *Cornish Studies: Second Series*, 15, Philip Payton, editor (Exeter: University of Exeter Press, 2008), pp. 141–63.

9. R.W. Raymond, *A Glossary of Mining and Metallurgical Terms* (Easton, Pennsylvania: Office of the Secretary, Lafayette College, 1881); Caroline Bancroft, 'Folklore of the Central City District, Colorado', *California Folklore Quarterly* (October 1945), pp. 315–42; Otis E. Young, Jr., *Western Mining* (Norman: University of Oklahoma Press, 1970), pp. 72–74; James C. Baker, 'Echoes of Tommyknockers in Bohemia, Oregon, Mines', *Western Folklore*, 30 (1971), pp. 121–22.

10. In addition to Wayland Hand's 'The Folklore, Customs, and Traditions of the Butte Miner', see his 'Folklore from Utah's Silver Mining Camps', *Journal of American Folklore*, 45 (1941), pp. 132–61; and see Hand, 'California Miners Folklore: Below Ground', *California Folklore Quarterly*, 1 (1942), pp. 127–53; and Bancroft, 'Folklore of the Central City District, Colorado'; Baker, 'Echoes of Tommyknockers in Bohemia, Oregon, Mines'. Lydia Fish, 'The European background of American miners' beliefs', in Goldstein and Rosenberg, editors, *Folklore Studies in Honour of Herbert Halpert*, pp. 157–71, repeats details from Hand and Bancroft but does not offer additional material.

11. Hand, 'California Miners Folklore: Below Ground', p. 129.

12. Ibid., pp. 128–31.

13. Hand, 'Folklore from Utah's Silver Mining Camps', pp. 142–43.

14. Hand, 'The Folklore, Customs, and Traditions of the Butte Miner', p. 5.

15. Ibid., pp. 5–8.

16. Bancroft, 'Folklore of the Central City District, Colorado', p. 322.

17. Baker, 'Echoes of Tommyknockers in Bohemia, Oregon, Mines', p. 121.

18. Ibid.

19. See, for example, *Virginia City Evening News*, 8 October 1884; and *Territorial Enterprise*, 21 January 1880; *Examiner* (San Francisco), 27 November 1887; *Daily Tribune* (Salt Lake City), 16 July 1885; and for the association of some of these primary sources with the tommyknocker, see, for example, Anthony Amaral, 'The Wild Weird World of the Tommyknockers', *Nevada Highways and Parks*, 25:3 (1965), p. 28.

20. Fisher Vane, 'Spooks, Spectres, and Superstitions in Mining', *The Mining Journal*, 21:1 (1937), p. 5, p. 40.

21. Writers' Program of the Works Projects Administration, *Arizona State Guide* (New York: Hastings House, 1940), p. 164.

22. Marguerite Humphrey, 'The Tommy Knocker', *Nevada: Official Bicentennial Book*, Stanley Paher, editor (Las Vegas: Nevada Publications, 1976), p. 123. The name Williams is either Cornish or Welsh. Census records provide support for the conclusion that he was Cornish, but his name is ambiguous.

23. George S. Baker, 'Cousin Jack Country', *Gold Prospector*, 16:3 (1990), pp. 10–12.

24. *Nevada Appeal* (Carson City, Nevada), 29 June 1992.

25. Ibid.

26. This material was gathered on 9 November 2013 from the website known as reddit (i.e. http://www.reddit.com), specifically from the 'subreddit' known as AskHistorians. The informant referred to herself as 'AlfredoEinsteino'; posts on the site are typically anonymous.

27. The source, having retrieved her secondary school paper, was able to make additions and corrections in a second post to the website on 3 November 2017.

28. Hand, 'California Miners Folklore: Below Ground', p. 128. Several studies have explored immigrant traditions about fairy-like supernatural beings; see Herbert Halpert, 'Pennsylvania Fairylore and Folktales', *Journal of American Folklore*, 58:228 (1945), pp. 130–34; and see articles by Gary R. Butler pp. 5–21 and Peter Narváez pp. 336–68 in Narváez, *The Good People*. And see articles by Peter Muise pp. 193–209, Simon Young pp. 210–21, and Chris Woodyard pp. 223–38 in Young and Ceri Houlbrook, editors, *Magical Folk*.

29. George Foster, *Traditional Societies and Technological Change* (New York: Harper and Row, second edition, 1973), pp. 35–36.

30. Ibid., p. 39.

31. Vane, 'Spooks, Spectres, and Superstitions in Mining'; Bancroft, 'Folklore of the Central City District, Colorado'. And consider the testimony of the Portuguese American miner in Golconda, Nevada who described tommyknockers in an abandoned level in the 1950s.

32. This conclusion is based on testimony collected by the author in May 1982 at the Geevor Mine and other locales in Cornwall. Informants knew of the tradition, but even the oldest miners, some of whom had worked almost sixty years, said that the references to knockers were 'long gone' when they first started in the mines. The European collectors of the early twentieth century write of the belief as archaic and increasingly inactive. Hunt, *Popular Romances of the West of England*, p. 347, wrote as early as 1881 that 'we rarely hear of the Knockers now'. Despite all of this, it is impossible to prove a negative, and one can ask whether belief in knockers in Cornwall will ever disappear entirely.

33. See the Skinner's Brewing Company website: http://www.skinnersbrewery. com/beers (accessed 25 January 2016). For the Colorado brewery and pub, see https://www.tommyknocker.com (accessed 25 January 2016).

34. Sveinsson, *The Folk-Stories of Iceland*; von Sydow, *Selected Papers on Folklore*, pp. 11–43; Christiansen, *European Folklore in America*; Dégh, 'Approaches to Folklore Research among Immigrant Groups', pp. 551–56. See also Wayland D. Hand, 'European Fairy Lore in the New World', *Folklore*, 92:2 (1981), pp. 141–48, and Briggs, *An Encyclopedia of Fairies*, pp. 6–8.

35. Robert B. Klymasz, 'From Immigrant to Ethnic Folklore: A Canadian View of Process and Transition', *Journal of the Folklore Institute*, 10:3 (1973), pp. 131–39.

36. Stephen Stern, 'Ethnic Folklore and the Folklore of Ethnicity', *Western Folklore*, 36:1 (1977), pp. 7–32.

37. Archie Green, 'At the Hall, in the Stope: Who Treasures Tales of Work?', *Western Folklore*, 46 (1987), pp. 153–70; and see his 'Working with Laborlore', *Labor's Heritage*, 1:3 (1989), pp. 66–75.

38. Anthony Fitch, *Ballads of Western Miners* (New York: Cochrane, 1910), pp. 15–16; Hand, 'California Miners Folklore: Below Ground', p. 129.

39. Hand, 'California Miners Folklore: Below Ground', p. 129. Spirits in the mines remain a motif in literature, continuing a tradition established by Hoffmann and Kingsley. See, for example, Daphne du Maurier, *Hungry Hill* (Philadelphia: Blakiston, 1944), p. 6, p. 31; and Louis L'Amour, *Comstock Lode* (New York: Bantam, 1981), p. 12, p. 180. It does not appear that Stephen King's bestseller, *The Tommyknockers* (New York: G.P. Putnam's Sons, 1987) is related to the Cornish immigrant tradition, but instead, it simply borrows the name.

Conclusion

1. R. Morton Nance, 'Folk-lore Recorded in the Cornish Language' (91st Annual Report of the Royal Cornwall Polytechnic Society, 1924, reprint: Penzance, Oakmagic, 2000), as quoted by McMahon, 'Folklore, Loss, and Social Change in Nineteenth Century Cornwall', p. 36.

2. Davey, 'As is the Manner and the Custom: Identity and Folk Tradition in Cornwall', p. 3. Davey became Grand Bard of the Gorsedh Kernow in 2015.

3. Almqvist, 'Irish Migratory Legends on the Supernatural', pp. 27–28. As noted previously, England shared Cornwall's predilection for legend rather than folktale: see Dorson, *The British Folklorists*, p. 160.

4. See the appendix for the tally. This number refers to ML 4050; ML 4075; ML 5006*; ML 5070; ML 5075; ML 5085; ML 6010; ML 6045; ML 6055; ML 6070A (see also ATU 113); ML 7015; ML 7060; ATU 365 (told in Cornwall as a legend); ATU 758 (normally told as a legend); and ATU 650A. Briggs identifies Cornish variants of ATU 650A. 'Strong Hans', but the classification is tenuous.

5. Almqvist, 'Irish Migratory Legends on the Supernatural', pp. 35–36.

6. Ibid., p. 36.

7. Dundes, *The Morphology of North American Indian Folktales*, pp. 22–24.

8. Ibid., p. 80, p. 100, p. 102.

9. Almqvist, *Viking Ale*, p. 25.

10. Ibid., p. 27.

11. Krohn, *Folklore Methodology*, pp. 13–15.

Bibliography

Aarne, Antti, and Thompson, Stith, *The Types of the Folktale: A Classification and Bibliography* (Helsinki: FF Communications No. 184, 1961; second revision, fourth printing, 1987).

Addy, Sidney Oldall, editor, *A Glossary of Words Used in the Neighbourhood of Sheffield* (London: English Dialect Society, 1888).

Agricola, Georgius, *De Animantibus Subterraneis Liber* (Basiliae: Apud Frobenium et Epicapium, 1549).

————, *De Re Metallica*, translated by Herbert Clark Hoover and Lou Henry Hoover (New York: Dover Publication, 1950; first published in translation, London: The Mining Magazine, 1912; page numbers refer to 1950 edition [1556]).

Almqvist, Bo, 'Of Mermaids and Marriages: Seamus Heaney's "Maighdean Mara" and Nula Ní Dhomhnaill's "an Mhaighdean Mhara" in the Light of Folk Tradition', *Béaloideas*, 58 (1990), pp. 1–74.

————, 'Irish Migratory Legends on the Supernatural: Sources, Studies, and Problems', *Béaloideas*, 59 (1991), pp. 1–43.

————, 'Crossing the Border: A Sampler of Irish Migratory Legends about the Supernatural', *Béaloideas*, 59 (1991), pp. 209–17, pp. 219–78.

————, edited by Éilís Ní Dhuibhne and Séamas Ó Catháin, *Viking Ale: Studies on Folklore Contacts between the Northern and the Western Worlds* (Aberystwyth: Boethius, 1991).

Amaral, Anthony, 'The Wild Weird World of the Tommyknockers', *Nevada Highways and Parks*, 25:3 (1965), pp. 27–29, p. 55.

Arnason, Jón, *Icelandic Legends*, translated by George E. J. Powell and Eiríkur Magnússon (London: R. Bentley, 1864).

Baker, George S., 'Cousin Jack Country', *Gold Prospector*, 16:3 (1990), pp. 10–12.

Baker, James C., 'Echoes of Tommyknockers in Bohemia, Oregon, Mines', *Western Folklore*, 30 (1971), pp. 119–22.

Ball, Kimberly, 'Legend as Metatradition', *Fabula*, 53:102 (December 2012).

Bancroft, Caroline, 'Folklore of the Central City District, Colorado', *California Folklore Quarterly* (October 1945), pp. 315–42.

Baragwanath, John, 'Pay Streak', *Cosmopolitan*, 60:5 (1936), pp. 56–57, pp. 78–82.

Baring-Gould, Sabine, *The Vicar of Morwenstow: A Life of Robert Stephen Hawker, M.A.* (New York: Thomas Whittaker, 1888).

———, *A Book of the West: Being an Introduction to Devon and Cornwall*, Volume 2 (London: Methuen and Company, 1899).

———, *Book of Folk-Lore* (London: Collins, 1913).

Basgov, Ilhan, 'Folklore Studies and Nationalism in Turkey', *Journal of the Folklore Institute*, 3:3 (December 1966).

Baughman, Ernest W., *Type and Motif-Index of the Folktales of England and North America* (Bloomington: Indiana University Folklore Series No. 20, 1966).

Baycroft, Timothy, and Hopkin, David, editors, *Folklore and Nationalism in Europe during the Long Nineteenth Century* (Leiden, Netherlands: Brill, 2012).

Bishop, Chris, 'Þyrs, ent, eoten, gigans—Anglo-Saxon Ontologies of "Giant"', *Modern Language Society*, 107:3 (2006), pp. 259–70.

Blight, John Thomas, *Ancient Crosses and other Antiquities in the West of Cornwall* (London: Simpkin, 1858, second edition [1856]).

———, *A Week at the Land's End* (London: Longman, Green, Longman, and Roberts, 1861).

Bois, G.J.C., *Jersey Folklore and Superstitions, Volume Two* (Central Milton Keynes: Author House, 2010).

Borlase, William, *Observations on the Antiquities of Cornwall* (Oxford: W Jackson, 1754).

———, *Natural History of Cornwall* (Oxford: W Jackson, 1758).

Borlase, William Copeland, *The Age of the Saints: A Monograph of Early Christianity in Cornwall with the Legends of the Cornish Saints and an Introduction Illustrative of the Ethnology of the District* (Somerset, UK: Llanerch, 1995 [1893]).

Borrowclough, David A., and Hallam, John, 'The Devil's Footprints and Other Folklore: Local Legend and Archaeological Evidence in Lancashire', *Folklore*, 119:1 (2008), pp. 93–102.

Boson, Nicholas, *John of Chyannor, or The three points of wisdom*, revised and translated by R. Morton Nance (Truro, UK: Cornish Language Board, 1969).

Bottrell, William, *Traditions and Hearthside Stories of West Cornwall* (Penzance: W. Cornish, 1870, first series).

———, *Traditions and Hearthside Stories of West Cornwall* (Penzance: Beare and Son, 1873, second series).

————, *Stories and Folk-Lore of West Cornwall* (Penzance: F. Rodda, 1880).

Bourke, Angela, *The Burning of Bridget Cleary: A True Story* (New York: Viking, 2000).

Bray, Anna Eliza, *Traditions, Legends, Superstitions, and Sketches of Devonshire on the Borders of the Tamar and the Tavy*, Volume 1 (London: John Murray, 1838).

————, *A Peep at the Pixies, or Legends of the West* (London: Grant and Griffith, 1854).

Brendon, Piers, *Hawker of Morwenstow: Portrait of a Victorian Eccentric* (London: Pimlico, 2002).

Briggs, Katharine, *The Fairies in Tradition and Literature* (London: Routledge and Kegan Paul, 1967).

————, 'The Fairies and the Realms of the Dead', *Folklore*, 81:2 (Summer 1970), pp. 81–96.

————, *An Encyclopedia of Fairies, Hobgoblins, Brownies, Bogies, and Other Supernatural Creatures* (New York: Pantheon Books, 1976).

————, *The Vanishing People: Fairy Lore and Legends* (New York: Pantheon, 1978).

————, *Folktales of Britain* (London: Folio Society, 2011 [1971]).

Bringéus, Nils-Arvid, *Carl Wilhelm von Sydow: A Swedish Pioneer in Folklore* (Helsinki: FF Communications No. 298, 2009).

British Archaeological Association, *Collectanea Archaeologica Communications*, Volume I (London: Longman, Green, Longman, and Roberts, 1862).

Bronson, Bertrand Harris, editor, *The Singing Tradition of Child's Popular Ballads (Abridgement)* (Princeton, New Jersey: Princeton University Press, 1976).

Brunvand, Jan Harold, *Too Good to be True: The Colossal Book of Urban Legends* (New York: W.W. Norton and Company, 1999).

Bryan, Eric Shane, 'The Moon Glides, Death Rides: Pejoration and Aborted Otherworldly Journeys in "The Dead Bridegroom Carries off his Bride" (ATU 365)', *Intégrité: A Faith and Learning Journal*, 16:1 (Spring 2017), pp. 13–30.

Burne, Charlotte S., 'Staffordshire Folk and their Lore', *Folklore*, 7:4 (December 1896), pp. 366–86.

————, 'Short Notice: Legends and Tales of North Cornwall', *Folklore*, 19:4 (1908), p. 508.

Burt, Roger, editor, *Industry and Society in the South-West* (Exeter: University of Exeter Press, 1970).

Calhoon, F.D., *Coolies, Kanakas and Cousin Jacks: and Eleven Other Ethnic Groups who Populated the West during the Gold Rush Years* (Sacramento, California: Cal-Con Publishers, 1986).

Carew, Richard, *Survey of Cornwall* (London: B. Law, 1769 [1602]; also F.E. Halliday, editor (Bath, UK: Adams and Dart, 1970; Documents of Social History)).

Child, Francis James, *The English and Scottish Popular Ballads* (Boston: Houghton, Mifflin, 1886–1898).

Christiansen, Reidar Th., *The Migratory Legends: A Proposed List of Types with a Systematic Catalogue of the Norwegian Variants* (Helsinki: FF Communications No. 175, 1958).

————, *European Folklore in America*, Studia Norvegica No. 12 (Oslo, Norway: Universitetsforlaget, 1962).

————, *Folktales of Norway* translated by Pat Shaw Iversen (Chicago: University of Chicago Press, 1964).

————, 'Some Notes on the Fairies and the Fairy Faith', *Béaloideas*, 39/41 (1971–1973), pp. 95–111.

Clark, John, 'Gogmagog Again', *3rd Stone*, 44 (Autumn 2002), pp. 38–43.

Cochrane, Timothy, 'The Concept of Ecotypes in American Folklore', *Journal of Folklore Research*, 24:1 (Jan–Apr 1987), pp. 33–55.

Conwell, Eugene A., 'On Ancient Sepulchral Cairns on the Loughcrew Hills,' *Proceedings of the Royal Irish Academy*, 9 (1864–1866), pp. 357–58.

Copeland, Louis Albert, 'The Cornish in Southwest Wisconsin', *Wisconsin Historical Collections*, 14 (1898), pp. 301–34.

Couch, Jonathan with additions by Couch, Thomas Quiller, *The History of Polperro: A Fishing Village on the South Coast of Cornwall* (Truro, UK: Simpkin, Marshall and Company, 1871).

Courtney, Margaret Ann, 'Cornish Folk-lore', *The Folk-Lore Journal* (1887) Volume 5, pp. 14–61, pp. 85–112, pp. 177–220.

————, *Cornish Feasts and Folk-lore* (Penzance: Beare and Son, 1890).

Courtney, Margaret Ann, and Couch, Thomas Quiller, *Glossary of Words in Use in Cornwall* (London: Trübner and Company, 1880).

Darwin, Gregory, 'On Mermaids, Meroveus, and Mélusine: Reading the Irish Seal Woman and Mélusine as Origin Legend', *Folklore*, 115:2 (2015), pp. 123–41.

Davey, Merv, 'As is the Manner and the Custom: Identity and Folk Tradition in Cornwall' (Exeter: University of Exeter, Doctoral Thesis, September 2011).

————, 'The Celto-Cornish Movement and Folk Revival: Competing Speech Communities', *Cornish Studies: Second Series*, 20, Philip Payton, editor (Exeter: University of Exeter Press, 2013), pp. 108–30.

Davies, Owen, *The Haunted: A Social History of Ghosts* (New York: Palgrave Macmillan, 2007).

Davies, Sioned, 'Storytelling in Medieval Wales', *Oral Tradition*, 7/2 (1992), pp. 231–57.

Deane, Tony, and Shaw, Tony, *The Folklore of Cornwall* (Totoway, New Jersey: Rowman and Littlefield, 1975).

———, *Folklore of Cornwall* (Stroud, Gloucestershire: Tempus, 2003).

Dégh, Linda, 'Approaches to Folklore Research among Immigrant Groups', *Journal of American Folklore*, 79 (1966), pp. 551–56.

Delargy, James H. (Séamus Ó Duilearga), 'The Gaelic Story-Teller with some notes on Gaelic Folk-Tales' (The Sir John Rhŷs Lecture, presented 28 November 1945; published 1946).

———, 'The Gaelic Story-Teller—No Living Counterpart in Western Christendom', *Ireland of the Welcomes*, 1:1 (1952), pp. 2–4.

Dorson, Richard, 'The Question of Folklore in a New Nation', *Journal of the Folklore Institute*, 3:3 (December 1966).

———, *The British Folklorists: A History* (Chicago: University of Chicago, 1968).

———, 'National Characteristics of Japanese Folktales', *Journal of the Folklore Institute*, 12:2/3 (August–December 1975).

Dundes, Alan, *The Morphology of North American Indian Folktales* (Helsinki: FF Communications No. 195, 1964).

———, editor, *The Study of Folklore* (Berkeley: University of California Press, 1965).

———, editor, *International Folkloristics: Classic Contributions by the Founders of Folklore* (New York: Rowan and Littlefield, 1999).

Dwyer, Richard A., and Lingenfelter, Richard E., *Dan De Quille, The Washoe Giant* (Reno: University of Nevada Press, 1990).

Earls, Brian, 'Supernatural Legends in Nineteenth-Century Irish Writing', *Béaloideas*, 60–61 (1992–1993), pp. 93–144.

Eminov, Sandra, 'Folklore and Nationalism in Modern China', *Journal of the Folklore Institute*, 12:2/3 (December 1966), pp. 257–77.

Evans-Wentz, Walter Yeeling, *The Fairy Faith in Celtic Countries* (New York: Citadel, 1990 [1911]).

Finucane, R.C., *Ghosts: Appearance of the Dead and Cultural Transformation* (Amherst, New York: Prometheus, 1996).

Fisher, John H., editor, *The Complete Poetry and Prose of Geoffrey Chaucer* (New York: Holt, Rinehart and Winston, 1977).

Fitch, Anthony, *Ballads of Western Miners* (New York: Cochrane, 1910).

Foster, George, *Traditional Societies and Technological Change* (New York: Harper and Row, second edition, 1973).

Foster, Michael Dylan, and Tolbert, Jeffrey A., *The Folkloresque: Reframing Folklore in a Popular Culture World* (Boulder: University of Colorado Press, 2016).

Frazer, James, *The Golden Bough* (London: Macmillan, 1912, third edition).

Garry, Jane, and El-Shamy, Hasan, editors, *Archetypes and Motifs in Folklore and Literature: A Handbook* (London: M.E. Sharpe, 2005).

Geoffrey of Monmouth, *The History of the Kings of Britain*, translated by Lewis Thorpe (London: Folio Society, 2010).

Glassie, Henry, *Passing the Time in Ballymenone: Culture and History of an Ulster Community* (Philadelphia: University of Pennsylvania Press, 1982).

Goldstein, Kenneth S., 'On the Application of the Concepts of Active and Inactive Traditions to the Study of Repertory', *The Journal of American Folklore*, 84:331 (Jan–Mar 1971), pp. 62–67.

Goldstein, Kenneth S., and Rosenberg, Neil V., editors, *Folklore Studies in Honour of Herbert Halpert* (St John's, Newfoundland: Memorial University of Newfoundland, 1980).

Golightly, Karen B., 'Who put the Folk in Folklore?: Nineteenth-Century Collecting of Irish Folklore from T. Crofton Croker to Lady August Gregory' (Carbondale: Southern Illinois University, 2007).

Green, Archie, 'At the Hall, in the Stope: Who Treasures Tales of Work?', *Western Folklore*, 46 (1987), pp. 153–70.

———, 'Working with Laborlore', *Labor's Heritage*, 1:3 (1989), pp. 66–75.

Green, Caitlin R., 'Tom Thumb and Jack the Giant-Killer: Two Arthurian Fairy Tales?', *Folklore*, 118:2 (2007), pp. 123–40.

———, 'Jack and Arthur: An Introduction to Jack the Giant-Killer', *The Arthuriad*: Volume 1: (http://www.arthuriana.co.uk/arthuriad/Arthuriad_ VolOne.pdf; accessed 9 April 2017).

Gregory, Cedric E., *Concise History of Mining* (New York: Pergamon, 1980).

Grimm, Jacob, *Teutonic Mythology*, translated from the fourth edition by James Stern Stallybrass (New York: Dover Publications, 1966 [1835]).

Grimm, Jacob, and Grimm, Wilhelm, *The Complete Grimm's Fairy Tales*, translated by James Stern with introduction by Padraic Colum and commentary by Josef Scharl (New York: Pantheon Books, 1944, seventh and final edition [1857]).

Grinsell, Leslie V., *Folklore of Prehistoric Sites in Britain* (Newton Abbot: David and Charles, 1976).

Grooms, John C., *Giants in Welsh Folklore and Tradition* (Aberystwyth: University of Wales, dissertation, 1988).

Haase, Donald, editor, *The Greenwood Encyclopedia of Folktales and Fairy Tales, Volume One* (London: Greenwood Press, 2008).

Hague, Abu Saeed Zahurul, 'The Use of Folklore in Nationalist Movements and Liberation Struggles: A Case Study of Bangladesh', *Journal of the Folklore Institute*, 3:3 (December 1966).

Hale, Amy, 'Rethinking Celtic Cornwall: An Ethnographic Approach', Philip Payton, editor, *Cornish Studies: Second Series*, 5 (Exeter: University of Exeter Press, 1997), pp. 85–99.

————, 'Genesis of the Celto-Cornish Revival? L.C. Duncombe-Jewell and the Cowethas Kelto-Kernuak', Philip Payton, editor, *Cornish Studies: Second Series*, 5 (Exeter: University of Exeter Press, 1997), pp. 100–11.

————, 'Gathering the Fragments: Performing Contemporary Celtic Identities in Cornwall' (Los Angeles: University of California Los Angeles, dissertation in Folklore and Mythology, 1998).

————, 'Whose Celtic Cornwall? The Ethnic Cornish Meets Celtic Spirituality', from David Harvey, et al., *Celtic Geographies: Old Culture, New Times* (London: Routledge, 2002), pp. 157–72.

————, 'Cornish' from *Celtic Culture: A Historical Encyclopedia*, Volumes 1–5 by John T. Koch, editor (Santa Barbara, California: ABC-CLIO, 2006), p. 761.

Hale, Amy, and Payton, Philip, editors, *New Directions in Celtic Studies* (Exeter: University of Exeter Press, 2000).

Halliwell-Phillipps, James Orchard, *Rambles in Western Cornwall by the Footsteps of the Giants, with Notes on the Celtic Remains of the Land's End District and the Islands of Scilly* (London: J.R. Smith, 1861).

Halpert, Herbert, 'Pennsylvania Fairylore and Folktales', *Journal of American Folklore*, 58:228 (1945), pp. 130–34.

Hand, Wayland D., 'Folklore from Utah's Silver Mining Camps', *Journal of American Folklore*, 45 (1941), pp. 132–61.

————, 'California Miners Folklore: Below Ground', *California Folklore Quarterly*, 1 (1942), pp. 127–53.

————, 'The Folklore, Customs, and Traditions of the Butte Miner', *California Folklore Quarterly*, 7 (1946), pp. 1–25.

————, 'European Fairy Lore in the New World', *Folklore*, 92:2 (1981), pp. 141–48.

Hansen, William F., *Ariadne's Thread: A Guide to International Tales Found in Classical Literature* (Ithaca, New York: Cornell University Press, 2002).

Harte, Jeremy, *Explore Fairy Traditions* (Loughborough, UK: Heart of Albion, 2004).

Hartland, Edwin Sidney, *English Fairy and other Folk Tales* (London: C.E. Brock, 1890).

————, 'Peeping Tom and Lady Godiva', *Folklore*, 1:2 (1890), pp. 207–26.

————, *The Science of Fairy Tales: An Enquiry into Fairy Mythology* (New York: Scribner and Welford, 1891).

Hartmann, Elisabeth, *Die Trollvorstellungen in den Sagen und Märchen der Skandinavischen Völker* (Tübingen: Eberhard Karls Universität Tübingen, 1936).

Hatto, Arthur Thomas, 'The Swan Maiden: A Folktale of North European Origin?', *Bulletin of the School of Oriental and African Studies*, 24:2 (1961), pp. 326–52.

Hawker, Robert Stephen, *Echoes from Old Cornwall* (London: Joseph Masters, 1846).

————, *Cornish Ballads with other Poems* (Oxford: Parker and Company, 1884).

————, *Footprints of Former Men in Far Cornwall* (London: J. Lane, 1903).

Hayward, Philip, 'Senara, Zennor, and the Mermaid Chair: Transplanting Cornish Folklore to a Fictional American Island', Garry H. Tregidga, editor, *Cornish Studies: Third Series*, 1 (Exeter: University of Exeter Press, 2015).

Hemmings, Jessica, '"Bos Primigenius" in Britain: Or, Why do Fairy Cows Have Red Ears?', *Folklore*, 113:1 (2002), pp. 71–82.

Henderson, Lizanne, and Cowan, Edward J., *Scottish Fairy Belief: A History* (East Lothian, Scotland: Tuckwell Press, 2001).

Hitchins, Fortescue, and Drew, Samuel, editor, *The History of Cornwall, From the earliest of Records and Traditions to the Present Time* (Helston, UK: W. Penaluna, 1824).

Hobsbawm, Eric, and Ranger, Terrence, *The Invention of Tradition* (Cambridge: Cambridge University Press, 1983).

Hoffmann, E.T.A., *Selected Writings of E.T.A. Hoffmann: The Tales*, Volume 1, edited and translated by Leonard J. Kent and Elizabeth C. Knight (Chicago: University of Chicago Press, 1969).

Hollander, Lee M., translator and editor, *The Poetic Edda* (Austin: University of Texas Press, 1962).

Hopkin, David, 'The Ecotype, Or a Modest Proposal to Reconnect Cultural and Social History', from Melissa Calaresu, Filippo de Vivo, and Joan-Pau Rubiés, editors, *Exploring Cultural History: Essays in Honour of Peter Burke* (Burlington, Vermont: Ashgate, 2012), pp. 31–54.

Hull, Eleanor, 'Legends and Traditions of the Cailleach Bheara or Old Woman (Hap) of Beare,' *Folklore*, 48:3 (30 September 1927), pp. 225–54.

Humphrey, Marguerite, 'The Tommy Knocker', *Nevada: Official Bicentennial Book*, Stanley Paher, editor (Las Vegas: Nevada Publications, 1976).

Hunt, Robert, *Popular Romances of the West of England or the Drolls, Traditions, and Superstitions of Old Cornwall* (London: Chatto and Windus, 1903, combined first and second series [1865]).

Ikeda, Hiroko, *A Type and Motif Index of Japanese Folk-Literature* (Helsinki: FF Communications No. 209, 1971).

Jackson, Kenneth Hurlstone, *The Oldest Irish Tradition: A Window on the Iron Age* (Cambridge: Cambridge University Press, 2011).

Jakobsson, Ármann, 'Beware of the Elf! A Note on the Evolving Meaning of *Álfar*', *Folklore,* 126:2 (July 2015), pp. 215–23.

James, Ronald M., 'Sven S. Liljeblad', *Halcyon*, 2 (1980).

————, 'A Year in Ireland: Reflections on a Methodological Crisis', *Sinsear: The Folklore Journal*, 4 (1982–1983), pp. 4–5, pp. 83–90.

————, 'Knockers, Knackers, and Ghosts: Immigrant Folklore in the Western Mines', *Western Folklore*, 51:2 (April 1992), pp. 153–76.

————, 'Defining the Group: Nineteenth-Century Cornish on the Mining Frontier', Philip Payton, editor, *Cornish Studies: Second Series*, 2 (Exeter: University of Exeter Press, 1994), pp. 32–47.

————, *The Roar and the Silence: A History of Virginia City and the Comstock Lode* (Reno: University of Nevada Press, 1998).

————, 'Home away from Home: Cornish Immigrants in Nineteenth-Century Nevada', Philip Payton, editor, *Cornish Studies: Second Series*, 15 (Exeter: University of Exeter Press, 2008), pp. 141–63.

————, 'Cornish Folklore: Context and Opportunity', Philip Payton, editor, *Cornish Studies: Second Series*, 18 (Exeter: University of Exeter Press, 2011), pp. 121–40.

————, '"The Spectral Bridegroom": A Study in Cornish Folklore', Philip Payton, editor, *Cornish Studies: Second Series*, 20 (Exeter: University of Exeter Press, 2013), pp. 131–47.

————, 'Curses, Vengeance, and Fishtails: The Cornish Mermaid in Perspective', Garry Tregidga, editor, *Cornish Studies: Third Series*, 1 (Exeter: University of Exeter Press, 2015), pp. 42–61.

Jenkin, A.K. Hamilton, *The Cornish Miner: An Account of his Life above and underground from Early Times* (London: Allen and Urwin, 1962 [1927]).

————, *Cornwall and the Cornish: Story, Religion, and Folk-Lore of 'The Western Land'* (London: J.M. Dent and Sons, 1933).

————, *Cornish Homes and Customs* (London: J.M. Dent and Sons, 1934).

Jewitt, Llewellynn, 'The Mermaid of Legend and of Art', *The Art Journal* (1875–1887), New Series, 6 (1880), pp. 117–20, 170–72 and 230–33.

Johnson, Marjorie T., *Seeing Fairies: From the Lost Archives of the Fairy Investigation Society, Authentic Reports of Fairies in Modern Times* (San Antonio, Texas: Anomalist Books, 2014).

Jones-Baker, Doris, 'The Graffiti of Folk Motifs in Cotswold Churches', *Folklore*, 92:2 (1981), pp. 160–67.

Keightley, Thomas, *The Fairy Mythology* (London: Bradbury and Evans, 1860).

Kent, Alan M., *The Literature of Cornwall: Continuity, Identity, Difference, 1000–2000* (Bristol: Redcliffe Press, 2000).

———, '"Drill Cores": A Newly-found Manuscript of Cousin Jack Narratives from the Upper Peninsula of Michigan, USA', Philip Payton, editor, *Cornish Studies: Second Series*, 12 (Exeter: University of Exeter Press, 2004), pp. 106–43.

Keyworth, G. David, 'Was the Vampire of the Eighteenth Century a Unique Type of Undead-corpse?', *Folklore*, 117:3 (2006), pp. 241–60.

Kickingereder, Stephanie, *The Motif of the Mermaid in English, Irish, and Scottish Fairy- and Folk Tales* (Diplomarbeit, Universität Wien; Philologisch-Kulturwissenschaftliche Fakultät; BetreuerIn: Franz-Karl Wöhrer, 2008).

Kiefer, Emma Emily, *Albert Wesselski and Recent Folklore Theories* (New York: Haskell House, 1973).

King, Stephen, *The Tommyknockers* (New York: G.P. Putnam's Sons, 1987).

Kingsley, Charles, *Yeast: A Problem* (London: J.M. Dent and Sons, 1851).

Kirk, Robert; see Stewart, R.J., editor.

Klymasz, Robert B., 'From Immigrant to Ethnic Folklore: A Canadian View of Process and Transition', *Journal of the Folklore Institute*, 10:3 (1973), pp. 131–39.

Kohn, Hans, *The Mind of Germany: The Education of a Nation* (New York: Harper and Row, 1960).

Kriza, János, Erdélyi, János, Pap, Gyula, et al., *The Folk-Tales of the Magyars*, translated by W. Henry Jones and Lewis L. Knopf (London: The Folk-Lore Society, 1889).

Krohn, Kaarle, *Folklore Methodology*, formulated by Julius Krohn; Roger L. Welsch, translator (Austin: University of Texas Press, 1971 [1926] as *Die folkloristische Arbeitsmethode*).

Kvideland, Reimund, and Sehmsdorf, Henning K., editors, *Scandinavian Folk Belief and Legend* (Minneapolis: University of Minnesota Press, 1988).

———, *Nordic Folklore: Recent Studies* (Bloomington: University of Indiana Press, 1989).

———, *All the World's Reward: Folktales Told by Five Scandinavian Storytellers* (Seattle: University of Washington Press, 1999).

L'Amour, Louis, *Comstock Lode* (New York: Bantam, 1981).

Lang, Andrew, *The Lilac Fairy Book* (London: Folio, 2012 [1910]).

Leavy, Barbara Fass, *In Search of the Swan Maiden: A Narrative on Folklore and Gender* (New York: New York University Press, 1995).

Lewis, C.S., *The Silver Chair* (London: Geoffrey Bles, 1953).

Liljeblad, Sven S., *Die Tobiageschichte und andere Märchen mit Toten Helfern* (Lund: Lindstedts, 1927).

———, *Introduction to Folklore* (self-published, 1966).

Lindow, John, 'Cats and Dogs, Trolls and Devils: At Home in Some Migratory Legend Types', *Western Folklore*, 69:2 (Spring 2010), pp. 163–79.

Lövkrona, Inger, *Det bortrövade dryckeskarlet: En sägenstudie* (Lund: Skrifter från Folklivsarkivet I Lund 24, 1982).

Lysaght, Patricia, *The Banshee: The Irish Death Messenger* (Boulder, Colorado: Roberts Rinehart, 1986).

Mac Cárthaigh, Críostóir, 'Midwife to the Fairies (ML 5070): The Irish Variants in their Scottish and Scandinavian Perspective', *Béaloideas*, 59 (1991), pp. 133–43.

MacKillop, James, *A Dictionary of Celtic Mythology* (Oxford: Oxford University Press, 1998).

Mac Philib, Séamas, 'The Changeling (ML 5058): Irish Versions of a Migratory Legend in their International Context', *Béaloideas*, 59 (1991), pp. 121–31.

McDonald, Neil, *Malta and Gozo: A Megalithic Journey* (Neil McDonald: Megalithic Publishing, 2016).

McGlathery, James M., editor, *The Brothers Grimm and Folktale* (Urbana: University of Illinois Press, 1988).

McMahon, Brendan, 'Folklore, Loss, and Social Change in Nineteenth Century Cornwall', *Tradition Today*, 2 (September 2012), pp. 33–49: http://centre-for-english-traditional-heritage.org/TraditionToday2/TT2_McMahon.pdf (accessed 22 November 2015).

———, 'Oedipus and identity in Victorian Cornwall: The Giant Stories', *Tradition Today*, 3 (December 2013), pp. 31–44: http://centre-for-english-traditional-heritage.org/TraditionToday3/TT3_McMahon_Giants.pdf (accessed 22 November 2015).

McQuiston, F.W., Jr., *Gold: The Saga of the Empire Mine 1850–1956* (Grass Valley, California: Empire Mine Park Association, 1986).

Maier, Bernhard, *Dictionary of Celtic Religion and Culture*, translated by Cyril Edwards (Woodbridge, UK: Boydell Press, 1997).

Manning, Paul, 'Jewish Ghosts, Knackers, Tommyknockers, and other Sprites of Capitalism in the Cornish Mines', Philip Payton, editor, *Cornish Studies: Second Series*, 13 (Exeter: University of Exeter Press, 2005), pp. 216–55.

Marshall, Peter, 'Ann Jefferies and the Fairies: Folk Belief and the War on Scepticism in Later Stuart England', from Angela McShane and Garthine Walker, editors, *The Extraordinary and the Everyday in Early Modern England* (Houndsmills, Basingstoke, Hampshire, UK: Palgrave MacMillan, 2010), pp. 127–41.

du Maurier, Daphne, *Hungry Hill* (Philadelphia: Blakiston, 1944).

Michaelis-Jena, Ruth, *The Brothers Grimm* (London: Routledge and Kegan Paul, 1970).

Milton, John, *The History of Britain* (London: Chiswell, 1695 [1670]: https://books.google.com/books?id=EA4-AQAAMAAJ&pg=PA3&source=gbs_selected_pages&cad=3#v=onepage&q&f=false, accessed 16 July 2017).

Monaghan, Patricia, *The Encyclopedia of Celtic Mythology and Folklore* (New York: Facts on File, 2004).

Motz, Lotte, 'The Rulers of The Mountain: A Study of the Giants of the Old Icelandic Texts', *Mankind Quarterly*, 20 (1979–1980), pp. 393–416.

———, 'Giants in Folklore and Mythology: A New Approach', *Folklore*, 93:1 (1982), pp. 70–84.

Murdoch, Brian, *Cornish Literature* (Woodbridge, Suffolk, UK: D.S. Brewer, 1993).

Murray, James A.H., editor, *A New English Dictionary on Historical Principals* (Oxford: Clarendon Press, 1888–1928; later volumes with additional editors; referred to as the *Oxford English Dictionary* after 1933).

Nance, Robert Morton, 'Cornish Beginnings', *Old Cornwall* (5:9) 1958.

———, 'Folk-lore Recorded in the Cornish Language' (91st Annual Report of the Royal Cornwall Polytechnic Society, 1924, reprint: Penzance, Oakmagic, 2000).

Narváez, Peter, editor, *The Good People: New Fairylore Essays* (Lexington: University of Kentucky, 1997).

Norman, Mark, and Hickey-Hall, Jo, 'Pixies and Pixy Rocks' from Simon Young and Ceri Houlbrook, editors, *Magical Folk: British and Irish Fairies 500 AD to the Present* (London: Gibson Square, 2018).

Ó Catháin, Séamas, 'A Tale of Two Sittings—Context and variation in a fairy legend from Tyrone', *Béaloideas*, 48–49 (1980–1981), pp. 135–47.

———, 'The Robbers and the Captive Girl: Ancient Antecedents and Other Elements of a Rare Irish Legend Type', *Béaloideas*, 62/63 (1994/1995), pp. 109–46.

Ó hÓgáin, Dáithí, 'Migratory Legends in Medieval Irish Literature', *Béaloideas*, 60/61 (1992/1993), pp. 57–74.

———, *The Lore of Ireland: An Encyclopaedia of Myth, Legend and Romance* (Cork: Boydell, 2006).

Olrik, Axel, 'Epische Gesetze der Volksdichtung', *Zeitschrift für Deutsches Altertum*, 51 (1909), pp. 1–12.

O'Reilly, Barry, 'River Claiming its Due and the Sod of Death Predestined (ML 4050 and MLSIT 4051): Two Legends of Fate in Irish Tradition', *Béaloideas*, 59 (1991), pp. 83–90.

Orwell, George, *The Road to Wigan Pier* (New York: Harcourt, Brace, 1958 [1937]).

Ó Súilleabháin, Seán, and Christiansen, Reidar Th., *The Types of the Irish Folktale* (Helsinki: FF Communications No. 188, 1967).

Padel, O.J., 'The Cornish background of the Tristan stories', *Cambridge Medieval Celtic Studies*, 1 (Summer 1981), pp. 53–81.

———, 'Geoffrey of Monmouth and Cornwall,' *Cambridge Medieval Celtic Studies*, 8 (Winter 1984), pp. 1–28.

Paris, T.C., *A Hand-Book for Travellers in Devon and Cornwall* (London: John Murray, 1851).

Parry-Jones, D., *Welsh Legends and Fairy Lore* (New York: Barnes and Noble, 1992 [1953]).

Paul, Wolfgang, *Mining Lore* (Portland, Oregon: Morris, 1970).

Paynter, William H., *The Cornish Witch-finder—William Henry Paynter and the Witchery, Ghosts, Charms and Folklore of Cornwall*, selected and introduced by Jason Semmens (St Agnes, UK: Federation of Old Cornwall Societies, 2008).

———, *Cornish Witchcraft: The Confessions of a Westcountry Witch-finder*, with a forward by Jason Semmens (Liskeard: Privately Printed, 2016).

Payton, Philip, *Cornwall* (Fowey: Alexander Associates, 1996).

———, *The Cornish Overseas: A History of Cornwall's 'Great Emigration'* (Fowey: Alexander Associates, 1999; reissued by University of Exeter Press in 2015).

———, 'Industrial Celts?: Cornish Identity in the Age of Technological Prowess', Philip Payton, editor, *Cornish Studies: Second Series*, 10 (Exeter: University of Exeter Press, 2002), pp. 116–35.

———, *Cornwall: A History* (Fowey: Cornwall Editions, 2004) (revised and updated edition, 2017, Exeter: University of Exeter Press).

———, 'Bridget Cleary and Cornish Studies: Folklore, Story-telling and Modernity', Philip Payton, editor, *Cornish Studies: Second Series*, 13 (Exeter: University of Exeter Press, 2005), pp. 194–215.

Pearson, Alan, *Robert Hunt, F.R.S. (1807–1887)* (Federation of Old Cornwall Societies, 1976).

Peate, Iorwerth C., 'Corn Ornaments', *Folklore*, 82:3 (Autumn 1971), p. 177.

Peppard, Murry B., *Paths through the Forest: A Biography of the Brothers Grimm* (New York: Holt, Rinehart and Winston, 1971).

Percy, Thomas, *Reliques of Ancient English Poetry: Volume III* (London: J. Dodsley, 1775).

Perrault, Charles, *Contes* (Paris: Editions Garnier Frères, 1967).

Peters, Caradoc, 'The Mermaid of Zennor—A Mirror on Three Worlds', Garry H. Tregidga, editor, *Cornish Studies: Third Series*, 1 (Exeter: University of Exeter Press, 2015).

Phillips, Carl, 'A "mystic message to the world": Henry Jenner, W.Y. Evans-Wentz and the fairy-faith in "Celtic" Cornwall', Philip Payton, editor, *Cornish Studies: Second Series*, 19 (Exeter: University of Exeter Press, 2012), pp. 123–39.

Pinson, Koppel S., *Modern Germany: Its History and Civilization* (New York: Macmillan, 1966).

Pitt, Moses, *An Account of one Ann Jefferies* (London: Richard Cumberland, 1696).

Pool, P.A.S., *The Life and Progress of Henry Quick of Zennor* (St Ives: W.J. Rowe, 1963).

Powell, T.G.E., and Daniel, G.E., *Barclodiad y Gawres: The Excavation of a Megalithic Chamber Tomb in Anglesey, 1952–1953* (Liverpool: Liverpool University Press, 1956).

Propp, Vladímir, *Morphology of the Folktale*, translated by Laurence Scott and revised and edited by Louis A. Wagner (Austin: University of Texas Press, 1968 [1928]).

Puhvel, Martin, 'The Legend of the Church-Building Troll in Northern Europe', *Folklore*, 72:4 (Winter 1961), pp. 567–83.

Purcell, William, *Onward Christian Soldier: A Life of Sabine Baring-Gould, Parson, Squire, Novelist, Antiquarian, 1834–1924* (London: Longmans Green, 1957).

Quiller-Couch, Mabel, *Cornwall's Wonderland* (London and Toronto: J.M. Dent and Sons, n.d., c.1914).

Ramm, Agatha, *Germany, 1789–1919: A Political History* (London: Methuen and Company, 1967).

Raymond, R.W., *A Glossary of Mining and Metallurgical Terms* (Easton, Pennsylvania: Office of the Secretary, Lafayette College, 1881).

Reed, Simon, *The Cornish Traditional Year* (London: Troy Books, 2011).

Rhŷs, Sir John, *Celtic Folklore: Welsh and Manx, Volume 1* (Oxford: Clarendon Press, 1901).

Roberts, Brynley F., 'Edward Lhwyd (c.1660–1709): Folklorist', *Folklore*, 120:1 (March 2009), pp. 36–56.

Roper, Jonathan, 'Review Essay', *Folk Life*, 45 (2007), pp. 124–27.

Rountree, Kathryn, *Crafting Contemporary Pagan Identities in a Catholic Society* (London: Routledge, Taylor and Francis Group, 2010).

Rowe, John, 'Cornish Emigrants in America', *Folklife: Journal for the Society for Folklife Studies*, 3 (1965), pp. 25–38.

————, *Hard Rock Men: Cornish Immigrants and the North American Mining Frontier* (New York: Barnes and Noble, 1974).

Rowse, A.L., *The Cousin Jacks: The Cornish in America* (New York: Charles Scribner's Sons, 1969).

————, *A Cornish Childhood* (London: Cardinal, 1975 [1942]).

Rule, John, *The Experience of Labour in Eighteenth-Century English Industry* (New York: St. Martin's, 1981).

————, *The Labouring Classes in Early Industrial England: 1750–1850* (New York: Longman, 1986).

————, *Essays in Eighteenth and Nineteenth Century Social History* (Clio Publishing: Southampton, 2006).

Sayers, Peig, *An Old Woman's Reflections*, translated by Séamus Ennis (Oxford: Oxford University Press, 1962).

————, *Peig: The Autobiography of Peig Sayers of the Great Blasket Island*, translated by Bryan MacMahon (Syracuse, New York: Syracuse University Press, 1974).

Sax, Boria, *The Serpent and the Swan: The Animal Bride in Folklore and Literature* (Blacksburg, Virginia, 1998).

Sébillot, Paul, *Traditions et Superstitions de La Haute Bretagne, Volume I* (Paris: Maison Neuve, 1882).

Semmens, Jason, '"Whyler Pystry": A Breviate of the Life and Folklore-Collecting Practices of William Henry Paynter (1901–1976) of Callington, Cornwall', *Folklore*, 116:1 (2005), pp. 75–94.

————, 'Bucca Redivivus: History, Folklore and the Construction of Ethnic Identity within Modern Pagan Witchcraft in Cornwall', Philip Payton, editor, *Cornish Studies: Second Series*, 18 (Exeter: University of Exeter Press, 2011), pp. 141–61.

Sikes, Wirt, *British Goblins, Welsh Folk-lore, Fairy Mythology, Legends and Traditions* (London: S. Low, Marston, Searle and Rivington, 1880).

Silver, Carole G., *Strange and Secret Peoples: Fairies and Victorian Consciousness* (Oxford: Oxford University Press, 1999).

Simpson, Jacqueline, *Icelandic Folktales and Legends* (Berkeley: University of California Press, 1972).

————, 'The Functions of Folklore in "Jane Eyre" and "Wuthering Heights"', *Folklore*, 85:1 (January 1974), pp. 47–61.

————, *British Dragons* (London: Batsford, 1980).

————, *Scandinavian Folktales* (London: Penguin Books, 1988).

————, 'Repentant Soul or Walking Corpse? Debatable Apparitions in Medieval England', *Folklore*, 114:3 (2003), pp. 389–402.

————, 'On the Ambiguity of Elves', *Folklore*, 122 (2011), pp. 76–83.

————, 'Fairy Queens and Pharisees', from Simon Young and Ceri Houlbrook, editors., *Magical Folk: British and Irish Fairies 500 AD to the Present* (London: Gibson Square, 2018), pp. 23–30.

Simpson, Jacqueline, and Roud, Steve, *A Dictionary of English Folklore* (Oxford: Oxford University Press, 2000).

Skjelbred, Ann Helene Bolstad, '"These Stories will not lead you to Heaven": An Encounter with Two Sami Narrators', *Folklore*, 112:1 (2001), pp. 47–63.

Smelt, Maurice, *101 Cornish Lives* (Penzance: Alison Hodge, 2006).

Smith, Elder and Co., editors, *Dictionary of National Biography* (New York: Macmillan, 1908, second edition).

Smith, James Elimalet, *Legends and Miracles and other Curious and Marvellous Stories of Human Nature* (London: B.D. Cousins, 1837).

Snorri Sturluson, *The Prose Edda: Tales from Norse Mythology*, translated by Jean I. Young (Berkeley: University of California Press, 1954).

Spence, Lewis, *Legends and Romances of Brittany* (Mineola, New York: Dover, 1997).

Spooner, Barbara C., 'Cornwall and the Church that was shifted', *Folklore*, 73:4 (Winter 1962), pp. 270–75.

————, 'The Giants of Cornwall', *Folklore*, 76:1 (Spring 1965), pp. 16–32.

————, 'Jack and Tom in "Drolls" and Chapbooks', *Folklore*, 87:1 (Spring 1976), pp. 105–12.

Spriggs, Matthew, 'Who was the Duchess of Cornwall in Nicholas Boson's (c.1660–70) "The Duchesse of Cornwall's Progresse to see the Land's End …"?', Philip Payton, editor, *Cornish Studies: Second Series*, 14 (Exeter: University of Exeter Press, 2006), pp. 56–69.

Stephen, Leslie, *Dictionary of National Biography* (London: Smith, Elder, and Co., 1887).

Stern, Stephen, 'Ethnic Folklore and the Folklore of Ethnicity', *Western Folklore*, 36:1 (1977), pp. 7–32.

Stewart, R.J., editor, *Robert Kirk: Walker between Worlds, a New Edition of The Secret Commonwealth of Elves, Fauns and Fairies* (Dorset: Element, 1990).

Suggett, Richard, 'The Fair Folk and Enchanters', from Simon Young and Ceri Houlbrook, editors., *Magical Folk: British and Irish Fairies 500 AD to the Present* (London: Gibson Square, 2018), pp. 137–50.

Sveinsson, Einar Ólafur, *The Folk-Stories of Iceland*, revised by Einar G. Pétursson, translated by Benedikt Benedikz, edited by Anthony Faulkes (London: University College London, 2003 [1940]).

Thomas, Calvin, *An Anthology of German Literature* (Boston: D.C. Heath, 1906).

Thomas, Charles, *Studies in the Folk-Lore of Cornwall: I. The Taboo* (Lowenac, Camborne, UK: self-published, 1951).

————, *Studies in the Folk-Lore of Cornwall: II. The Sacrifice* (Lowenac, Camborne, UK: self-published, 1952).

————, 'Present-day Charmers in Cornwall', *Folklore*, 64 (1953), pp. 304–5.

————, *Gathering the Fragments: The Selected Essays of a Groundbreaking Historian*, Chris Bond, editor (Waterthorpe, Sheffield: Cornovia, 2012).

Thomas, Keith, *Religion and the Decline of Magic* (London: Folio Society, 2012 [1971]; second edition in 1991, minor changes in the 2012 edition).

Thomas, Neil, *Diu Crône and the Medieval Arthurian Cycle* (Cambridge, UK: D.S. Brewer, 2002; Arthurian Studies I).

Thomas, Peter W., and Williams, Derek R., *Setting Cornwall on its Feet—Robert Morton Nance 1873–1959* (London: Francis Boutle, 2007).

Thompson, Stith, *The Folktale* (Berkeley: University of California Press, 1977 [1946]).

Todd, Arthur Cecil, *The Cornish Miner in America* (Glendale, California: Arthur H. Clark, 1967).

Tolkien, J.R.R., *The Hobbit* (London: George Allen and Urwin, 1937).

————, *Farmer Giles of Ham*, edited by Christina Scull and Wayne G. Hammond (London: Harper Collins, 1999 [1949]).

Tregarthen, Enys, *The Piskey-Purse: Legends and Tales of North Cornwall* (London: Gardner, Darton and Co., 1905).

————, *North Cornwall Fairies and Legends* (London: Gardner, Darton and Co., 1906).

————, collected by Elizabeth Yates, *Pixie Folklore and Legends* (New York: Avenel, 1996; originally published as *Piskey Folk: A Book of Cornish Legends*).

Udall, Nicolas, translator. *The Apophthegmes of Erasmus* (London: Kingston, 1564; reprinted, Boston, Lincolnshire: Robert Roberts, 1877).

Uí Ógaín, Ríonach and O'Connor, Anne, '"Spor ar An gCois Is gan An Chos Ann": A Study of "The Dead Lover's Return" in Irish Tradition', *Béaloideas*, 51 (1983), pp. 126–44.

Uther, Hans-Jörg, *The Types of International Folktales (Parts I–III)* (Helsinki: FF Communications No. 284, 285, and 286, 2011).

Vane, Fisher, 'Spooks, Spectres, and Superstitions in Mining', *The Mining Journal*, 21:1 (1937), p. 5, p. 40.

von Sydow, Carl Wilhelm, 'Studier i Finnsägnen och besläktade byggmästar-sägner', 1. *Fataburen*, 2 (1907), pp. 65–78, pp. 199–218.

————, 'Jätterna I mytologi och folktro', *Folkminnen och folktankar VI* (1919), pp. 52–96.

————, 'Geography and Folk-Tale Oicotypes', *Béaloideas*, 4:3 (1934), pp. 344–55, reprinted in von Sydow, *Selected Papers on Folklore*.

————, *Selected Papers on Folklore*, Laurits Bødker, editor (Copenhagen: Rosenkilde and Bagger, 1948).

Waugh, Arthur, 'The Folklore of the Merfolk', *Folklore*, 71:2 (June 1960), pp. 73–84.

Westwood, Jennifer, and Simpson, Jacqueline, *The Lore of the Land: A Guide to England's Legends, from Spring-Heeled Jack to the Witches of Warboys* (London: Penguin Books, 2005).

Williams, Derek R., *Henry and Katharine Jenner: A Celebration of Cornwall's Culture, Language and Identity* (London: Francis Boutle, 2004).

Wilson, William A., 'The *Kalevala* and Finnish Politics' *Journal of the Folklore Institute*, 3:3 (December 1966).

Worth, R.N., *West Country Garland: Selected from the writings of the poets of Devon and Cornwall* (London: Houlston, 1875).

Wright, Elizabeth Mary, *Rustic Speech and Folk-Lore* (New York: H. Milford, 1913).

Wright, Joseph, *The English Dialect Dictionary: Volume II. D–G* (London: Henry Frowde, Amen Corner, 1900).

Wright, William Henry Kearley, *West-Country Poets: Their Lives and Works* (London: Elliot Stock, 1896).

Writers' Program of the Works Projects Administration, *Arizona State Guide* (New York: Hastings House, 1940).

Young, Otis E., Jr., *Western Mining* (Norman: University of Oklahoma Press, 1970).

Young, Simon, 'Five Notes on Nineteenth-Century Cornish Changelings', *Journal of the Royal Institution of Cornwall* (2013), pp. 51–79.

————, 'Some Notes on Irish Fairy Changelings in Nineteenth-Century Newspapers', *Béascna*, 8 (2013), pp. 34–47.

————, 'Against Taxonomy: The Fairy Families of Cornwall', Philip Payton, editor, *Cornish Studies: Second Series*, 21 (Exeter: University of Exeter Press, 2014), pp. 223–37.

————, 'Pixy-Led in Devon and the South-West', *The Devonshire Association Transactions*, 148 (June 2016), pp. 311–36.

————, 'The Phantom Cornish Browney', *Devon and Cornwall Notes and Queries*, 41:10 (Autumn 2016), pp. 323–27.

————, '"Her Room Was Her World": Nellie Sloggett and North Cornish Folklore', *Journal of Ethnology and Folkloristics* (2017; http://www.jef.ee).

————, 'Fairy Holes and Fairy Butter', from Simon Young and Ceri Houlbrook, editors, *Magical Folk: British and Irish Fairies 500 AD to the Present* (London: Gibson Square, 2018), pp. 79–94.

————, and Houlbrook, Ceri, editors, *Magical Folk: British and Irish Fairies 500 AD to the Present* (London: Gibson Square, 2018).

Zimmermann, George Denis, *The Irish Storyteller* (Dublin: Four Courts Press, 2001).

Zipes, Jack, *Breaking the Magic Spell: Radical Theories of Folk and Fairy Tales* (Austin: University of Texas Press, 1979).

————, *The Brothers Grimm: From Enchanted Forests to the Modern World* (New York: Routledge, 1988).

————, translator and editor, *The Original Folk and Fairy Tales of the Brothers Grimm: The Complete First Edition* (Princeton: Princeton University Press, 2014).

————, editor, *The Oxford Companion to Fairy Tales* (Oxford: University Press, 2015, second edition).

Websites

https://en.wikisource.org/wiki/The_Times/1887/Obituary/Robert_Hunt (accessed 1 May 2010).

http://www.reddit.com (accessed 9 November 2013 and 3 November 2017).

https://www.skinnersbrewery.com/our-beers/ (accessed 25 January 2016).

http://www.storylines.org.uk/2013/05/21/the-cornish-tradition-of-crying-the-neck/ (accessed 29 July 2016).

http://www.strangehistory.net/2011/08/27/cornish-mermaid-half-priest-half-fish/ (accessed 28 September 2017).

http://www.tommyknocker.com (accessed 25 January 2016).

http://www.voicesfromthedawn.com/loughcrew/ (accessed 20 May 2017).

Index

CPSIA information can be obtained
at www.ICGtesting.com
Printed in the USA
BVHW031243100219
539890BV00001B/1/P